David L. Edwar_ _h have been well received. "_____ once again", wrote a reviewer, "is that marvellous fluency and lucidity, that ability to present complex and conflicting facts and situations completely fairly, those magisterial judgements which combine penetrating insight and down-to-earth common sense, and with it all a sheer readability" (*Church Times*). "I stand back in admiration of a man who, if the world could be saved by books alone, would already have saved the world six times over" (*Methodist Recorder*). His most recent books include three volumes of a history of *Christian England* (revised as one volume in 1989). In 1990 he was honoured by a Lambeth Doctorate of Divinity.

Now Provost of Southwark Cathedral in London, he was formerly a Fellow of All Souls College, Oxford, Dean of King's College, Cambridge, Sub-Dean of Westminster and Dean of Norwich. He has served the ecumenical movement as Editor of the SCM Press and Chairman of Christian Aid. While at Westminster Abbey he was the Speaker's Chaplain in the House of Commons.

Books by the same author include

A REASON TO HOPE
A KEY TO THE OLD TESTAMENT
JESUS FOR MODERN MAN
CHRISTIAN ENGLAND
(three volumes in one)

(Collins)

RELIGION AND CHANGE
THE FUTURES OF CHRISTIANITY
ESSENTIALS: a dialogue with John Stott
TRADITION AND TRUTH
CHRISTIANITY AND CONSERVATISM
(edited with Michael Alison)

(Hodder and Stoughton)

THE CATHEDRALS OF BRITAIN

(Pitkin Pictorials)

WHAT ANGLICANS BELIEVE

(Mowbrays)

Christians in
a New Europe

David L. Edwards

Collins
FOUNT PAPERBACKS

To Helen, Kathy, Clare, Martin
and their generation

William Collins Sons & Co. Ltd
London · Glasgow · Sydney · Auckland
Toronto · Johannesburg

First published in Great Britain in 1990 by Fount Paperbacks

Fount Paperbacks is an imprint of
Collins Religious Division,
part of the Collins Publishing Group
8 Grafton Street, London W1X 3LA

Copyright © 1990 David L. Edwards

Printed and bound in Great Britain by Cox & Wyman Ltd,
Reading, Berks.

CONDITIONS OF SALE

This book is sold subject to the condition that it shall not,
by way of trade or otherwise, be lent, re-sold, hired out or
otherwise circulated without the publisher's prior consent in
any form of binding or cover other than that in which it is
published and without a similar condition including this condition
being imposed on the subsequent purchaser

CONTENTS

	Preface	9
1.	Prelude to Europe	11
2.	Twelve Cheers for the Community	29
3.	The Wider Europe	66
4.	The Christian Contributions	85
5.	After the Empires	122
6.	Towards the Union	152
7.	Twelve Stars in the Night	169
8.	A Single Market in Religion	195
9.	'Come Over and Help Us'	246
	For Further Reading	248
	Index	251

Preface

IN 1990 there seems to be a need for a short book which tries to discuss the immense changes which have begun to make a new Europe, in the light of history and from a Christian viewpoint. This is such a book. It may be that I have understood something, or (more probably) that I have amateurishly assembled the insights of experts. But if this book only brings into focus the reader's disagreement with the opinions offered, it will have served a purpose. The discussion about the agenda for Christians in a new Europe is going to be a long one, and while I have been working on this book I have been told of many initiatives which others have taken – although so far as I know this book is the first of its kind.

I attempt to consider the fears which surround the development of the European Community into the European Union – and the feeling that religion has nothing to do with it. But I offer twelve down-to-earth reasons (or groups of reasons) for welcoming this development – reasons which, I suggest, should appeal to Christians among others. After the intensely dramatic changes of 1989, I also discuss briefly the wider Europe which seems to be drawn to the magnet of the Community where democracy is combined with prosperity. I try to summarize the contributions which Christians have already made to Western and Eastern Europe in a long history, before considering what might be their contributions in the future. Europe's relationship with the other continents – which has transformed the world but is still burdened by colonialist guilt – needs a more positive reassessment. Now that the European Union is coming to birth, new objectives for society need clarification and agreement. Finally I suggest that we need a fresh look at the European Churches, at their own diversity and their own union. It may help to think of them as a "single market in religion", so that a deepening and widening communion between them may lead to a Christian *perestroika*, reconstructing a Church which will be worthy to be the heart of the union of the states of Europe.

I am very much an Englishman and more of an historian than a prophet. But I have had the benefit of comments on a draft of this book, in whole or part, from Dean John Arnold, Dr Henry Chadwick, Richard Hay of the European Commission, Marc Lenders of the European Ecumenical Commission for Church and Society, Canon W.J. Milligan who eased my path in Strasbourg, Bishop Patrick Rodger, Edwin Robertson, Elizabeth Salter and Bishop Kallistos Ware. I am very grateful for the advice of such experts in European affairs. Bishop Rodger's comment in a letter summed up what I am sure is the right message: "In a sense we all have to start again – but we have a great opportunity to start, and to start together."

London, Easter 1990 D.L.E.

1

Prelude to Europe

Watching a birth

IN the 1990s it seems that the union of the states of Europe is at last being born – slowly, painfully but in reality. Here are difficulties and dangers together with vast prospects for life, liberty and the pursuit of happiness. "Our destiny is in Europe", Margaret Thatcher declared in Bruges in 1988, "as members of the European Community." If she said it, we may well believe it. It has also become reasonable to expect the Community to deepen into a union – and to widen by including Eastern Europe and other nations no less European. And the nearness of AD 2000 is a reminder that for almost two thousand years Christianity has been a spiritual force shaping this continent's history. It is still the main religion of those Europeans who are religious, and it appears to have outlived the most systematic and the most brutal rivals it has ever had, Nazism and Communism. Heartened by this victory, many Christians are responding to the Pope's initiative in calling for the 1990s to be a "decade of evangelism" in preparation for the third millennium AD. What, then, should Christians (the "Easter people") think about the new Europe, and contribute to it?

By "union" I do not mean anything much like the USA, for the peoples of Europe remain very touchy about national identity and culture, and any European Union or USE will have to be a new form of political organization which needs to be invented by us or our children. If a transatlantic comparison is wanted, the uneasy federation of Canada may be more relevant than the USA. But much Eurofederalist talk has been counter-productive, because it alarms patriots and obscures the real possibilities. It is indeed an irony that a few enthusiasts should be urging the nations which make up the EC to become a unitary state at the very time when the Soviet Union appears to be breaking up or at least becoming a looser union. It seems that we have to go back to words agreed at the end of the first European Assembly in Strasbourg in 1949: "the aim and goal is the creation of a European Political Authority with limited functions but real powers." That was the spirit of the Treaty of Rome which constituted the European Community in 1957, and I do not find it impossible to believe that Europeans, who have invented so many things over so many years, will invent a good future along these lines.

By "Europe" I do not mean something restricted to the present membership of the European Community. If they will accept the conditions, other Europeans have as much right to belong to the Community as its founders have. Many of them are becoming more and more closely associated with the EC in economics. All of them already share most of the ideas and values of the peoples in the EC. In this context, full of dramatic changes, President Gorbachev has famously spoken of "Europe, our common home", and President Bush of "Europe whole and free" as part of a "new era in world affairs". And the amazing changes as the 1980s became the 1990s have made such phrases more than talk. The cold war is over. The melting ice has left behind torrents of confusion but also seed growing in many fields; and it may be that the most important change will not result from the growth of free markets.

By "Christianity" I do not mean anything less than the whole company of Christians – which was the earliest meaning of the word that became in English "Christianity". Christians in Europe are almost as diverse as their non-Christian neighbours and they have no reason to regret it. Just as pluralism deserves to be celebrated since it is part of the true

Prelude to Europe

wealth of Europe, so its own diversity is part of the strength of the Christian tradition. Nowadays no one in Europe really wants uniformity in politics or religion, although some accuse others of seeking it. But something unprecedented, something pregnant with the future, is happening in Europe before our eyes, and it pulls us together, making us ask freshly and urgently what it is that we have in common as Europeans. So I want to explore the meaning of this new reality for those of us who by inheriting Europe's Christian tradition in one shape or another have inherited a great fortune – a fortune which we long to increase and to share with our neighbours. And the new reality of a uniting Europe makes Europe's Christians ask what they already have in common as Christians, and what is the stronger unity which they ought to want now. It is often said that Christian unity is one of the gifts which Christians could offer to a divided world and a divided Europe. Actually, the success of attempts to achieve the visible reunion of Christians has been very limited – far more limited than the success of the economic union between the nations. In 1948 two great conferences were held in Dutch cities. In Amsterdam the World Council of Churches was inaugurated. It has done something to bring the churches together into visible unity, but far less than its founders hoped. In The Hague a Congress of Europe was held, to advocate the continent's cultural, economic and ultimately political unity. Despite problems and setbacks, that cause has prospered. History seems to have been saying: ecumenical, no – economic, yes. Have Christians, then, been pursuing an unrealistic aim in the ecumenical movement? What spiritual unity is possible as our contribution to the ending of Europe's quarrels and the beginning of a new age? I shall be asking: should the Christian aim now be a spiritual unity, a communion, which (do not laugh) may be curiously like the European Community's single market?

Obviously the emergence of this colossal market is one of the changes creating the new Europe. It was promised (or threatened) for many years. Eventually we were told that it would be created by 1992, then by the end of 1992. Now it is clear that the change will take many more years to complete before it amounts to the totally free movement of goods, services, people and money from one end of the Community to another. At the beginning of 1990, 142 "directives" had been accepted in theory by the governments as necessary – but only fourteen had been enacted as national laws throughout the EC. However, it is also obvious that the single market is coming. What will it bring? It may bring disaster. Let me outline the fears about it as I understand them.

Competition in this single market is a game which must end with losers as well as winners. So every one of the twelve nations in the Community asks what will be the costs and benefits. Patriots ask whether the outcome of the new politics will be plus or minus. Consumers ask what goods will be dearer or cheaper. Workers ask whether wages and conditions will improve or will be sacrificed to competition. Employers ask what profits and losses are possible. Many nations and "interest groups" eye each other and bargain with each other. And this anxious reckoning only intensifies the character which the EC has had from the beginning.

The Community has always been a tough-minded bargain between competitors who reckon that they may gain by a practical arrangement. Things were like that when the Community was being planned in the 1950s. France, still recovering from the European wars and burdened by the expense of futile colonial wars, wanted help for its farmers and peasants – guarantees for their markets and money to modernize their farms, often small and old-fashioned. At that stage it also thought that the development of nuclear power ("atoms for peace") needed an international effort. West Germany wanted respectability in the eyes of other nations. It also wanted secure markets for its industrial exports already booming. Italy and the three "Low" Countries (already bound together in the Benelux Community) wanted advantages for their own agriculture and industry but they also wanted places at the table when Germany and France were making their historic pact. And all these nations knew that if their own social systems could not bring their peoples increasing prosperity, Communism advertised an alternative way. It controlled half Europe with claims which had not yet been totally discredited. So a bargain was struck between six non-communist nations.

During the competitive game which began then, there has been rough play. Governments have failed to keep their parts of bargains by failing to enforce the decisions to which they agreed while at the council table in Brussels. Interest groups have made sure that they have gained at the expense of others. The chief criticism has been directed against the Common Agricultural Policy, which absorbed almost three-quarters of the Community's budget in 1985 before its reform. Criticism has been of the kind expressed (although without specific reference to the CAP) in *Our Common Future*, the 1987 report of the UN World Commission on Environment and Development (the Brundtland Report). "Subsidies have encouraged the overuse of soil and chemicals, the pollution of both water resources and foods with these chemicals, and the degradation of the countryside. Much of this effort has produced surpluses and their associated financial burdens. And some of this surplus has been sent at concessional rates to the developing world, where it has been undermining the farming policies of recipient nations" (p.12). To these quietly devastating words should be added the fact that the CAP has been subjected to extensive fraud. The EC's Social and Regional Funds have been exploited similarly. Indeed, it has sometimes been said that Europe has been on the fiddle.

Where there has not been cheating, there has been fear. In Britain, for example, many seem to have felt that the French veto on the original application for membership (in 1963) ought to have been accepted as final. Although the 1975 referendum gave continuing membership of the EC a majority (of almost 17.5 million to 8.5 million), unofficial public opinion polls showed a majority against membership from 1978 to 1985, including a majority of two to one against in 1980. When the leading pro-marketeers had left the Labour Party to form the Social Democrats, Labour's manifesto for the 1983 election promised to take the country out of the EC, and Labour's MPs voted against the Single European Act in 1986. Although Mrs Thatcher remained in the Community she gave the persistent impression of doing so with a bad grace, "I want my money back" being perhaps her best known phrase in this connection. In a 1989 poll although 64 per cent thought that their children would feel "more part of Europe" than they did, 95 per cent thought that nothing discussed in the European Parliament during the previous year had affected them personally, and 55 per cent were against transferring more power to it.

This picture of a half-convinced nation is easily explained. "Europe" has alarmed all the extremists in British politics. Many on the Left and the Right, deeply divided in their own ideological visions of a desirable society (particularly if they belong to "the New Left" or "the New Right"), have feared that the EC would be dominated by the enemy. It has been strangely possible to predict *both* a ruthless capitalism's arrival by kicking in the front door *and* (it was another of Mrs Thatcher's phrases) the sinister infiltration of "Socialism by the back door". On closer inspection, the crusaders of the Left and the Right in Britain have all been alarmed to discover that nowadays most of the rest of the EC see and do things in an essentially pragmatic third way. Most electorates and most politicians in the Community have rejected any idea that there ought to be a profound ideological chasm or class war between "Christian" Democracy and "Social" Democracy. The bulk of the British electorate also seems to be for pragmatism and against extremism, but the extremes of the Left and the Right have been strong enough to maintain the tradition that the

Government and the Opposition ought to be connected not by dialogues but by insults, the purpose being to defeat the other team.

Many of the British, without being activists in any form of politics, have been conservative. They regret the many changes in daily habits. The shilling has gone; the gallon, the ounce and the ton, the inch and the mile, are going, to be followed by the fathom and the therm. The British weather has to be talked about in unfamiliar degrees of temperature. Greenwich Mean Time is to be sacrificed to Continental Time, and perhaps even the pound and the pint are under threat. One day, will motorists have to use the right side of the road? More seriously, many deplore the damage which British membership of the Community has done to the Commonwealth, that legacy of history's greatest empire; and they are deeply sad that so much of the sovereignty of the Crown in Parliament has moved to Brussels. "It means", as Hugh Gaitskell warned at the Labour Party Conference in 1962, "the end of a thousand years of history". And many are fearful about the future. A row about the excessive British contribution to the EC budget dragged on until 1984. The UK's balance of trade with the rest of the EC has been in deficit since the country "went into Europe" (a phrase often used in defiance of geography), and many fear that the country will be unable to compete after 1992. Will it be flooded by imports and outclassed in exports? Michael Heseltine, who among Conservatives in Britain has been conspicuous for his constructive attitude to the EC, called his 1989 book *The Challenge of Europe: Can Britain Win*? He left the answer in doubt. What seems more likely is that Germany will "win" – a curious epilogue to the world wars and one not attractive to those who thought that they had won those wars.

As the British do not always acknowledge, there have been roughly similar anxieties in other countries. One reason why the formation of the EC was delayed was that the Socialist parties in West Germany and Italy opposed it, and the French

Left was largely suspicious of it, for it seemed to offer capitalism under American supervision. The Party Conference of the German Socialists objected even to the creation of the powerless Council of Europe and the limited Coal and Steel Community. "No to all conservative, clerical, monopolistic-capitalist attempts to create a Europe...", they said in 1950; "an organization of Western Europe on the basis of the interests of heavy industry would be a fatal blow to democracy." In Eastern Europe in the 1990s there is a renewal of anxiety among Socialists, as they count the social cost of the changes needed if they are to fit into the Community. But within the Community the anxieties are now chiefly of a different sort, for the worry now is that the Community may not be a sound commercial proposition.

Kevin Featherstone's 1988 study of *Socialist Parties and European Integration* noted that "by the mid-1980s a fragile consensus had appeared amongst the Socialist Parties of the EC to accept membership" (p. 3). The consensus that the EC is going to be good for business is, however, equally or more fragile. The Community can be described as a "level playing field" for the competitive games which businessmen play. But in these games it is easy to get hurt, particularly if you are small. Nations such as Ireland or the Benelux countries may get hurt as the giants compete. Although Denmark accepted the Single European Act after a referendum, its public has been even more resistant than the British to any prospect of the European Union. Alone among the Scandinavian countries it has joined the EC – but almost entirely in order to be able to sell its agricultural products to Britain and Germany.

German industry knows that its largest new markets lie outside the EC, in Eastern Europe, and that is where it most wants to invest. West Germany's aim, clearly stated in its Basic Law at its foundation, was always reunion with East Germany, and in the 1990s its heart is in the completion of that rebirth of the fatherland rather than in the birth of any western union. It asks whether it can afford to invest in the east, and in particular to subsidize the reconstruction of East Germany, *and* to pour money into the development of poorer nations and regions elsewhere in the EC. It is in any case anxious that its proud economy should not be dragged down by the more feckless economic behaviour of its partners in the EC where it has been the chief paymaster, contributing almost a third of the budget. Indeed, as a highly regulated society it is generally anxious now that it has to be generally entangled in a Europe which is far more relaxed and permissive. Like other high-wage industrial nations it is worried about competition from low-wage industrializing countries such as Spain. Yet it does not wish to insist that conditions of work must be made uniform throughout the Community, with a rigid development of the Social Charter – for it must make allowances for East German backwardness. So West Germany, the tallest giant in Europe, has headaches.

Germany's neighbour France – so often treated in an unneighbourly fashion – is the nation which invented superpatriotic "chauvinism" and which produced Charles de Gaulle, the Margaret Thatcher of the 1960s. As the 1990s begin France, remembering three wars, worries about a Germany with a greater strength than ever. Remembering the glories of its history (specially of Paris), it resents not being the completely acknowledged light of Europe. The suggestion that in order to balance German strength the *entente cordiale* with Britain must be revived arouses no enthusiasm, for after its history France feels little cordiality in that direction. Its determination to keep its own nuclear *force de frappe*, and its obstinate reliance on nuclear energy for electricity, are highly symbolic.

To the south, the Mediterranean countries large and small ask whether their own rural poverty can be cured by the EC as France's was. Or will it actually grow worse as they are marginalized by the new technologies concentrated in the already rich areas – and by the new calls for investment coming from the ex-communist east? And will their own industries, often in a fragile infancy, be crushed by the new competition? Their fears have already made them slow to implement the Community's regulations and slack in hunting down fraud. The Greeks and the Portuguese still feel a long way from the centres of wealth and power, and richer Italy still wants to subsidize and protect its state-owned industries.

Because hesitations and fears have been so widespread and so deep, many tasks which might be thought suitable for a European Community had proved too difficult for effective bargaining before the end of the 1980s. Perhaps these were limitations accepted sensibly; perhaps they were chances missed. The countries' legal systems remained different, so that a company law for the "transnational corporations" likely to flourish in the single market was delayed. Even co-operation between the national police forces was delayed: at the end of 1989 it was admitted that the computer systems of the French and West German police were still incompatible. Educational and training systems remained very different, and the teaching of foreign languages was almost everywhere inadequate. All that could be arranged was some exchange of students and some recognition of other countries' diplomas. VAT and taxes on personal incomes and company profits varied from country to country. So did immigration policies (a problem specially acute in countries to which a North African can take a ferry), although the citizens of the nations in the EC were eventually allowed free movement across its own frontiers. The protection of the worker and of the environment was left almost entirely to national governments. The Community was unable to develop a coherent transport policy although this was expected at its foundation. Lorries were still delayed by "customs" (a word with a double meaning) when permitted to cross frontiers. Different governments had different policies for the overdue modernization of their railways, and because of a lack of competition air fares in Europe were the world's highest per mile. By the end of the 1980s the EC had not done much to encourage energy saving. Nor was there an effective energy policy. The Community was founded in the age of coal, with the prospect of cheap oil and with optimism about cheap nuclear power. When its own coal became more expensive than imported coal, when oil prices shot up and then down, and when nuclear power became unpopular because unsafe (except in France), the Community could not unite the nations in any agreed strategy although there were of course discussions and gestures. Since most of Europe's oil has been imported (with calamitous results in the mid-1970s), this problem shows how difficult it was to co-ordinate foreign policies. The co-ordination of military security was impossible. There has been no President of Europe able to talk on equal terms with the White House or the Kremlin while Europe's fate has been under discussion between the superpowers: on summits, there has been room for two. Had a European President existed, he could not have commanded a single soldier. The budget of the EC, although often attacked as money grabbed by a Brussels bureaucracy, was about three per cent of the total of the budgets of the national governments.

There is no one European language, as almost 3,000 translators employed by the EC to cope with nine official languages (and about 900,000 pages of documentation a year) bear witness. Europe is a "geographical expression", said Bismarck (adding that an appeal to the interests of "Europe" always made him watch out for a nationalist manoeuvre), but the expression is imprecise. The Atlantic fixes one end of it, but where is the other end? In the nineteenth century geographers began to end Europe at the Ural river and mountains in Russia, thus assigning about eight per cent of the world's land surface to this continent, but their decision only dramatized the well-known problem of whether Russia is, or is not, European. It is not surprising that the geographers of the ancient world did not think much of "Europe". The word was seldom used. It might refer to Greece as distinct from Asia, or it might point vaguely to a north populated by barbarians. Aristotle's *Politics* observed that "those who live in a cold climate and in Europe are full of spirit, but wanting in intelligence and skill; therefore they keep their freedom, but have no political organization."

Since Aristotle's day the Europeans have learned something about politics. They developed the tribal kingdom, the medieval society, the nation state, the parliamentary democracy. They paid for their lessons in politics by blood, sweat and tears. It is not surprising that they hesitate when asked to welcome the newfangled European Community and a European Union which may turn out to be no more than a daydream and which could become a nightmare.

However, for those Europeans who are prepared to consider new possibilities a very searching question must arise. Would a whole-hearted membership of the European Union be an economic, political or moral disaster in comparison with what has been achieved in this century by the politics of unfettered national sovereignty? The British experience is instructive. Those leaders of Britain who pressed the three applications to join the EC (over ten years from 1962) argued that the country was declining in isolation – and they could not be contradicted. When the EC was formed, in 1957, Britain was richer than any member. But when Britain was eventually accepted as a member, in 1972, among the existing members only Italy was poorer. Since joining Britain has not been able to catch up in wealth (Gross Domestic Product per head in 1989) with West Germany, Denmark, France, Belgium, Italy or the Netherlands (in that order of wealth). About half Britain's exports now go to EC countries, and the contemplation of what might have been if it had *not* joined that market is horrendous. Michael Heseltine's question "Can Britain win?" is a painfully real one. But the question "Can Britain leave?" would be unreal.

So, in pursuit of their own interests and full of hesitations, governments have committed peoples to membership of the European Community and to the development of the

Community into the Union. No nation's membership has ever been cancelled and probably never could be. Perhaps the main motive has been the fear of being left out, but once a nation has "gone in" it has always found itself thoroughly in. It has grumbled, it has regretted, it has been afraid, but it has stayed in; like a swimmer after a dive, it has had to swim however cold the water. Six governments signed the Treaty of Rome, with its vision: "Determined to lay the foundations of an ever-closer union among the peoples of Europe, resolved to ensure the economic and social progress of their countries by common action to eliminate the barriers which divided Europe...." Twelve governments (including even the Greek Socialists) signed the Single European Act of 1986, committing themselves irreversibly to a single market and to political co-operation. Even so, governments have of course been slow to abandon their powers. They have attempted to stop capital leaving their countries and to stop foreign investors buying up their industries. They have tried to protect or subsidize non-competitive firms which provided employment. But eventually they have agreed to take their Euromedicine, surrendering, transferring or "pooling" (the most tactful word) many precious forms of sovereignty. It has become clear that, whether they like it or not, the common destiny of many Europeans is in Europe, as members of the European Union. A shrewd columnist in a British Conservative newspaper wrote in 1990 that "the movement in Brussels favouring political integration, far from being a dream of Community enthusiasts, is a realistic reflection of the mood of every capital within the Community except London" (Ronald Butt in *The Times*, 11 April). And the hopes of many nations not in the European Community as the 1990s begin have begun to include membership. It is hoped that what the EC has done for an Ireland now fairly prosperous it could do for Poland; that what the EC has done for a Spain now thoroughly democratic it could do for Romania. "There is one thing stronger than armies," said Victor Hugo, "an idea whose hour has come."

A thousand years before Christ, Greek mythology told the story of Europa, a beautiful princess of Tyre who was taken from Asia to Crete on the back of a bull. The animal was in fact Zeus in disguise: the father of the gods was ferrying the princess into her future. Europa was no doubt alarmed. But she was on her way to wealth as well as to motherhood, Crete being the place where European civilization began. There seems to be a lesson in the old story for Europe's nations as they approach AD 2000. They will have to embark on a new voyage, and risk drowning, if they sincerely want to grow richer.

Nothing to do with religion?

Ought a Christian to be interested in such a blushing voyage to European wealth? Many people are surprised if religion is ever mentioned in the debates about the European Community. When the British Council of Churches published a pioneering report on *Christians and the Common Market* in 1967, a Conservative Central Office leaflet was quoted: "The Common Market was set up by the Treaty of Rome. This has nothing to do with the Pope or the Vatican. The Treaty just happened to be signed in Rome. The Common Market has nothing to do with religion." One of the best informed of recent writers in this field, Ernest Wistrich, who was a director of the British section of the European Movement for seventeen years until 1986, wrote in *After 1992* (1989, p.143): "the European Movement, which is primarily an umbrella organization for all types of organizations with an interest in European affairs, keeps in touch with associations of individuals in every sector of society.

This includes political parties, industry, commerce, trade unions, employers' associations, most professions, educational establishments and special interest organizations.'' Here was a deafening silence about the churches.

In Europe it often seems easier to associate religion with private life rather than with the news. At its widest religion may seem to sanctify a small unit – the family, the village, an ethnic group such as the Bretons or a nation such as Poland. The image perhaps is of grandmothers going to church in peasant costumes, or of immigrants in a strange city glad to use their own language in a church, temple or mosque, and critics may talk about religion as folklore or opium, but it has to be admitted that this ethnic or tribal religion flourishes quite easily. In contrast, official religion usually finds it hard to find a public place in large modern institutions such as international organizations. Churches and similar bodies often endorse the ideals of the United Nations, etc., and may be welcomed into the fringes of their discussions as "non-governmental organizations" (the Vatican having the advantage of being able to claim the seat as a sovereign state), but it is not easy for religious institutions to arrange a continuous and effective presence. Perhaps there is a feeling that the deity worshipped by a particular religion dislikes these organizations which must be neutral between the creeds and which may seem to ignore all creeds – a feeling suggested by the Genesis story of the divine displeasure against the multicultural Tower of Babel. The United Nations headquarters in New York has a meditation room, but its furnishing, which avoids any suggestion of a particular religious commitment, hints how difficult it is to agree on the relevance of any one of the world's faiths to the world's quarrels and compromises once there is movement beyond generalities about justice, peace and the environment. The headquarters of the European Community in Brussels, although named after a convent which used to be on the site (the Berlaymont), has no chapel, only a similar room. The group of civil servants that meets regularly for Bible study and prayer is small. The nearby Ecumencial Centre where Protestant, Orthodox and Anglican churches jointly sponsor some studies and discussions in a modest office, seriously underfinanced. The Catholic Centre (OCIPE) is also modest. And although these embassies of the Churches ought to be strengthened, no one wants them to lose their modesty. So far as I know, no one has written a hymn about a Christian triumph in the EC (although Beethoven's setting of Schiller's "Ode to Joy," the finale of his Ninth Symphony, is used as an anthem); and no one has proposed that the twelve stars in a circle on the blue European flag should be rearranged as a cross.

When the Christian religion is thought to be relevant to public affairs in modern times and even to international organizations, the Church is often told that it should avoid any tendency to bless the rich. Its "preferential option" must be a bias towards the poor. Its support must be given not to the activity called "wealth creation" but to warnings such as those endorsed in the statement issued by the officers of Europe-wide church agencies based in Brussels and Strasbourg before the European Parliamentary elections of 1989. "We wish to build an open Europe, a Europe open in its dealings with its own citizens and the rest of the world", they said. "We seek a Europe that is transparent and democratic, not dominated by concentrations of economic, social and political power – a Europe that looks not inward, but outward to the needs of the Third World, immigrants, refugees, the hungry, poor and oppressed everywhere – a Europe that is united, East and West, and is securely at peace with itself and with all of planet Earth."

This Christian defence of the poor and of the planet is both correct and courageous. It is more Christian to be identified with the poor than to be allied with the powerful, and much of the history of Christianity (which suggests the opposite) is a history of sin. But I am also claiming in this book that the Christian may applaud the arrival of a European Union which in comparison with others is a rich society likely to grow richer – as the Christian may applaud the liberation of the masses of Latin America (for example) from grinding poverty, or the empowerment and enrichment of the black majority in South Africa.

I shall outline a dozen reasons for applauding the EC. And I do not apologize that those reasons involve the creation of wealth. The Christian religion conveys God's good news for the poor but it does not teach them that they should remain poor if they can work for a better living honourably and in harmony with their natural environment. On the contrary, Christianity inherits the teaching of the Hebrew Scriptures that a just society is blessed by a peaceful prosperity (*shalom*) – and *shalom* is what a just individual deserves even if he does not always get it (*shalom* is what Job enjoys before and after his sufferings). The New Testament does not offer much comfort to the rich: it concentrates on warning them against the fascinations and cares of wealth, against complacency, avarice, selfishness and oppression. But it also does not offer much comfort to the poor who are idle. Taken as a whole, the Christian Bible, which includes two Testaments, proclaims God's creation of nature, which is to be respected for God's sake, but it does not advocate a back-to-nature escape from an adult, informed, responsible and fruitful dominion over nature. It blesses work and says that the Father is at work. It affirms that man does not live by bread alone but adds that the Father knows that his children need bread plus a little wine. Therefore words such as "materialism" and "greed" should not be used too readily as stones to throw at neighbours using their God-given talents to work in the God-given vineyard. Christians ought to resist the temptation to be holier than God.

Many Christians have made Europe materially richer. Perhaps the long tradition began with Lydia, according to the Acts of the Apostles (16:14) the first European to be baptized as a Christian. She was a dealer in purple fabric, a manufacture for luxury. In about 540 the *Rule* of St Benedict (who was to be venerated as a patron saint of Europe) prescribed for his monks manual labour lasting about six hours a day, and later Benedictines achieved the great improvement of agriculture in many countries. Cathedrals soared, partly in order to advertise the wealth of towns. Venice, Florence and Bruges are still monuments to the church-going and church-building habits of medieval and Renaissance merchants. The spirit of Protestantism and the spirit of capitalism were married (for better, for worse) in Amsterdam, London, Glasgow and Hamburg. European civilization has had material foundations and, generation after generation, Christians have strengthened them. They have done so while always being reminded that God alone is to be worshipped, not Caesar or Mammon. They have thought that they were creating wealth in collaboration with the Creator. Why, then, should Christians object if in the twenty-first century AD Europe becomes wealthy enough to remove finance from the problems of education, health care, culture and religion, to banish poverty from its own extensive territory, and to be quite easily open and generous, sharing the fruits of growth in a world of a probably growing poverty and a deepening environmental crisis? Could such a world afford a poor Europe?

2

Twelve Cheers for the Community

1. A CHRISTIAN cannot fail to notice that the European Community is a community of peace. The people who walked in darkness have seen a great light.

When Britain joined the EC on the first day of 1973 it was a significant moment in that peacemaking which Christians call the Kingdom of God. I was then one of the clergy of Westminster Abbey, and we put the national flags of the EC around the grave of the unknown warrior, a place where more than forty million deaths caused by the two greatest wars among Europe's many wars are remembered. In that moment those who had died and those who had been bereaved seemed to have a reward. In the setting of the bloody history of Europe it is astonishing that the member states of the EC cannot now go to war with each other. The city of Brussels has many attractions, but the most thought-provoking is the location of the Community's headquarters so close to the battlefield of Waterloo. The cathedral of Strasbourg is a marvel, but it is a greater marvel that the European Parliament should meet in a city which Germany seized in one war and after another had to return to France, which had seized it in 1681. One President of that Parliament had the tattoo marks of a concentration camp on her body as she made sure that the peaceful debates were in order. Even as memories of Europe's wars fade, friendship between Frenchmen and Germans as the powerhouse of the EC (with a formal network of regular consultations established by the treaty of 1963) must still seem a major miracle.

Equally momentous and marvellous is the end of the cold war between Western and Eastern Europe and the superpowers behind them. Forty-five years of terror on both sides of the Iron

Curtain – for both sides lived on the brink of the nuclear abyss – are being ended as I write; unless negotiations fail the numbers of nuclear warheads are being halved, and conventional forces are being reduced drastically. One factor in the miracle is obvious. The peaceful prosperity of the EC has made its own member states far less vulnerable to aggression, and has acted as a magnet to the nations of Eastern Europe as they move into freedom and prosperity. And although Britain may be at some distance from continental emotions, it must be relevant to the islanders that Europe is now giving birth to a union instead of to another world war in which each side would have had ten thousand nuclear warheads.

There is a precious possibility that this union of Europe will help to heal tribal enmity between Catholic and Protestant in Northern Ireland by reducing the power of the old equation: Catholic equals poor. By the end of the 1980s membership of the EC had brought up living stndards in the Republic of Ireland, partly through new subsidies but mainly because it had greatly increased trade with countries other than Britain. The majority in Ireland in favour of joining the EC in the 1972 referendum (a majority of five to one) had been justified: the country was still poor in comparison with most nations in the EC, but the image of an underdeveloped ex-colony, still dependent and deeply resentful, was slowly being replaced. And with modernity, as understood in Europe, goes a monitored respect for human rights, meaning in this context that Catholic must not impose the Church's moral teaching on the whole nation and Protestant must not treat Catholic as an inferior breed. On such a basis there might one day be a federation of all Ireland. It is difficult to think of any other end to the agony.

A greater anxiety accompanies the British fear that the enmity in Northern Ireland will never be eased. It is anxiety about German power dominating Europe. For many centuries Britain very expensively organized, subsidized and fought alongside alliances against the powers which sought the mastery of "the Continent" - Philip of Spain, the France of Louis XIV or Napoleon, the Germany of the Kaiser or Adolf Hitler, Stalin's Soviet Union. Only if there was a "balance of power" could Britain be free enough to prosper - as it did. Now the question arises: what other power could balance the economic might of a reunited Germany which has a population some twenty million more than any other EC country, and which has added Eastern Europe to the areas which are hungry for its know-how, its goods and its loans? And it is also questioned, even more fearfully, whether despite all the assurances such a Germany can for ever be stopped from reclaiming its historic territory assigned to Poland in 1945. Chancellor Kohl sent shivers down many spines when he entered the 1990s claiming that Germany's eastern frontier had not been finally settled.

The realistic answer begins by saying that the policy of building up military alliances to restrain Germany is outdated. As the 1990s begin no military power on earth can stop Germany being the biggest and strongest of the European nations. One has only to ask whether Britain is supposed to build up an alliance with France and Russia against Germany, as it did before 1914, to see that Europe has changed irreversibly. As the 1990s end no power will be able to deprive the Germans of their place at the head of Europe because they will be at the top of the league of European economic performance. But there is a strength which is greater than any one nation's power and its name is European union. In the 1990s that seems an ideal which is accepted by the bulk of the German people, still ashamed of the Nazi or Communist past, still wanting to begin anew. Seldom in history - if ever - has a nation done as much harm to its neighbours (and to many of its own residents) as the German nation in the twentieth century. Seldom in history - if ever - has a nation so completely changed its mind, in what Christians call repentance. And if idealism is discounted, the single European market brings solid profits to

German exporters. But if this European union is cemented, it will make any idea of a revival of German militarist nationalism perpetually impossible, leaving to those who do not like German economic superiority the challenge to compete in that non-violent field. Washing machine must be pitted against washing machine, hi-fi against hi-fi. And it is difficult to think of any other way of ending a threat which is felt by most Germans (who are well aware of the curse which they have inherited) as well as by their nervous neighbours. Since Germany cannot be locked up, it must be locked into a Europe at peace; and almost everything in the German record since the 1950s encourages the hope that this comfortable and dignified future will be welcomed. As Jacques Delors said in April 1990, "the solution of a European Germany rather than a German Europe is possible".

Tensions in Eastern Europe were the causes or pretexts of World Wars One and Two. As the 1990s begin problems over frontiers remain – and remain capable of exploding in conflicts unless a fresh unity can be achieved after the loosening of Soviet military control and Communist ideology. Many languages are spoken and it is rarer than in Western Europe to find people who are multilingual. Much of the map of Eastern Europe was drawn when war had put an end to the unity imposed by the Ottoman and Habsburg empires, but the principle of "national self-determination", proclaimed as a gospel by President Wilson when he tried to sort out Europe's problems, was not easy to translate on to the map. In 1990 the unity of Serbs, Slovenes and Croats in Yugoslavia is far from stable and the unity of Czechs and Slovaks is far from perfect, because the post-1918 map threw nations together. Other nationalities are also uncertain. After the Second World War new frontiers between Poland, Romania and the Soviet Union, and between Romania and Hungary were all decreed by the victors. They have all remained disputable despite the forcible movement of populations by Stalin. To the south Bulgaria, Greece and

Turkey constitute a triangle of historic enmities. In this whole region the easiest public emotion to arouse is nationalism, but because the divisions between nations are dangerously unclear there is a prospect of trouble if frontiers remain important. One hope is that all the people will wish to be drawn increasingly into the orbit of the EC – into its interlocked economies, its common ideas and its frontier-transcending peace. Already in 1990 a Czech President (Havel) has proposed a loose union between Poland, Czechoslovakia and Hungary, saying: "Before us is a historic opportunity to fill a large political vacuum created in Central Europe after the fall of the Habsburgs." Thus the end of the Communist empire has revived the dream of the 1840s that the Habsburg Empire might be replaced by a democratic Danube Confederation. Insurance against a reunited and expansionist Germany is not the only motive. The example of the European Community is infectious: in unity is strength, but "unity" need not mean another empire. And probably the Central European Union, if it can be formed, will, when it is stronger economically, follow Austria into full membership of the EC.

Marking the fiftieth anniversary of the outbreak of World War Two, in September 1989, Pope John Paul II wrote: "Yesterday, this continent exported war. Today, its role is to be a peacemaker. Europe, all eyes are on you!" On Christmas Day that year he was able to speak about "the very special moment in history – a true *kairos* [Greek for crisis] of God's providence, which the world is now experiencing as if awakened from a nightmare and opened to a better hope." But what is this "Europe" to which humanity should look for peace? Many people would like to see a peacemaking community bigger and better than the present EC. Many projects have been advocated or launched to suggest how such a unity might be reached, from Dante's *De Monarchia* six centuries ago through William Penn's *Essay towards the Present and Future Peace of Europe* (1694) to the Conference on Security and Co-operation in Europe (CSCE) begun in the 1970s and revived in the 1990s. Many of these projects are still worth pursuing – the Conference in particular, for realistically it involves the USA and the Soviet Union in the future of Europe and it includes every European nation except Albania. But the European Community – an unglamorous affair of bargains which may take all night to reach – has one advantage over all of the great ideas and over the CSCE. As a force in economics and politics, making shared decisions, it exists. It employs a staff, raises taxes and enforces laws. It makes war impossible. It makes peace pay. For these purposes, it wields power.

2. A Christian sees that in the EC power is dispersed – and remembering the crimes of dictatorships of the Right and of the Left in this often ghastly century, a Christian must be relieved that the formation of the EC has done so much to stop George Orwell's nightmare about the further advance of tyranny through technology to the climax of *1984*. It is unlikely that anyone reading this book will hope that it will offer a detailed guide to the institutions of the EC, but these institutions are worth a look because they are so often misrepresented in debates and so often have misleading images in public opinion. It will be enough to draw from a few facts the conclusion that power is dispersed.

As the 1990s begin the national governments still have the decisive say. That is inevitable when three nations with a population of around fifty-six million – France, Italy and Great Britain (in that order of wealth) – eye the larger and richer Germany and are in their turn eyed by less powerful members. The Treaty of Rome made no provision for regular private meetings between all the supreme political leaders of the member states, presumably because it was not expected that the road to union should be quite so full of problems. Nowadays, two or three times a year the "European Council" of heads of state or government meets, and almost three times a year the media alarm us by talk about a crisis at the summit – only to report that an agreement, or at least a compromise, has been reached. The less dramatic Council of Ministers gets down to work in Brussels more often, with its membership varying according to the task in hand. It is prepared for, and advised by, the work of diplomats on the Permanent Representatives' Commitee. Enthusiasts for the European Parliament have often spoken as if that body alone is capable of giving the Community "democratic legitimacy", and they attack the Council of Ministers because it meets behind closed doors and has its business arranged by people who have never been elected to their posts (the Permanent Representatives plus the Commissioners and their civil servants). But the national governments are themselves elected by their peoples and so far the peoples have paid much more attention to these elections than to any arguments about the Community deployed in elections to the European Parliament – although this tendency has decreased in recent years. The power of the nations in the Council of Ministers embodies the principle which was accepted in the Parliament's own Draft Treaty for European Union (1984) – that the Union should "only act to carry out those tasks which may be undertaken more effectively in common than by the member states acting separately." There is also much to be said for excluding the media from the actual work of these councils. That somewhat reduces the temptation which a politician has to play to a nationalist gallery.

On most matters the ministers representing their governments can nowadays take decisions by a "qualified" majority, but the weighting of the votes suggests the real distribution of international power. France, West Germany, Italy and Britain have ten votes each, Belgium, Greece, the Netherlands and Portugal five, and Denmark and Ireland three. Spain has eight and Luxembourg two. Even more suggestive is the comparison between the strength of the national economies reflected in the agreed composition of the basket of currencies known as the

European Currency Unit or ecu. In 1989 West Germany provided approximately thirty per cent of the value of the Ecu, France nineteen, Britain thirteen, Italy ten, the Netherlands nine, Belgium seven, Spain five, Denmark three, Ireland and the rest less. It will be interesting to see whether a united Germany adheres to the policy of not demanding more votes in the Council. If it does, the renunciation of power will be remarkable.

Every four years the governments nominate the Commission, whose President has to work with the governments' nominees as the sixteen other Commissioners. However, the Commission has real corporate powers as the executive. It expresses opinions which are often important initiatives, and successive Presidents have been farsighted statesmen. It alone has the authority to recommend legislation to the Council of Ministers and it administers or monitors the execution of the agreed plans. It is advised by the larger Economic and Social Committee representing employers, trade unions, farmers, academics and consumers. Commissioners are expected to be loyal to the Community, not to their own nations, and on the whole they have been that, partly because they have a well qualified permanent civil service (in 1990 about 10,000 strong) to guide them through work which is mostly technical although often controversial. This "Brussels bureaucracy" is tiny in comparison with national civil services, although it may suit national politicians to blame it for decisions which are in fact taken by the Council of Ministers.

The Community is governed by this dialogue between the Council of Ministers and the Commission, both working in Brussels. The European Parliament has much less power. This seems to have been indicated by locating its full sessions in Strasbourg. The Council and the Commission send envoys to report to these full sessions (held for the inside of a week every month), and to the eighteen specialist committees, but they are not at all fully accountable: this odd process is known as "co-operation". Most of the usefulness of the Parliament is in fact informal. Its comments improve proposals and its pressures maintain ideals. It assembles 518 members who sit and work in international "groups" or parties, not in national blocs. To a surprising extent they develop a common spirit, needing to construct coalitions in order to obtain majorities, criticizing the Council and the Commission rather than each other, and defending "Europe" against the nationalism which probably prevails back home. The Parliament receives petitions and debates the world's current problems, reaching conclusions which have some influence. Its formal powers enable it to amend or reject decisions which some members of the Council of Ministers have already opposed; the Council has to be unanimous if it wishes to reaffirm the decision. The Parliament can make the Commission reconsider part of its budget; its tendency has been to press for more expenditure. In theory it could dismiss the Commissioners as a body (but not individually). Its consent is necessary for any extension of the membership and for any comprehensive trading agreement with a state which wishes to be "associated".

The European Court of Justice in Luxembourg tries complaints against governments brought under the Community's treaties and legislation. The European Court of Auditors detects fraud, waste and mismanagement connected with the Community. It is widely agreed that they and the larger institutions all need changes. But no change is likely to be acceptable which is not based on the principles that power is safest when dispersed, and that progress is made through a dialogue between people and institutions. That agreement about principles is itself a very striking advance in political organization, with enormous knock-on effects.

3. A Christian also observes that the EC is a community of the free. "Freedom" is a word with many meanings. In many countries freedom from want is understandably valued more

highly than free speech, and liberation from an early death is reckoned more important than the freedom to vote in free elections. Such societies may turn to – or may accept – strong regimes which promise what matters most to hungry people. But in the EC many kinds of freedom are thought to be compatible with each other and to support each other.

Here is political freedom, symbolized in and since 1979 by the direct elections to the European Parliament – in a continent where at the beginning of 1945 democracy existed only in Britain and Ireland. The emotions with which West Germany and Italy helped to found the Community in the 1950s have not yet died down completely. Greece, Spain and Portugal could not join until they had got rid of their own Fascist regimes in 1974-77, and membership still means to them a larger, cleaner world. In 1990 the President of the European Parliament is a Spaniard who was imprisoned under Franco because he believed in democracy. Eastern European countries could not contemplate association with the Community until they had overthrown their Communist regimes in 1989. This freedom deserves frequent celebration, increased by the thought of how near it was to death. Hitler might have incorporated all Europe in the Third Reich had he not declared war on the Soviet Union and the USA before he had finished off Britain. Stalin might have incorporated much more of Europe into the Union of Soviet Socialist Republics had he not been deterred by the American nuclear missiles and by the American willingness to station here a large and heavily equipped army. And without the example of Western Europe it might have been impossible to keep alive in Eastern Europe, right up to the elections of 1989-90, the hope which Stalin cynically endorsed at the Yalta Conference: "the earliest possible establishment through free elections of governments responsive to the will of the people."

Here in the EC is freedom of speech, proved by the zest with which the peoples criticize their elected leaders and their elected bodies criticize each other. Here, indeed, is the wider freedom to do as one likes, provided that one's neighbour is not harmed – and one of the things one can do freely is to worship (or not worship) according to one's own conscience. But it is believed that all these freedoms are supported by the freedom to buy and sell in a free market. One of the fundamental provisions of the Treaty of Rome was the prohibition of practices or agreements which "have as their object and effect the prevention, restriction or distortion of competition within the common market". Each individual can sell competitively labour, knowledge, skill and the use of savings. Each can choose among goods (for example, washing machines) and services (for example, mortgages) offered by competing producers. Producers want to compete because by doing so they can earn profits for themselves, but the theory of the free market, confirmed by much (not all) of its practice, is that wealth is created for the benefit of all: "the tide rises and all the boats float".

A community of the free, where freedom is thus understood, is going to be an untidy and tough society in which some competitors will find more success or luck than others. That is why in a humane society, particular in a democracy, limits must be set to the operation of "market forces". But the economic statistics of the twentieth century show that a market-oriented society is going to be a richer society – which is what most of those called Socialists or Social Democrats in most European countries have come, or are coming, to accept. The supply of goods and services will be encouraged because the largest profits will be gained by the producers who deliver most efficiently, most attractively and most cheaply. Waste will be discouraged because it is costly. Dishonesty will be punished because in the long run it is not the best for sales. Research and risk-taking will be encouraged, as attentive and courteous service will be. Suppliers will be stimulated to direct all their operations with the purpose of satisfying their neighbours, the customers. When making their choices customers will have to decide for themselves within the financial resources available to them, and will thus develop their personalities. If their purchases are durable, the customers will have the dignity, responsibility and joy of ownership – and they can keep profits to augment their private property. At the beginning of the 1990s this system was still in dramatic contrast with the system of the Soviet Union, where despite talk about markets about eighty-five per cent of the property was owned by the state, where about ninety per cent of the output of farms and factories was distributed by the state, and where savings were hoarded not invested, partly because there were too few goods to buy. Free people can prosper. Such a society deserves some praise for the life which it fosters. It can be said seriously that this is the least bad society which humanity has so far been able to invent.

4. The EC is, however, not a mere playing field for competitors, not a mere free trade area, not a mere customs union, not a mere common market. It is a community; indeed, precisely because it respects the freedom of people who want to live in communities, it is a Community of communities. The Christian approves because his religion places so much emphasis on the incorporation of individuals into fellowships. In the terms used in Catholic philosophy, "personalism" (a concept developed by the French philosopher Emmanuel Mounier in the 1930s, meaning more than individualism) has a twin – "solidarity" (an idea given legs and teeth by the Poles in the 1980s).

Throughout the work of European institutions such as the EC there is emphasis on retaining the identity of each nation and neighbourhood. On no other basis would Europeans accept any union. In such a setting the standardization of goods and services faces many obstacles, but Europeans care more about conserving their own traditions and satisfying their own tastes than about the problems of Europe-wide enterprises hoping to take advantage of the single market. One result is that standardization has been easier to achieve when it simply means adopting something from the USA (perhaps something that originated in Europe, such as jeans from Genoa). The international youth culture has had a flavour as American as Coca-Cola. The future will produce more Europroducts by Eurocompanies and it will be fascinating to see whether the language difficulties can be overcome in spoken or written culture. What will be the appeal of Europrogrammes on the new high-definition TV by satellite or cable? Already commerce and tourism provide many incentives to learn languages. Europeans whose mother tongue is English or French are the laziest learners, but may not be punished as they deserve, since these two languages are already used in almost all of the daily business of the EC and are the only two official languages in the Council of Europe. Already the language of music, classical or pop, is international. But mainly what unites Europe is – and is likely to remain – competition with goods or ideas which are thoroughly and proudly characteristic of a nation or a neighbourhood. That is what lies behind the very expensive principle of the EC that people representing the member states must be able to read and speak in their own languages. That is what avoids the bland uniformity of big business or big government which Europeans notice when visiting the USA or the Soviet Union. Europe is a tapestry.

In every sphere of life it is increasingly the practice to learn by asking: how and why do other Europeans do this? It has become almost the first question to ask. (Why do the French spend so much more on health care than the British? Why do the Germans drive so much faster than the Italians? Why do the Danes worry so much more than the Dutch about pollution?...) And then Europeans compete. Competition in commerce thrives by finding parts which other goods cannot reach. Competition in sport receives incessant publicity because it is such a huge source of interest and pleasure. Competition in food has deliciously increased the pleasures of the table as Greek yogurt vies with Belgian chocolate, French wine with Scottish whisky, Italian pizzas with German sausagemeat, Danish bacon with English lamb.... Competition in tourism means that the European with a bit of money can choose between Spain and Greece, between sand and snow, between the modernity of the young crowd in the disco and layer upon layer of historic culture. Competition within Europe is all the time raising standards and increasing choice and fun, as is proved by the history of coffee or ice cream. Europe is open to other continents which enrich the quality of life – wide open, and not only in its restaurants. But to find a lifetime's pleasure in competitive diversity, and to find that one has then barely tasted the banquet, the European does not have to leave Europe.

In *Forum*, the magazine of the Council of Europe (2/89), Frédérique Hébrard recalled a childhood in the 1940s, spent in a castle where the masterpieces from the Louvre had been sent for wartime safety.

> I grew up with civilization all around me, as if I were living in some fragile yet impregnable greenhouse, and I came to know Europe, thanks to the genius of its painters, before I could traverse Europe for myself. Through the works of Canaletto and Ruysdael I travelled from Venice to the Netherlands. I sprang from Goya to Watteau, I glided over the waters painted by Turner to go and greet the trees and ravens of Caspar David Friedrich. I knew all about Holland thanks to Rembrandt, about Death because of Albrecht Dürer, about Beauty because of Botticelli, while behind the smile of the Mona Lisa I sensed that the world would be mine if I loved it enough.

Salvador de Madariaga, who presided over the cultural commission of the Congress of Europe in 1948, wrote in his Foreword to Kenneth Lindsay's prophetic *Towards a European Parliament*:

Above all, we must love Europe, our Europe, sonorous with the roaring laughter of Rabelais, luminous with the smile of Erasmus, sparkling with the wit of Voltaire; in whose mental skies shine the fiery eyes of Dante, the clear eyes of Shakespeare, the serene eyes of Goethe, the tormented eyes of Dostoevsky; this Europe to whom La Gioconda for ever smiles, where Moses and David spring to perennial life under Michelangelo's marble, and Bach's genius rises spontaneous to be caught in his intellectual geometry; where Hamlet seeks in thought the mystery of his inaction, and Faust seeks in action comfort for the void of his thought; where Don Juan seeks in women to meet the woman he never found, and Don Quixote, spear in hand, gallops to force reality to rise above itself; this Europe where Newton and Leibniz measure the infinitesimal, and the cathedrals, as Musset once wrote, pray on their knees in robes of stone; where rivers, silver threads, link together strings of cities, jewels wrought in the crystal of space by the chisel of time...this Europe must be born. And she will, when Spaniards will say "our Chartres", when Englishmen "our Cracow", Italians "our Copenhagen", when Germans say "our Bruges", and creep back horror-stricken at the thought of laying murderous hands on it. Then will Europe live, for then it will be that the Spirit that leads History will have uttered the creative words: *Fiat Europa!*

To many Europeans, however, the purple passages which I have just written or quoted would seem too complacent, too interested in the pleasures of the cosmopolitan able to study in several universities, to speak and read several languages, to enjoy with discrimination the music and art of many cultures, to shop around for cheap air fares and perhaps to end up preferring to keep a business appointment in another country by eating a delicious lunch on board a high speed train. There has been a very widespread feeling that beneath the glamorous surface the quality of European life is being disastrously damaged – or at least, is at risk. Fear grips the heart that the pollution and exhaustion of natural resources may destroy the environment; that nuclear weapons and even the use of nuclear power for peaceful purposes may destroy civilization; that the modernization of economies and the mass media may destroy the little communities in which people used to find their identities; that the new technologies mean mass unemployment, particularly for the unskilled; that family life is being wrecked by the new individualism; that the rootlessness, loneliness and boredom must inevitably cause the addictions to various drugs, the spread of crime and the cult of violence. So protests are made and alternative societies are imagined. And certainly the ugly side of European modernity is real enough to terrify. But at least it can be said that these problems have not been kept secret. On the contrary, the protests and pleas are often heard within the Community's democratic institutions, particularly in its own Parliament. Here, for all its faults, is a Community which is not lacking in anxiety or self-criticism. Indeed, that self-critical spirit is the greatest of its resources. And again and again the heart of the answer to these self-criticisms turns out to be: become more of a Community of communities on a human scale!

The EC is already a Community of nations which are themselves communities of regions. Indeed, the idea of the European Community has a special appeal for many people with a special feeling about the local community, for such people like the thought that the nation state is not going to be the only tier of government. In the United Kingdom many communities are keen to assert their identity against London and the south of England. The majorities against "devolution" in the 1979 referendum did not end the pressures in Scotland and Wales for cultural distinctiveness accompanied by some kind of political voice. The use of the word "Unionist" by Protestants in Northern Ireland has not by any means indicated a complete willingness to obey the wishes of the Westminster government. In post-Franco Spain the seventeen "autonomous communities" include Basques who have taken separatism to the point of terrorism, and Catalonians who are tempted to do so. These regions have their own governments and parliaments and are determined to restrict the power of the central government in Madrid. That is also the attitude of the twenty-two regions in Italy, where a long tradition persists of not wasting money by paying taxes to politicians in Rome. The ten *Länder* of West Germany have been guaranteed more power than any of the subordinate societies already mentioned, for the nation which they constitute is a Federal Republic, which as I write in 1990 is about to be enlarged by the inclusion of East Germany, bringing with it almost half a century of life under a radically different social system. The national unions of Germany and Italy were completed only at the beginning of the 1870s. There is still a reaction against the centralization imposed by Hitler and Mussolini. In Spain, Germany and Italy there is now a constitutional obligation to seek economic equality between the regions, and to some extent the practice corresponds with the theory. In France there is a longer national history and a stronger centralization (thanks largely to Napoleon) but de Gaulle had the feelings and needs of the ninety-five *départements* in mind when he complained that France made three hundred and sixty-five cheeses. His successors in Paris have had to delegate more power and resources to regional councils. The Netherlands has had a long history of communal tensions, reflected (as in Northern Ireland) in divisions between Catholic and Protestant; it was only in 1977 that the Catholics and the two Calvinist parties, combined as the Christian Democratic Appeal, became a partner in a coalition government. Even tiny Luxembourg has had its division between the rural north and the urban south. And it is appropriate that the headquarters of the EC should be in Belgium, a nation divided between French- and Dutch-speaking areas, with regionalism given a new strength by the 1980 constitution.

Such is the fragmented background to the patchwork of nations consituting the European Community – and it is no accident that the strengthening of regional loyalties has coincided with the development of the EC as an authority above the nations. To some extent, the nation state which was the idol is now the sick man of Europe. Yet obviously each nation can still command loyalties because it embodies memories and hopes. People are still ready to die for the nation: they need say no more. The EC must be, in the Gaullist phrase, a *Europe des patries*, whether or not the General's brand of nationalism is admired, for few Europeans would admit to being unpatriotic. (That is also true of those who passionately reckon that Scotland or Corsica or the land of the Basques is a nation.) Within the EC these rival patriots pay a price for their freedom to bargain and dissent: almost all their decisions are slow to achieve and many are not fully honoured in practice. But as an alternative to the empires and military alliances which have imposed unity in the past, this approach to problems can be reckoned a morally admirable way of being *communautaire* – a way which preserves a rich diversity of communities in the European Community.

5. These nations have chosen to form this Community because they see that modernity both enables and demands largeness. In politics the Right often has a feeling for the individual defying the bureaucracy or the trade union, for the entrepreneur or craftsman who relies on his own inventiveness and hard work, for the small business. On the Left it is protested that small is beautiful, that minorities have rights, that what is best is what is closest to nature. And in the EC these feelings surface. There are many self-employed and many small businesses: it is reckoned that about two-thirds of employment is in businesses with fewer than five hundred employees. There are many practical demonstrations of the sincerity and power of

the belief in smallness close to nature. But the EC also represents the realism that is equally characteristic of Europe.

There has always been a tension in the area of research between the recognition of the need to do together the projects that not even the richest of governments or firms was willing to undertake separately, and the wish to keep the results of research to oneself when they might have commercial applications. This handicapped the Euratom Community, created with the Economic Community in 1957, as the peaceful uses of nuclear energy became clear. The research side of the Community has lurched from crisis to crisis, although there now seems to be a greater consensus on a programme with a reduced nuclear component. On the other hand, the vastly expensive project into the all-important possibility of producing nuclear power by the safe fusion of atoms (JET) has been successfully carried forward in the context of the Community – it is located in Britain, at Culham near Oxford – because it is very far from commercial development. And the need to develop a European capacity in informatics to match US and Japanese competition has also been a motor for the successful European Strategic Programme for Research and Development in Information Technology, launched only in 1984 but since developed as European firms and governments have become enthusiastic. In parallel, outside the Community framework other initiatives have taken place – the European Space Agency formed in 1975, the Concorde, Tornado and Airbus aircraft (the last achieving a real market in world aviation although not denting American dominance). EUREKA was launched as a European answer to the US Star Wars programme. All in all, it seems that there is growing recognition of the scope for common action as mutual confidence grows.

Life in the EC has encouraged largeness in firms in situations where only large firms can prosper. Mergers or looser alliances result. Although this creates problems for a Community which has set its face against monopolies and price-fixing cartels, often firms do need largeness if they are to compete with each other and with firms outside the EC. They need large amounts of capital to provide high technology and further research. They need large markets if their prices for single items are to be low because production runs are large. They need large organizations to reach and serve those markets. Natural suspicions about the motives of these giants should not be allowed to outweigh the facts that large firms can mean secure jobs for employees and good products at good prices for consumers. But in the EC it is agreed that the giants must not be allowed to govern the rest of us. Already many "transnational corporations" have revenues larger than those of some governments seated in the United Nations. Who shall discipline these giants who can so easily switch resources and operations from one country to another, who could perhaps if pressed bully or bribe a local government? Again and again in discussions about this growing problem, the answer is clear. The transnationals ought to be governed in the public interest by an authority which itself crosses the frontiers.

6. Free competition between producers does not mean that the EC is a boxing ring for businessmen without any referee. It means that regulations must set common standards and technical specifications – the rules of the game. A new, bigger market means new regulations which may well be stricter. Community law must take precedence over national law in detail after detail. For Britain that was made absolutely clear by the European Community Act of 1972. A new process began in 1979 when the European Court of Justice ruled that the West Germans could not prevent the sale in their country of a French blackcurrant liqueur (*Cassis de Dijon*), which satisfied French standards, merely because it did not meet their own regulations. That process has already pushed far into a new understanding of what justice means for Europeans. It does not mean *laissez faire*, unbridled competition, or the justice of the

jungle. It means a large body of legislation – of treaties, of "regulations" applied to the whole Community; of "decisions" issued by the Commissions to governments, firms or individuals; and of "directives" which require governments to work out their own methods of achieving agreed results – all as interpreted by the Court of Justice if there are disputes. In order to implement the Single European Act creating the single market the Commission had to propose two hundred and seventy-nine "directives". When new states apply to join the Community their governments have to study thousands of pages of legislation, the *acquis communautaire*.

In a modern community what justice means has to be worked out in relation to levels of taxes. Within the nations disputes about taxing the rich or increasing public expenditure are often conducted on moral grounds. In the single market of the EC the Commission has sought agreement about the level of Value Added Tax (a French invention) if there is to be fair competition at the point of sale. There need not be complete uniformity; the sales tax varies by up to five per cent between the states of the USA. But moral reasoning has been produced in defence of variations greater than that. Britain, for example, developed a tradition of exempting food, children's clothing and books from VAT, and Denmark and Greece a tradition of imposing VAT in order to triple (almost) the cost of buying a car. As moral disagreements of this nature are sorted out or maintained, what justice means for Europeans has been clarified.

In the 1980s the pressure has grown that the rights of citizens should be clarified and enforced as being parts of justice. One simple way of achieving much would be for the EC to adhere corporately to the European Convention on Human Rights, making that document of 1950 (with additions) part of Community law taking precedence over national legislation. Britain, Ireland and Denmark have resisted the move.

What justice now means may be further illustrated by the success of the EC's joint action in areas where overproduction was dangerous. From 1974 onwards the world's production of steel was exceeding demand for it. Europe's steel mills had to be closed or restricted in output and sales, and modernized with fewer workers. All that might have been done by cut-throat competition aided by competing national subsidies. Instead the EC managed the transition with less pain than had been expected. At about the same time there was alarm about the dangers of overfishing in Europe's waters, now measured as all the sea within two hundred miles of the coasts. There could have been many fights at sea, as in the Britain v. Iceland cod war of 1975. Instead there were grumbles and occasional displays of anger when in 1983 the EC allocated fishing rights by zones and conserved fishing stocks by quotas. It was justice, however rough.

7. The EC has always talked about "economic and social progress" and much more ambitiously in the Single European Act it began to talk about "economic and social cohesion". It is quite often said that it must become the Europe of the people, the Europe of citizens and workers. Even those who regard it as no more than a level playing field for commercial competition have to acknowledge that if the competition is to be fair a referee is needed. There must be efforts to reduce the advantages to be gained by the competitor who starts with lower standards in "labour costs" – which means, in the treatment of Europeans at work. And even those who strongly criticize the trade unions for resisting the introduction of new technology have to acknowledge that in a democracy the people will demand that if labour-saving technology makes sense in economics, Europeans who then become redundant must be saved from the scrap heap by social security and retraining. The level of long-term unemployment caused partly by technology in the 1970s and 1980s is felt by the overwhelming majority of Europeans to be such a waste of human life that it is unacceptable morally – and therefore, in the long run, politically.

Imposing standardization on working conditions and social security is more obviously dificult than most other efforts in the EC, and in places it is less obviously desirable. It suits some workers to get low pay and long hours with poor social security benefits rather than no job at all. It also suits some managers to maintain that workers need to be managed without consultation, otherwise there will be no profits. The rights of the employed were therefore exempted from the Single European Act's provision for decisions by majorities in the Council of Ministers (as was the right of people seeking work to move into the Community). But the movement of the EC over the years has been into a common understanding of what Europeans deserve – equal pay and rights for women and men, adequate training and wages, working hours which allow for leisure and paid holidays, health and safety at work, protection from unfair dismissal, sickness and unemployment benefits, security in old age and the rights to join (or not to join) a trade union, to be consulted about working conditions (at least), and to strike. The West German example of "co-determination" (*Mitbestimmung*) in the workplace, with the equal representation of employees and shareholders on supervisory boards, and with formal discussions about everyday problems on works councils, is suspect in a country such as Britain with its tradition of confrontation between management and trade unions – but it is an example set by Europe's strongest economy applauded by many successful managers elsewhere.

So the EC has encouraged a new understanding of what the worker deserves, in contrast with the theory that labour is a mere "factor of production" to be employed for the shortest periods, at the lowest wages and in the meanest conditions that it will tolerate in order to survive.

Nothing less than a high estimate of human rights (reinforced by electoral considerations) lies behind the aim to make the Community as attractive to workers as it is to enterprising businessmen. And this aim has not merely produced idealistic talk about the "Social Market" philosophy in a "People's Europe". It has produced the Social Fund to help young people and others in job creation and in training for new jobs. Evolving from the social charter accepted by the Council of Europe in 1961, the EC's own Social Charter adopted in 1989 has set standards in employment which are bound to influence practices, whether or not they are embodied in legislation. The British government was in the position of being the one dissentient, although actually the agreed standards would be more of a challenge to the practices of the Community's newest and poorest members and of the nations moving into the Community's orbit and out of the Soviet Union's.

8. Consumers need to be protected from goods and labels which are dangerous or misleading, and are specially anxious that food should be safe. The environment needs to be protected from businessmen who might be happy to rape it. National governments have for many years intervened to offer such protection, but with varying thoroughness and success. Past complacency is indicated by the omission of the environment from the Treaty of Rome, which called for the "continuous and balanced expansion of economic activities". But the success of the EC, multiplying the volume and variety of goods including food on sale, greatly increasing both industrialization and traffic, generating about 2,000 million tonnes of waste a year, has extended the problems. Consequently there have been demands from 1972 onwards for energetic "action programmes" to protect the consumer and the environment.

That challenge to the EC has had an inescapable logic, in that pollution, like disease, does not respect frontiers. When criticized for being dirty, the Dutch used to reply that about three-quarters of their pollution began outside their territory. Europe's aerosols and refrigerators were destroying the ozone layer, and emissions from Europe's cars were helping to melt the Arctic. The fallout from the nuclear accident at Chernobyl, and acid rain from British power stations, blew across Europe, possibly to meet over the filth that flowed down the Rhine to join the sewage and toxic industrial waste in the North Sea. All Europe's visible heritage was in danger. The Black Forest was turning yellow, Venice was being destroyed by the adjacent industries, the cathedrals were crumbling, the Parthenon was being eaten by smog, the Mediterranean was being used as a cesspool and a dump for oil. And lead in petrol was damaging the nervous systems of Europe's children. Although he presided over many of the worst environmental disasters in Europe, Mikhail Gorbachev voiced a continent's concern when introducing his 1987 book, *Perestroika*: "We are all passengers aboard one ship, the Earth, and we must not allow it to be wrecked. There will be no second Noah's Ark."

Not nearly enough has been done (of course), but Environmental Impact Assessments were agreed in 1985 to be an essential part of many applications for planning permission for new developments. Much else has been achieved by the Community's co-ordination of national governments and by its own direct actions, so that the standards already achieved in the EC have been envied in Eastern Europe – where the motto "the polluter pays" has not been very useful, for the chief polluter has been the state itself, claiming that it cannot afford any alternative to the use of pollutants such as brown coal (lignite), the standard fuel in East Germany. Because they often profit handsomely by pleasing customers, producers of the EC can be made to stop displeasing nature. They can be subjected to strict regulations made by authorities who are not desperate to get economic growth at more or less any price. They can be fined for offences and they can be taxed for projects to restore the environment. And governments which are still complacent can be awakened by pressure from the EC. The British government at the end of the 1980s had to raise fresh capital for the water and electricity industries (and did so by privatization). One reason was that it had to respond to the EC's pressure for higher standards of cleanliness in the supply of water, and to protests by EC partners against the sulphur dioxide pouring out of Britain's power stations.

9. Left to itself, capital flows most easily into the regions where it is easiest to make a profit – the regions which have the advantages of geographical position, skilled labour, good communications and developed financial services. Just as market forces once favoured the industrialization of the North and Midlands of England because they were near coal and water, so the market forces of the new Europe create a golden triangle, Birmingham – Milan – Dortmund. That leaves out not only some areas where prosperity is no great problem (as in parts of Spain) but also underdeveloped rural areas and regions blighted by the decay of the old industries – the areas of mountain, scrub and rust. In a democracy such regions must be assisted if their inhabitants are to be at all happy about the market forces and at all able to take advantage of them. And that has developed as the policy of the EC, although it was not clearly stated in the Treaty of Rome. Progress from Rome had to include progress in Italy's deprived south, in the Mezzogiorno and Sicily – and it was not acceptable to say that the only realistic road was the road of the peasant becoming a factory worker in Milan or Turin.

Since 1958 the European Investment Bank has helped modernization in these regions. Grants from the EC's Regional Development Fund have been made since 1974, and since 1984 they have been given a high priority. These grants have never been adequate in relation to the needs. (The main reason why the British contribution to the EC's budget had to be renegotiated so painfully was that regional grants were much smaller than was hoped for at the time of entry.) It is also a fact that these grants have been used for national governments as reimbursement for their own grants, not for additional projects. But the policy is established and its direction has been stressed by the willingness of the EC to admit into membership relatively underdeveloped countries such as Ireland (1973), Greece (1981) and Spain and Portugal (1986). So far from excluding competition from producers with the advantages of low costs for wages in these countries, the Community funded an expensive new programme to help Mediterranean countries which had relied on the sale of olive oil, wine, fruits and vegetables to modernize their farms and to create many new jobs in industries and services. The EC has also accepted as a fact of life that Portugal and Greece would be the worst offenders in the practice of failing to pull down barriers to competitive trade despite agreement about the theory of the single market. Without its social, regional and Mediterranean policies the Community might have complacently reflected in its own membership the North/South, Rich/Poor division in the world. But as it is, the doubling of expenditure on these "structural funds" (agreed in 1988, to be achieved by 1993) was a great step forward in helping the poorer member states. In addition the EC appears to be ready to work and spend towards equalization with the ex-communist east – a Herculean task, too great for the Community alone (as was shown by the composition of the Development Bank in 1990) but too European to be refused. It is right to compare such programmes with the Marshall Aid poured into Western Europe by the USA to rescue war-ravaged nations in the 1940s.

10. The history of the EC has also proved some willingness to help the poorer peoples of the world by trade and aid. The Community had to take an attitude because it is the world's biggest trading bloc (now with double Japan's share of world trade). It has imported more from the rest of the world than it has exported, but on its own terms – for it has been a customs union, fixing all customs duties on all imports.

The Treaty of Rome decreed that no member state could import just what it liked. However, many exceptions to the agreed rules have been made in order to allow for "transition" while other countries found substitutes for their European markets. More systematically, in the 1950s France insisted that its ex-colonies should be allowed preferential trading terms. It wanted to maintain its own links in imports and exports for its own advantage, but to have abandoned these new, underdeveloped, nations would have meant denying the theory that as colonies they had virtually been departments of France. Other ex-colonial powers have also wanted ex-colonies to be favoured. The result has been the unlimited admission to the EC of almost all non-agricultural imports from African, Caribbean and Pacific countries numbering sixty-nine in 1990, with a fund to stabilize their export earnings in more than forty commodities. The Yaoundé Convention and four Lomé Conventions have been negotiated as parts of a large involvement with these privileged nations. In Asia, Latin America and North Africa food aid, technical assistance and investment loans have benefited other developing countries, whose exports to the EC have been exempted from customs duties within quotas. India has been included in this subsidiary arrangement.

The EC has not done nearly as much as it could have done to help the poor in other continents. Its help has by no means cancelled out the effects of two tendencies – "developed" nations are likely to buy manufactures from each other, and poorer nations which have commodities to sell are unlikely to achieve high and stable prices. On average, world commodity prices halved between the mid-1970s and the mid-1980s. In the 1980s the EC's trade with "developing" nations decreased, and Africa (in particular), because it could not earn its living, slithered deeper into poverty and debt. European banks were among those who demanded from developing nations interest sometimes five times larger than the original loan. But the Community has done something to establish dialogue and cooperation, in contrast with patronizing attitudes elsewhere. Governments of developing nations often complain that when they have to call in the International Monetary Fund and the World Bank they receive advice (amounting to conditions for any loans) which ignores non-economic factors. They are told to cut their budgets, raise interest rates, concentrate on exports and admit fewer imports – all policies which may be sensible in economics but which carry enormous human costs, particularly if imposed in a hurry. The EC has basically the same economic philosophy, but it does listen. It shows a degree of sensitivity when it calls its aid – as it names the dialogue between its own institutions – "co-operation". It gives almost all its aid as grants, not loans. It can fairly point out that the USA (for example) imposes duties on developing nations' exports, and has no international dialogues about trade which may be compared with argumentative negotiations and reviews surrounding successive Lomé Conventions. This matters because trade is three times more important than aid in supplying the foreign exchange which developing countries need vitally, and about two-thirds of their exports go to the industrial nations. And recently the average of aid given officially by member states of the EC year by year has been just above 0.50 per cent of the Gross National Product, as compared with the average for the USA of just under 0.25 (the UN target being 0.70). Aid given through the EC has recently been only one-fifth of the aid given by national governments but has amounted to some £1.5 billion a year, about the same as the aid budget of the British government. The renegotiation of the Lomé Convention in 1989 pledged aid of £8.5 billion over five years, an increase of about forty per cent.

11. A defence of the EC's Common Agricultural Policy can be offered – if the objections are considered first.

Some of the objections have come – very loudly – from the "Third" World whose human importance is better indicated if it is called the "Two-Thirds" World. Obviously the contrast between European worries about slimming and African worries about starving has been stark and deeply disturbing, but apart from emergencies which call for "food aid", the real problem has been the failure of comparatively rich nations such as those in the EC to enable and encourage Two-Thirds World farmers to grow more food and to develop the capacity of Two-Thirds World consumers to buy that food. The EC has contributed to the difficulties here. By guaranteeing prices above the world market levels to its own farmers up to high production levels the Community acquired the problems connected with storing and selling off the surpluses which the farmers eventually produced. Often these surpluses, particularly of dairy products and cereals, were used as gifts to poorer nations. Or they were sold at prices lower than the USA offered: between the EC and the USA, there was something like a trade war. This could damage the poorer nations' hopes of selling their own exports at good prices and could mean bad prices for their own farmers. As President Kaunda of Zambia observed in 1988, "food aid without assisting us to improve our production is fertilizer for a rich crop called hunger." Yet food aid has accounted for about a third of all spending on aid by the EC, and although it has met some genuine needs (most obviously in the gifts of grain in emergencies) it has done damage. Large surpluses of sugar beet (for example) have been accumulated and dumped on the world market at a time when the cane sugar producers of the Caribbean, Mauritius and Fiji desperately needed to sell in the European market. The damage done has not been put right by guaranteeing a market at EC prices for some sugar entering Europe. What is needed is a new agreement to set a world minimum price for all sugar. Poorer nations not favoured by the Lomé Conventions have also had many causes to complain. Cattle farmers in Latin America (for example) could sell beef at almost half the price guaranteed to the EC's producers but have been largely excluded from the European market, where until recently each cow in the farm was receiving each year a subsidy more than the average income of a farmer in the Two-Thirds

World (although only about half the subsidy enjoyed by a cow in the USA). The Lomé countries account for only twelve per cent of the population of the Two-Thirds World, since Latin America and Asia have been largely excluded.

The anger of the other continents has not been the only criticism of the Common Agricultural Policy. Within Europe there have been many protests against the damage to the environment. Pesticides have killed off more than pests, fertilizers have poisoned rivers with nitrates, the standardization of crops by agribusinesses has exhausted the soil, factory farming has been cruel to animals and fowls, the destruction of hedges and walls has been an ecological disaster. There have also been strong protests against the costs of maintaining stocks of surplus produce – the grain and sugar mountains, the milk and wine lakes – while the food in the shops cost more than world market prices. These complaints about the CAP have grown more bitter as the extent of fraud has been revealed. There have not been enough checks on claims that produce had been added to the surpluses or sold off outside the EC. Racketeers have acquired little mountains of the taxpayer's money. Apart from such fraud, the violence of farmers' opposition to proposals for reform (for example, the 1969 Mansholt proposals) left a bad impression.

But some other points about the CAP deserve attention. The EC is not isolated in wishing to protect and subsidize its farmers. The farmers of the USA, for example, have been subsidized more heavily, the farmers of Japan much more heavily. Within the EC, national governments have often given additional benefits to farmers even after the establishment of the CAP. It may seem more sensible to support the incomes of farmers, rather than guarantee the prices of their products (as was the policy of Britain before it joined the EC), but the common European expectation in the 1950s was that the price of food would be largely fixed by the government, and farmers thought it both more dignified and more secure to depend on this than to have to rely on social security. This attitude was influential partly because in the countries forming the EC the political parties of the Right and Left tended to be more or less evenly balanced in their appeal to the cities and towns: votes in the countryside could be decisive. But the rural constituencies of Europe had stronger arguments than that. To almost everyone it seemed obvious: the more food, the merrier. The world's population was known to be increasing: let Europe feed it. Within Europe memories of wartime shortages, and of the nearness of famine in the winters after the war, were still vivid. West Germany was worried about the disappearance of fertile agricultural regions, traditionally its breadbasket, behind the Iron Curtain. It was willing to pay high prices for food, including large imports from the USA. In fact the new Community was a net importer of food – and about a third of its population still lived on the land. As things turned out, the rundown of this agricultural workforce was to be orderly, thanks in large measure to the cushioning provided by the CAP. (In France, the rural population dropped without much pain from seventeen million in 1960 to eight million in 1980.) But the later enlargement of the Community to include Ireland, Denmark and Mediterranean countries revived the situation of dependence on agriculture. Finally it is fair to note that the surpluses produced by the CAP did not become a major problem before the 1980s. When the Treaty of Rome was signed there was general agreement about the aim "to increase agricultural productivity by promoting technical progress..." (Article 39), but the "green revolution", transforming the fields by mechanization, chemistry and improved seeds and genes, was not fully expected. Indeed, the financial decisions which were to support the surpluses generated by "technical progress" were not made before 1962-65.

These decisions could not be reversed until the Community had been changed; first by the accession of Britain which strenuously objected to subsidizing other countries' "inefficient" farmers, and then by the arrival of Mediterranean countries more interested in subsidies for their industrialization. But change has come. Painful reforms such as stricter quotas for milk production have been effected and (as I briefly discuss later) it has been possible to plan new ways of helping the EC's present rural community, where jobs in farming have been cut to about forty per cent of their number in 1960. It ought also to be possible to face the greater challenge of integrating the farms of the ex-communist east (in 1990 sometimes almost medieval in their methods) into Europe's agriculture.

12. Although many uncertainties still surround the project of monetary union in the EC, most experts seem agreed that it is both irreversible and, on the whole, desirable. Basically anyone who has had to change money – and to pay some of it to the changers – in order to visit another country, or do business in it, knows why.

Monetary union has been a very slow process and it seems ludicrous that the heads of government in 1972 declared their intention to "transform the whole complex of their relations into a European Union" by 1980. Every change in the EC tends to take longer than expected. But monetary union in Europe has been desirable ever since the collapse in 1971 of the Bretton Woods system which anchored the world's currencies to the US dollar, anchored in its turn to the gold stored in the USA. The fluctuating values of the currencies have made it harder for businessmen to strike international bargains. They have also annoyed tourists. National governments have tried to control the fluctuations but have often been defeated by the international character of modern capitalism. Immense sums of money can be transferred electronically across frontiers and around the world in order to make more money by the speculation that a particular currency is about to gain or lose in value. So governments have had to choose between possible policies. They could impose exchange controls which are a further hindrance to international trade. They could defend the currency against speculators by ordering the central bank (such as the Bank of England) to intervene and buy. But they could also club together so that many currencies support each other.

A wise preference for the third policy led to the experiment of the "snake" as a co-ordinator of currencies in 1972-4, and to the beginning of the European Monetary System in 1979. The EMS established a common "currency unit", the ecu, for optional use in international transactions, the value of the ecu depending on the value of an agreed combination of the national currencies. As a second stage in monetary union the EMS also established an exchange rate mechanism for these currencies. They were to be allowed to fluctuate in relation to each other by 2.25 per cent, but larger revaluations must be agreed by all the participating countries. In a further stage not yet reached as the 1990s begin, the currencies of these countries become totally convertible and capital can flow where it pleases, to be deposited in any bank or invested in any firm – but the currencies are locked together. The completion of these three stages in monetary union was proposed in the Delors Report of 1989. A single currency for the EC was not proposed but was the logical consequence. In a monetary union people and firms will wish to hold their assets in the strongest currency and to make their international dealings as simple as possible. No one national currency (not even the Deutschmark) would be strong enough to perform this role throughout the EC or would be politically acceptable in this role. If the ecu was readily available it would become popular because useful, although in order to preserve national traditions national terms like "pound", "mark" or "franc" could still be used as the fixed equivalent of so many ecus. The ecu as a mere basket of national currencies seems bound to yield to the ecu as Europe's money.

Obviously it is painful to national governments when they have to yield the ultimate control over their currencies to some international authority. It would be painful to the economically successful West German government, for example, as well as to the relatively unsuccessful British government. If the government controls the central bank which decides how much money to issue (in cash or credit), it can at least attempt to control the economy. In particular it can try to control the international value of the currency, for it can make the central bank buy or sell the currency massively. Life would therefore be more difficult for national governments if the control were to be vested in a European System of Central Banks run by a committee of central bank governors and other government nominees appointed for a fixed term. That was proposed in the Delors Report and it would be the Central Bank of Europe under a less alarming name. But for the peoples of Europe the pain may be less than it would for governments. Reviewing the first ten years of the European Monetary System, Michael Heseltine justly observed: "the fact is that the EMS has been more successful than could have been hoped or imagined in achieving its primary objective of exchange rate stability and sustaining confidence in the currency markets" (*The Challenge of Europe*, p. 72). Being largely outside this system, the pound fluctuated from a value of $2.45 in 1981 to $1.04 in 1985.

Under any system whereby politicians have to appeal to electors to re-elect them, a government is tempted to order its central bank to issue money, or to revalue the currency, in order to win an electoral advantage. And if the government yields to the temptation, the people will suffer. It is a tradition in British politics (for example) that both Conservative and Labour governments controlling the Bank of England are attracted by the idea of creating or promising a boom by cuts in taxes or increases in public expenditure with an eye on a general election. But they find that a boom which does not correspond with any increased production of goods produces inflation when those with something to sell raise their prices as too much money chases too few goods. Inflation causes or threatens unemployment. Then the temptation is to devalue the currency by a single decree or by merely allowing it to happen, so that the higher domestic prices do not price the country's exports out of foreign markets and so that it is more expensive in the domestic market to buy imports from foreign producers. Such has been the story of the weakening economy in the recent history of Britain – and the problems of Britain are not unique. (This was also the French experience in 1981–3.) Inflation has other causes but this one is not negligible.

A European currency would not be so exposed to the temptations of national politics, since European councils and officials are not in the same position of having to woo electorates. It seems probable that a Central Bank of Europe would be distanced from governments although its governing body would be appointed by them and ultimately accountable to the Council of Ministers and the Parliament. That is the character of the EC Commission at present. It is also the character of the Federal Reserve System in the USA, and in the post-war reconstruction of West Germany the Bundesbank was set up with a similar independence, helping to make it the most cautious, most successful and most important bank in Europe, constitutionally committed to an inflation rate as near zero as possible. And if the volume of imports is a problem, there would be less danger of damage to the currency – if the imports came from another nation in the EC with the same currency, but also if the imports came from outside the Community but the ecu still commanded confidence. If the problem is to be one of recession, it is hoped that more prosperous states in the EC would help by financing the EC's own budget which could relieve the troubled nation's budget through the Regional and Social Funds.

These matters are debated by expert economists and it is healthy for moralists to remember that for many years it appeared to be morally desirable to place central banks under political, and therefore "democratic", control. The dangers of government interference were not fully foreseen. It is also healthy to remember that there is a strong case for *some* "printing of money", meaning the creation of credit by central banks in advance of increases in production in order to stimulate the economy. But the bitter experience of "democratic" politics leading to inflation has advertised the benefits of a monetary discipline which comes more easily to bankers than to politicians. At the end of the day it is the duty of a government to govern, in a democracy when the electorate has spoken; and this includes governing the economy. It was significant that in 1990 the Bundesbank reluctantly accepted its government's policy for the conversion of East German marks into its own much stronger currency on terms which were extremely generous to salaries, wages, pensions and small savings (a one-for-one exchange), and in general risked inflation. But actual or proposed interventions by governments in the economy have often been foolish. One example was the West German Chancellor's strong hint that he would secure a one-for-one exchange rate for all East German marks, when he was successfully electioneering for the Christian Democrats in the east. Governments and central bankers need to have a relationship which illustrates the European principle that wisdom comes from dialogue.

3

The Wider Europe

The Community as a magnet

IT seems that the head of the European Union is slowly emerging out of the womb of economics. No one can foresee the mature shape of this unprecedented creature, but it is not too early to begin thinking. Nor is it premature to begin trying to imagine a European unity wider than the present membership of the EC.

Here again the problems are great. There are problems for the EC. Any widening of the membership will in due course encourage other countries to compete with the present twelve, either by better products or by lower wages – and the competition will not always be to the advantage of the existing members. It is a real question whether a Community with twenty members or more could retain its identity and cohesion. Equally real is the question whether the Community can afford to make all the necessary concessions, and to give all the necessary subsidies, in order to include nations to the east, the north and the south. It must be a temptation for the EC to postpone any "widening" well beyond 1993, which has been generally agreed as the earliest possible date. Yet ever since Greece became the first European "associate" member in 1962, and ever since France withdrew its veto on Britain's applications to join, one of the decisions of the EC has been not to be exclusive. That is in keeping with the Treaty of Rome, which called on other European peoples who shared the founders' ideals – yes, ideals – to join their tasks. And in the 1990s there are many nations actively interested in membership or in various kinds of "association".

Some nations of Europe have been – or have wanted to be – more or less cut off from the rest of the continent in recent times, although without creating any Iron Curtain between them and their neighbours. Switzerland has been famous for its mountainous aloofness from Europe's wars and recessions. It does not want more foreign workers or lorries and it insists that controversial legislation should be subject to a referendum in each canton. Three islands are distant from the mainland and may not even be reckoned as nations – Iceland, Malta, Cyprus. Norway is the one country where a referendum has reached a conclusion against joining the EC (in 1972), largely because the ocean which had been crossed by the Vikings had more recently promised independent wealth from oil. Sweden, once the ruler of an empire crossing the Baltic, then became the envy of the world for its combination of a booming economy with a comprehensive welfare state. To live in a neutral and prosperous peace has also been the recent ambition of Austria, which once had its own empire along the Danube. And Finland, like Austria, has barely escaped from being included in the Soviet empire, the price of independence being neutrality.

However, all these nations now depend on trade with countries in the EC. Two-thirds of Finland's exports go that way. Even Sweden has run into economic difficulties while on its own. Even the Swiss franc has had to be devalued in step with the mighty Deutschmark. Six of these nations belong to the European Free Trade Area which Britain founded in 1959 as a rival to the EC and then left. EFTA covers trade in industrial goods without tariffs – but nothing much else. So in 1989 Austria applied for full membership of the EC, with Soviet acquiescence – a sign that neutrality means much less now that the cold war is over. Other countries hitherto considered detached or neutral began elaborate negotiations to enter a very close but not complete relationship with the EC. The European Economic Space, linking them with the EC, will have its own institutions. Since the nations will have to agree to becoming a single market with the free movement of goods, services, people and capital to and from the EC, but will not have a full share in the EC's decision-making, it seems likely that they will in due course choose full membership – with the exception of Switzerland, an exception which may not be permanent. If these Europeans so choose, and are willing to pay the price, nations which have signed the Treaty of Rome cannot logically reject them. It is impossible to ignore the portents – "Scanlink" which joins Norway, Sweden and Denmark to the rest of Europe by high speed trains, or the great new tunnels which join south and north through the Swiss Alps.

Nor can the EC ignore the Turks. By the year 2000 there will be about a hundred million of them. For long their empire was one of the realities defining Europe, as the Soviet empire has stimulated the formation of the EC more recently. The Turks were at the gates of Vienna in 1683 and were compelled to grant independence to Bulgaria as recently as 1878. Today a small portion of Turkey still lies in Europe, and about two million Turks are "guest workers" in West Germany and other European countries; opportunities for trade grow; and many Turks are anxious to be modern, welcoming European goods and ideas, thinking of themselves as Europeans and certainly not as Arabs. Turkey therefore applied for full membership of the EC in 1987 as the fulfilment of its association since 1965. It was already a member of the Council of Europe. But here special problems make it probable that full membership will be delayed. By European standards Turkey is very poor (with income per head less than half that of the poorest EC country, Portugal) and EC countries who are themselves plagued by unemployment do not want more unskilled "guest workers". They are severely critical of the record of Turkish governments on human rights (specially the rights of prisoners and Kurds), and they sympathize with the Greek case against Turkish aggression. They are worried that many less Westernized Turks do not accept the pluralist democracy that is the culture of

Europe. But if these economic and political problems were ever to be solved, there would not be a widespread demand from Christians or others to keep the Turks out simply because those who are religious are Muslims. Neither Christianity nor European culture in general nowadays wishes to be intolerantly exclusive. The crusades are over. If at times it seems that Islamic fundamentalism is about to launch a counter-crusade against Europe and its pluralism, it must also appear attractive to contemplate detaching Turkey from the Middle East. And if Turkey becomes more European, what about Israel, Egypt, Tunisia, Algeria, Morocco...? Could these lands, already tied to Europe economically, also be tied to its faith in freedom and its child, pluralism?

The problems about relationships between the EC and the countries lying between West Germany and Turkey are such that they will probably take many years to resolve. The European Cultural Foundation's attempt to predict *Europe 2000* concluded in 1977 that "prospects for fundamental change in Eastern Europe appear almost non-existent" (p. 29). At the time, that was the conventional wisdom. In the event, however, Soviet military control of this region was to end well before 2000, and its end was to be the beginning of changes second to none in the shaping of the Europe of the third millenium.

The Eastern European countries were organized under the Soviet hegemony into an economic bloc co-ordinated by COMECON, recently known as the Council for Mutual Economic Assistance. Superficially it looked somewhat like the EC. In fact arguments were cut short by Soviet orders; currencies were not readily convertible; trade with the outside world earning hard currency was small compared with a system of barter within the CMEA area; within each state, a rigid Communist control of the economy was imposed; until about 1953 the confiscation of goods and equipment for transfer to the Soviet Union was considered payment for liberation by the Red Army. Although after that date the costs of the Soviet empire in

Eastern Europe were probably greater than its economic benefits (a familiar story in the history of imperialism), countries within the empire were also damaged (another familiar story). The basic damage was done by the isolation of this bloc from the competitive energy, the innovations and standards, of the advanced industrial nations. In the 1930s Czechoslovakia had a standard of living equal to France, and East Germany was not very much poorer, although it was less industrial, in comparison with West Germany. But all the Eastern European nations (with Hungary a partial exception) were dragged down by Communist commands. Technical and managerial developments in the West were ignored. Exports were directed to the Soviet Union, making up the increasing failures of that economy. In exchange oil, gas, coal and raw materials arrived because at the time these could be spared – but they fed industries which, on the whole, paid low wages and produced second-rate goods with a great deal of polluting filth. Farmers lacked incentives to grow for the market although their commanded production for the state inflicted environmental damage through the careless use of fertilizers and pesticides. Thus Communist rule piled up effects which were to prove disastrous for its credibility in the 1980s. It could not pay or feed the people.

During the years of military and economic division an Iron Curtain of ideology also cut the continent in two. To the East the virtues of "Socialism" were incessantly extolled, and many people consoled themselves for the economic inefficiency of Communism, and for the lying, the spying and the brutal harshness of the Communist police state, with the sincere belief that it was morally superior to the "elbow society" of capitalism in the West. Even during and after the revolutions of 1989 the future was widely seen as a development within "Socialism". What finally moved the peoples in all the revolutions of 1989 which had their climax when the Berlin Wall was dismantled was not only economic discontent or misery. It was a hunger for freedom and a disgust at the cruel tyranny and personal corruption of many in the old leadership. It was often hoped that the "Socialism" which such leaders had betrayed might at last be given "a human face" and an honest one. Yet as the 1990s begin the rejection of political parties labelled Socialist in East Germany's and Hungary's first free elections has marked the end of an era. It seems probable that the European Community's understanding of freedom as involving the freedom to innovate, to risk and to compete economically will appeal to the peoples in the east as the results of this understanding of freedom become known and become thought to be attainable. Peoples hungry for the fruits of economic freedom will want an economic revolution to follow the political one. It remains to be seen what of "Socialism" will survive now that the Berlin Wall has been sold off as souvenirs and the Soviet Union offers no clear alternative to poverty and chaos.

The experience of the Soviet Union in the 1980s showed that *perestroika* (restructuring) does not mean prosperity while it keeps almost all of the economy under the daily control of the bureaucracy. *Perestroika* does not work if in order to conserve Socialism it denies the peasants the right to own their land, makes it very difficult for businessmen to obtain permissions and finances and limits co-operatives to small enterprises. Such a severely limited recognition of a free market does not give the official market its opportunity to increase production and to lower prices through vigorous competition. What happens instead is inflation as a few more goods, often of better quality, come on the market, and purchasers, many with accumulated cash, compete for the privilege of buying. Then farmers who sell daily necessities through the private markets, and even the officially recognized co-operatives, become branded by public opinion as profiteers. In the Soviet Union at the end of the 1980s a frightened leadership announced a return to the "administrative command" system of running the economy. But a few months later further steps towards a market economy were authorized and the expansion of Gorbachev's presidential power meant the expansion of these steps. Such steps were being taken more rapidly in the ex-communist countries of Eastern Europe, because there the example and influence of the EC were greater, and it could be acknowledged more candidly that *perestroika* leads either to an EC-type market or to a mess (although in Romania and Bulgaria "Socialism" is more conservative).

On its side the early response of the EC to the new Eastern Europe has been nervously positive. The EC has already welcomed poorer Mediterranean countries into membership. Enormous problems were presented and enormous grants had to be promised to modernize those economies. But the decision was made – because these countries were already fellow Europeans and because they were, actually or potentially, trading partners. Greater problems have arisen in relation to Eastern Europe (not least because the Mediterranean countries see attention switching from their needs), but again the attitudes dominant in the EC have been encouraging. In 1989 food aid, technical assistance and development loans began to pour across the demolished Iron Curtain, much of it co-ordinated by the EC. A factor in this response was a feeling for the spiritual and cultural unity of Europe. Deep runs the emotion that Europe is Europe and ought not to be subjected to what Marx categorized as Oriental Despotism. This European solidarity surfaced when, in almost his last spasm of madness, Romania's Communist tyrant had ordered the destruction of many of the villages. The Europe-wide protest, which was broadcast into Romania, was started by young people in Belgium. After that tyrant's fall another shock was recorded throughout Europe when the plight of Romania's orphans was made known. But irreversible economic pressures are likely to help the growth of the wider unity in Europe, as they have helped the development of the EC in the west. The attraction of the EC's economic success is the latest proof of the wisdom of Marx's observation that social realities reflect economic realities.

West Germany has become more impressive than the Soviet Union and is now poised to throw its energies into the huge potential market which exists in the east for its goods and services. From the Middle Ages to the end of Hitler's Third Reich *Mitteleuropa* was the German sphere of influence and rewards will be much greater in the twenty-first century if Eastern Europe can develop modern appetites and modern purchasing power. France also has traditional links with Russia and the Balkans. Other nations begin to see the possibilities of trade. The investors and the salesmen of the EC are beginning to swarm over Eastern Europe. With them go the ideas.

1689 – 1789 – 1989

If we ask what has been the movement of the European spirit amid all these changes, one answer may be put briefly like this: there has been a movement into freedom, the freedom of the people which Christians along with others have learned to accept and demand.

In 1689 John Locke published the first of his *Letters on Toleration*. This English philosopher had been greatly influenced by his time in the Netherlands, then unique in Europe for its religious tolerance. What Locke advocated, in these letters or in other writings, was limited. Although he did not want anyone to be persecuted, he could not see how any atheist, not believing in eternal rewards and punishments for morality and immorality, could be a good citizen; and he could not think it possible for a Roman Catholic to be a loyal subject. But within these considerable limits, he urged an explicit policy of religious toleration, basing himself firmly on his own belief in the "reasonableness" of Christianity. This was a daring novelty (and to safeguard himself Locke wrote at first in Latin and anonymously). For many centuries almost all governments had felt themselves obliged to defend and spread the local religious faith. They still did; in 1685 Louis XIV had revoked the limited toleration of Protestants granted by the Edict of Nantes. But Locke argued that governments ought to confine their energies to securing lives, liberty, health and possessions, leaving the salvation of souls to religious bodies whose only sanction should be excommunication. That novel argument prevailed in England, where the persecution of non-Anglican Protestants ceased. It justified the "Glorious" Revolution which drove out James II, asserting that a Parliament was entitled to dethrone a king thought likely to imitate Louis XIV. And in other countries, some took note. A slow movement to toleration began. Among Protestants, it was not complete until Finland's decision in 1923. Disabilities for Protestants in Catholic and Orthodox lands continued even then. But the reasoned advocacy of religious toleration in 1689 was a landmark on Europe's road to freedom.

The French Revolution of 1789 set in motion processes which have been of central importance in the creation of a modern and united Europe. The key idea went beyond Locke's plea for toleration. It was the idea of the will of the people, expressed through elected representatives and tending towards equality. That very revolutionary idea has prevailed over the strong and long tradition that a country ought to be run by a governing class and largely for the benefit of that class. The idea of the liberty of the people – "the rights of Man and the citizen" – has prevailed over the traditions of religious persecution, intellectual censorship, arbitrary arrests and inequality before the law. Eventually it has been seen to involve human rights for women as well as men and for foreigners as well as citizens. The idea of the unity or "fraternity" of the people, expressed in a common language and a common taxation, has prevailed over the stranglehold of feudal obligations and local traditions. Devices such as the metric system have been adopted for the sake of economic rationality.

For many years such ideas seemed to have been ruined by the French Revolution's lapse into violence, terror and deeper poverty, so that order had to be restored and the army which the revolution had created was used by Napoleon. Looking back in exile, that emperor liked to picture himself as a good, indeed entirely benevolent, European – almost as if he would have been in his element as President of the Commission in Brussels. But in reality his was a French empire depending on force, and other nationalisms (Germany's, for example) arose in response to it. Later in the nineteenth century other reactions crushed anything that looked like a revolution.

All over Europe the hierarchy of the Roman Catholic Church put itself at the head of these reactions. The most eloquent of all the statements of reaction was, however, written by a member of the Church of England, Edmund Burke, the author of *Reflections on the Revolution in France* (1790). His book has remained a classic of conservatism and we may pause for a moment to look at it.

Two centuries after it was written, it seems a classic of complacency, defending a social order which meant unfreedom and poverty for the many. Burke loved a "manly, moral, regulated liberty" and proved it by defending Americans, Indians and Irish under English rule. He was willing to see some changes, since "a state without the means of some change is without the means of its conservation". He wisely perceived the dangers in the French Revolution, "the most astonishing thing that has hitherto happened in the world". But he failed to understand the forces which have made so many Europeans think that 1789 and later revolutions have made progress. To him, "a spirit of innovation is generally the result of a selfish temper and confined views". In the French Revolution it had produced the idea of equality, "that monstrous fiction which, by inspiring false ideas and vain expectations into men destined to travel in the obscure walk of a laborious life, serves only to aggravate and embitter that real inequality, which it never can remove". Against that idea of equality he defended government by hereditary monarchs; without that, "the glory of Europe is extinguished for ever". Monarchy should be tempered by institutions such as the unreformed House of Commons, voted for by a narrow and corrupt electorate but, Burke claimed, "filled with every thing illustrious in rank, in descent, in hereditary and in acquired opulence, in military, civil, naval and politic distinction, that the country can afford". That, he reckoned, was infinitely better than rule by men of "a sordid mercenary occupation" inspired by "short-sighted coxcombs of philosophy" unable to see that "the will of the many, and their interest, must very often differ". He was sure that there must be imposed on the people "a sufficient restraint upon their passions". In England at that time, that meant savage punishments for anything that could be called theft or riot. "A perfect democracy", he declared, "is the most shameful thing in the world." "Nothing is more certain", he proclaimed, "than that our manners, our civilization and all the good things that are connected with manners, and with civilization, have, in this European world of ours, depended for ages upon two principles – and were indeed the result of both combined; I mean, the spirit of a gentleman and the spirit of religion."

Burke's reflections on 1789 deserve to be recalled because so many Europeans, including Christians, have in part shared his own conviction that they are Christian thoughts. Voters who consulted their clergy have been likely to vote conservatively. But in the history of Western Europe the defeat of government by hereditary monarchs and a richly privileged ruling class has been overwhelming. It has been a moral defeat, a defeat by the conscience of Europe. The dangers in the revolutions have been answered not by less, but by more, democracy. And Christians have slowly seen that the defence of religion need not mean the defence of privilege.

In 1989 the best ideas of 1789 triumphed in Eastern Europe: President Mitterand was right when he said that. But first it had been necessary for the peoples (including the churches) of Eastern Europe to go through the purging fires of great suffering. The powers of emperors, monarchs, dictators, landlords and capitalists had been broken – only to be replaced by the regimes installed by Stalin and his heirs. The wars were over – only to be followed by a cold war. For long there appeared to be some reality in Brezhnev's rhetoric of "democratic centralism, Socialist internationalism and mutual assistance" – the rhetoric which sent Soviet tanks into the demonstrations for freedom. But at last in the 1980s the actual peoples effectively defied the regimes in so-called "People's Democracies", as anger replaced fear. When Gorbachev by his *glasnost* and *perestroika* began to transform the Soviet Union from 1985 onwards, and when he allowed Eastern European and Soviet peoples to force the Communist Party out of its monopoly of power, Europe seemed to be becoming a "common home" where the best ideas of 1789 were at home in every room and even in Europe's pulpits.

Addressing the Parliamentary Assembly of the Council of Europe in 1989, Gorbachev preached these ideas. He declared that

> The Europeans have a truly unique chance to play a role in building a new world, one that would be worthy of their past, of their economic and spiritual potential.... The Europeans can meet the challenges of the coming century only by pooling their efforts. We are convinced that what they need is one Europe – peaceful and democratic, a Europe that maintains all its diversity and common humanistic ideals, a prosperous Europe that extends its hand to the rest of the

world, a Europe that confidently advances into the future. It is in such a Europe that we visualize our own future. *Perestroika*, which seeks to renew Soviet society radically, determines our policy aimed at the development of Europe precisely in that direction. We are firmly and irreversibly embarked on that road. You and your governments, your parliaments and peoples will soon be dealing with a totally different Socialist nation than has been the case before. And this will have, and cannot but have, a favourable impact on the entire world process.

Christians learned to see good as the outcome of these revolutions and to support the spread of their best ideas. In the early years many of them were dismayed by the rapidity and cruelty of the changes, mourning the end of churches' old privileges and sentimentalizing about the death of the old order in society. But before the second millenium of their history ended most Christians in Europe could see that it had been wise – or that it would have been wise – to support the humanitarianism of the revolutions while protesting against the frequent inhumanity of the regimes which claimed a "revolutionary legitimacy". Christians could think that in the revolutions God had moved his "left hand" (a Lutheran phrase), inspiring people who often did not acknowledge him to execute his judgement on an *ancien régime* which, like the monarchies of Ancient Israel and Judah, had ceased to serve his purpose.

In Western Europe the change most obviously necessary in the twentieth century was that Roman Catholics should no longer feel obliged to support, or yearn for, an authoritarian regime of the Right which denied many freedoms to the people but won the Church's favour by large subsidies, by imposing the Church's teaching about personal morality on the public by force of law, and by making the nation's schools provide a religious education approved by the clergy. Laws enforcing the Church's teaching have not been repealed everywhere: in 1973 the Irish Parliament rejected a proposal to allow the sale of contraceptives to married couples, and in 1986 a referendum decided against legalizing divorce. But step by step Roman Catholics have found a new role for themselves – a role of service and of spiritual influence within the freedom and pluralism of a genuine democracy.

The bishops assembled in the Second Vatican Council in the 1960s blessed the idea of religious freedom which a Pope had cursed in the 1860s. "In matters religious", said the bishops, "no one is to be forced to act in a manner contrary to his own beliefs." John XXIII's *Pacem in Terris* (1963) announced that even Marxism in practice (not in theory) contained elements which were "good and worthy of approval". However, developments in particular nations have often depended on the laity being more ready than the bishops for the Church to be moved out of its privileged position. In the 1930s the movement known as Catholic Action was explicitly designed to offer lay support to the bishops, often in defence of the Church's privileges. Thirty years later the movement had become, or was becoming, a definitely lay movement with a commitment to democracy and often with a willingness to collaborate with Socialists and even Communists. Many public opinion polls showed a new strength of feeling that bishops ought not to presume to tell electors how to vote. For their own electoral credibility the new Christian Democratic parties had to show that, unlike the Catholic parties of previous years, they were not controlled by the bishops. The motto of Catholic Action, "see, judge, act", produced insights, judgements and actions which placed many political activists whose religion was Catholic on the Left of the hierarchy and of the bulk of the non-political faithful, but the conservative reaction among Catholics was remarkably mild. The Italian movement *Communione e Liberazione* could be criticized as too conservative, but its main emphasis was spiritual not political. Its very title showed that it lived in the climate created by the Second Vatican Council. And the influx of Catholic people and values into the Left also had an effect on the Left. It greatly strengthened the electoral appeal of Socialism in Spain, for example, or France. It greatly helped the redefinition of Socialism as social justice not necessarily involving the ownership of most of the economy by the state. In this way, which the bishops who had served in Pius XII's crusade against Communism had never intended, Catholicism prevailed over Marxism.

In France the situation inherited by the 1990s was in almost complete contrast with the relationship between the Church and the Republic before the 1890s. Now there was no Catholic party; there was little memory of the reactionary political Catholicism of the Action Française movement which had been condemned by Pius XI in 1926; movements such as *Jeunesse Agricole Chrétienne* or *Jeunesse Ouvrière Catholique* had much in common with the remaining Communists. In Spain the church leadership, which had secured immense privileges in the 1953 concordat with the Franco regime, distanced itself from the ageing dictator and watched many church-related organizations becoming centres of opposition, working-class, intellectual or regionalist, to the extent that by 1968 Catholic Action as a movement controlled by the bishops had disintegrated, and it proved impossible to organize a large Christian Democratic party. Although the *Opus Dei* movement, which was remarkably conservative amid the new Catholicism, originated in Spain, on the whole the Church accepted both its reduced position under the 1978 consitution and the withdrawal of state subsidies, to be complete by 1991. Similar abolitions of old privileges were accepted in Italy under the new concordat between Church and State in 1984. Most of the Italian bishops, led by the Vatican, tried to resist the subsequent legalization of contraceptives, divorce and abortion. It is to their credit that they fought harder in these moral issues than in the defence of their financial or educational privileges. But in the 1974 referendum on divorce, only forty-one per cent of Italians voted as the bishops wished, and in the 1981 referendum on abortion only thirty-two per cent.

One cause of these revolutionary changes was secularization. By the 1990s only about a quarter of the Italians attended Mass every week; in the early 1950s two-thirds had been regular. The figures for Spain have been roughly similar. But another cause was a growing acceptance of a pluralist democracy among the actively faithful, specially among those who were also active in politics. Introducing a collection of studies of *Religion in West European Politics* in 1982, the American sociologist Suzanne Berger observed:

> The religiously observant populations of Western Europe have been among the staunchest supporters of right-wing politics. There have been exceptions to this alliance of religion with the defenders of the *status quo*, or of reaction, and some of the deviant cases have been very important: French Protestant support of the Republic; radical millennarian movements in Italy; Catholic support for Irish nationalism; and so forth. But the dominant pattern has been of a tight association between religion and the Right.... The essays in this volume tell a common story: that those old and close ties between religion and conservatism are unravelling and that possibilities for new politics are beginning to unfold.

Since 1982 this tendency has gathered momentum, particularly as the contrast has grown between this Christian support of pluralism and the totalitarian denial of freedom in Islamic fundamentalism.

And nowhere was the shift in Christian opinion more dramatic than in Eastern Europe, where the churches were transformed within the lifetime of the cardinal aged ninety who was still in office when democracy triumphed in Prague. Before 1945 they had, on the whole, supported the pre-Communist regimes of the Right verging into Fascism (Czechoslovakia being unusual in its passion for democracy). Now they faced cruel questions of conscience. Were they to cling to the past or to send their hearts to the other side of the Iron Curtain, even while dragging out their lives as the "Church of Silence" under Communism? Or were they to be "Christians within Socialism"? If so, what degree of co-operation with the new regimes did that entail? Was it to extend to the sycophancy of the Orthodox bishops of Romania? It was easy to make mistakes in this wilderness of temptation and mistakes were made. But at the end of the 1980s the Christians emerged using for the most part language of human rights and pluralist democracy. On the lips of Christians such language, which had been used in the west against regimes more or less Fascist, from Mussolini through Hitler to Franco, now helped to bring down tyrannies of the Left. And Christians who had lived under Marxism while scarcely daring to hope for any alternative had been able to draw on the experience of Christians who had resisted Nazism. In the wilderness they had found food.

Let Europe arise!

"Let Europe arise!" cried Churchill in Zürich in 1946. He even looked forward to "a kind of United States of Europe". The speech has often been regarded as an example of an old cigar-smoker's rhetoric, somewhat like the vague proposal by the French politician Aristide Briand in 1929–30 to which it referred – for Churchill did not propose that the British empire should arise and join. When he recovered political power in 1951, he remained aloof. Ernest Bevin, Labour's great Foreign Secretary, has been ridiculed for telling the House of Commons in 1948 that "the conception of the unity of Europe and the preservation of Europe at the heart of Western civilization" had been "accepted by most people" – for Bevin, too, held aloof from the communities in which other Western European states expressed their unity. It was one of the greatest mistakes in British history, for Britain missed the chance of leading Europe, probably for ever. But Churchill and Bevin spoke more wisely than they acted. Since the 1940s Europe has indeed arisen. It seems that most people have accepted that Britain and Denmark, for all their reluctance, will have no future outside it. Ten other nations already in the Community positively welcome the process of an "ever closer union". At least a dozen other nations seem likely to be very closely associated with it or to end up as members.

The slow birth of this new Europe has made most of the thinking of the Christian centuries about "Church and society" outdated. A new age demands new thought – as it did when St Paul led Christianity into the Gentile world, or when the Church first had an emperor as its patron, or when St Augustine looked beyond the fall of the Roman empire, or when Eastern Orthodoxy had to come to terms with the fact that there was no emperor in Constantinople, or when cathedrals of stones and cathedrals of ideas could be built after the Dark Ages, or when a host of powerful minds asked what should come after the Middle Ages, or when Christians were excited by the "new order of the ages" as the British empire ended in America, or when other Christians saw that the end of all the European empires left them with roots in all six continents and with a mission to them all. What, then, is to be the Christian significance of the new Europe?

A preliminary clue to an answer may be found in the poems which are collected in the Hebrew Scriptures in the middle of the book of Isaiah (chapters 40–55). More than five hundred years before Christ, a prophet hailed Cyrus King of the Persians as a liberator, as God's "anointed" (in Hebrew *messiah*). To compare Cyrus with Mikhail Gorbachev is not completely ridiculous, for Gorbachev has enabled peoples to go their own ways and the Persian empire which conquered Babylon was the first empire in history to have a deliberate policy of respect for the identities of the peoples within it. This Jewish prophet looked back over the great suffering of his people in defeat and exile, before Cyrus had been raised by God; and he composed songs which Christians have used about the suffering of Christ. To apply these sacred songs to the suffering of Jews and others under Nazism or to the suffering of Christians and others under Communism need not be blasphemous. But the prophet celebrated the patient faithfulness of God who had mysteriously supported people "despised and rejected" – people who had despised and rejected themselves. The power of God, the Creator and the Saviour, had been found amid that degradation. To say that this has also been the experience of modern Europeans is not unrealistic. Many Europeans have found God as a light shining when all other lights had gone out. The prophet who brought good news to the exiles in the time of Cyrus announced that God had poured out justice, righteousness, peace and prosperity on his suffering people, and to hold the ancient Bible alongside Europe's newspapers with their good news will not seem silly unless it is believed that the Creator stopped acting when men stopped writing the Bible. Often in 1989, therefore, the most profound commentary on the news came from the "word of the Lord" in Isaiah 43:18–19:

> Cease to dwell on days gone by
> and to brood over past history.
> Here and now I will do a new thing;
> this moment it will break from the bud.
> Can you not perceive it?

4

The Christian Contributions

The values of a society

AS I repeat that question about what Christians could think and do, I am aware that I have not yet shown that it is relevant to the decisive realities of Europe. Everyone knows that Christians matter in the dramas of Latin America, for example, or South Africa. But do they matter in Europe? Christianity is no longer Europe's only faith. If Christian Europe once defined itself as Christendom against Islam, European Christianity now has to remember that there are millions (probably three) of Muslims in France and that about three per cent of the populations of Britain and West Germany is Muslim. And as everyone knows, Christian faith has been challenged in Europe's modern history by a biting scepticism, and more recently rivalled by two value-systems as all-embracing as Islam – Communism as a version of Socialism and consumerism as a version of capitalism. But if we compare Christianity, Islam, scepticism, Communism and consumerism, we see that the new Europe will witness a competition more momentous than any rivalry in the market place. If Islam is ruled out as being "foreign" in a profound sense, the competition will not be over. One of the other four rivals will provide the main value-system in the new Europe that is being born. And "Which one?" is now Europe's most important question.

The rivalry between these value-systems has this importance because as Europe becomes more and more united economically it becomes ever clearer that it will be a single market for ideas. Europe will be pluralist, particularly if – as is to be hoped

– the nations of the EC enter into a close relationship with the Socialist nations of Eastern Europe. The freedom of individuals, of groups and of peoples must be respected if Europe is to become European and that must mean "pluralism" if that now fashionable word means freedom under laws which interfere as little as possible with freedom. But it is impossible to build a society on a foundation of a "pluralism" amounting to anarchy, whether physical or psychological. That becomes obvious once one considers Europe's main competitors. None of them is a spiritual vacuum. Islam takes a pride in being the opposite, and even if the tide of fundamentalism is rolled back in the next few centuries there is not going to be anarchy. Since 1917 the Soviet Union has developed a very strong character of its own as a result of the dominance exercised over more than a hundred nationalities and fifteen republics by the Communist Party, which in 1990 has nineteen million full members, and by the Russian Republic which stretches from Leningrad to Vladivostock. It seems unlikely that this character will be totally obliterated by the new thinking of *perestroika*, or by ethnic pressures against the discredited centre, although Soviet society is bound to be changed in many ways. The USA also has its identity. The sacredness of its flag would be sufficient proof if proof were needed. Its great diversity from Maine to New Mexico is subordinated to the "American way of life" through the schools, the TV and the standardization of so much in commerce. Despite the well known problems, the Blacks and the Hispanics now seem to be joining earlier immigrants in the jump (or jog) into the melting pot. Japan has perhaps the strongest national character in the world, admitting foreign influences only on its terms and putting the psychology of its people into its all-conquering exports. If India or China ever becomes an economic competitor for Europe, the world will know who is competing. Surrounded by such rivals, Europe cannot be the only society in the world to have no character except a "pluralism" meaning that it has indeed no character.

Religion is easily corrupted when its spokesmen and officers deny pluralism and control a community. The love of God then often takes second place to the love of privilege, and the love of neighbour is twisted into a "loving" determination to make the neighbour conform to orthodoxy. For such reasons many Christians are glad that in the emerging Europe the Christian churches seem likely to remain minorities (if frequent attendance at church is counted) and to be subject to many criticisms. It is easier to keep clean in hot water and it is easier to be truly Christian amid pluralism. But religion can contribute powerfully to the values, and therefore to the character, of a community, which is wider than the religious institutions. The founders and great teachers of religion have claimed to be speaking the truth about reality. They have spoken in pictures, paradoxes, epigrams, myths and rituals, but always they have sought to point to what is really there, not to be suggesting some game of make-believe. And whole societies and civilizations have arisen out of religious teachings, like harvests after the planting of hidden seeds. Christianity is no exception to the general rule that religions create history.

Christianity's construction of Europe

The story of Christianity in the old Europe was assessed by J.M. Roberts in his *Pelican History of Europe* (1988, p. 255). He wrote that this religion

> grew up within the classical world of the Roman empire, fusing itself in the end with its institutions and spreading

through its social and mental structures to become our most important legacy from that civilization. Often disguised or muted, its influence runs through all the great creative processes of the last fifteen hundred years; almost incidentally, it defined Europe. We are what we are because a handful of Jews saw their teacher and leader crucified and believed that he rose again from the dead.

Long before the faith of the Christians became influential or even respectable, what they could contribute to Europe could be glimpsed. In the second century AD the anonymous author of the *Epistle to Diognetus* claimed that they were to the world as the soul is to the body.

> They dwell in their own fatherlands as if sojourners in them, they share all things as citizens and suffer all things as strangers. Every foreign country is their fatherland, and every fatherland is a foreign country.... They love all men and are persecuted by all men. They obey the appointed laws, and they surpass the laws in their own lives. They are unknown and they are condemned. They are put to death and they gain life.

Christians in Britain have good reason to remember that this is the story of the conversion of the Irish and Scots by missions which began in the survival of the Roman empire's Christianity in Wales. It is the story of the conversion of Anglo-Saxon England, influenced by the Christian civilization of the Franks and leading to the conversion of the Vikings. It is the story of the conversion of the German and Scandinavian lands (with some English missionaries such as St Boniface of Crediton, the apostle to Germany). It is the earlier story of the conversion of the emperor Constantine, baptized just before his death in 337. He was the founder of Constantinople (Byzantium), the New Rome where the sunshine fell on the marble and the mosaics of the great churches; and from Gibraltar to the Danube,

Romanized peoples were drawn into this story. It is the story that followed the baptisms of Clovis King of the Franks in 496, and of Vladimir King of "Rus" and Mieszko King of Poland some five hundred years later. It is the story of Catholic Spain after the conversion of the Visigoths in 589. It is the story of the Christian cultures of the Slavonic and Magyar peoples, begun by Cyril, Methodius and Stephen. It is the story of the Orthodox Empire of Byzantium over eleven centuries, and of the Holy Roman Empire which lasted (at least in outward appearances) until 1806 and was inaugurated by the coronation of Charlemagne in Rome on Christmas Day 800. And very often it is an international story: one of Charlemagne's chief agents was an English monk, Alcuin of York.

By the end of the fourteenth century all of Europe had been converted, at least superficially, to the Christian faith, the last country to join that religious community being Lithuania. Indeed, the usual word for the continent became "Christendom" or its equivalent in non-English languages; Europe was the place where Christ reigned. The unity of Christian Europe was never complete. The schism between Western and Eastern Christians, looking to Rome or Byzantium, became final in 1054; within Western Christendom there was no single political authority; not even the religion of the West was uniform and for a time there were two or three Popes. But in the Middle Ages what united European Christians was far more significant than what divided them – and for most of them, this was expressed in a common spiritual allegiance to the Pope, in a common participation in the Catholic form of the Church, and in a common use of the Latin language by educated men. When "European" was used, it was often in connection with the fact that Islam had overrun many of the lands where Christianity had been established, from the Holy Land and the Bible's seven cities of Asia to Spain. The first use of *Europeenses* as an adjective in Latin has been traced to a reference by a Spanish monk describing the army which defeated the Muslims at the battle of

Tours in 732. The first major enterprise by a European community was the first Crusade, launched by Pope Urban II in 1095. He put emotional power into the geographers' division of the world into Asia, Africa and Europe, for the enemies of the cross had overrun Asia and Africa and "there remains Europe, the third continent" (as he was reported to have said). Another Pope, Pius II, seems to have invented the word *Europaei* to refer to those who dwelt in the *Respublica Christiana*. He had travelled widely over the continent and he, too, concentrated his thoughts on a crusade as a counter-attack against Islam before his disappointed death in 1464.

After the ending of the Middle Ages in 1450–1550, when Constantinople had fallen to the Turks and Rome had been rejected by the Protestants, "Christendom" was less of a reality and less of a word. Christians now preferred to speak of "Europe". Various hopes of uniting Europe followed – the hopes of the Habsburg, Bourbon and Napoleonic dynasties, of the "enlightened" in the eighteenth century, of the royal and reactionary Holy Alliance after 1815, of liberals rebelling in 1848, of Free Traders or Socialists. But these hopes that Europe might recover its unity never possessed the substance that had been given to Christendom by Christianity.

The story of Christian influence in a less Christian and less unified Europe has continued. The peoples of "early modern" and of modern Europe would have been very different had they not been deeply influenced by the religion that inspired El Greco and Rembrandt, Palestrina and Bach, Cervantes and Shakespeare, Milton and Handel, Pascal and Kierkegaard, Dostoevsky and Tolstoy, Florence Nightingale and Mother Teresa, Bonhoeffer and Hammarskjöld. But instead of embarking on that story, it may be more relevant to observe that in times when church attendance has fallen because it is no longer compulsory or fashionable, religion in the shape of "Christian values" has continued to mould Europe.

In the background of the Treaty of Rome of 1957 stood three

godfathers, all strong Christians (and Roman Catholics): Robert Schuman, Foreign or Prime Minister of France 1948-52, Alcide de Gasperi, Prime Minister of Italy 1945-59, and Konrad Adenauer, Chancellor of West Germany 1949-63. They all had a passionate sense of Europe's unity, partly because they all came from Europe's disputed frontier regions - Schuman from Lorraine, de Gasperi from the Tyrol, Adenauer from the Rhineland. But they were also tough and determined politicians. They had collaborated in the European Coal and Steel Community from 1952. The coals of fire which warmed their commitment to the reconstruction of Europe in unity had been left in their hearts by the experience of the defence of "Christian civilization" or "Christian principles" or "Christian values" against Nazi, Fascist or Communist evils. The pre-war Right had been discredited by Hitlerism, the pre-war Left by Stalinism. The steel which sustained their backbones when their pioneering project seemed impossible was the strong political grouping which in Italy and West Germany was called the Christian Democratic Party. Of course the popularity of that party should not be exaggerated: in Italy the anticlerical backlash against the Catholic Church has remained strong, and in West Germany coalition governments have been the norm. Nor should the party's cohesion be exaggerated: in West Germany it has been more conservative than in Italy, although not so conservative as its usual partner in coalitions, the Christian Social Union of Bavaria. It has always been easier to say what Christian Democracy has been against than to say what it has been for in politics (and Italian cynics add that it is only for power). In France these factors have meant that the *Mouvement Republican Populaire* (Robert Schuman's party) soon got lost in the maze of politics. But the Christian Democrats did play an indispensable role in the post-war reconstruction of Western Europe. They have created Europe's most successful economy; they have written the constitutions of West Germany and Italy, with Constitutional Courts to uphold the citizens' rights; they have always backed the federal idea of a European Union; and they remained the largest group in the European Parliament until the Socialists took over in 1975. The word "Christian" in their title has most obviously meant "attempting to reconcile".

The social and political influence of Christians has remained substantial in Europe. It could be illustrated by naming many successors to the EC's godfathers in the leadership of the Community. The argument about the future of the EC at the end of the 1980s was led by Margaret Thatcher and Jacques Delors. Neither the British Prime Minister nor the French President of the Commission is a Christian Democrat, but the Conservative and the Socialist, the Protestant and the Catholic, are both definite Christians, willing on occasion to show how religion and politics are connected in the background to a controversial policy. What that shows is not that either politician has got the mixture of religion and politics infallibly right, but that religion can still inspire politics.

This Christian influence in the shaping of society has been surprisingly and movingly strong in Eastern Europe outside Albania and Turkey. It accounted in part for the difference between two events of 4th June 1989 – the victory of Solidarity in the Polish general elections, and the massacre of the students demonstrating in favour of democracy in China. The difficulties faced by Christians in Eastern Europe have been immense. Under Communist rule if churches "registered" with the state, or even accepted an "alliance" with it, they were invited or compelled to pay a price: religious activities must be confined to within the church walls and the houses of believers, religious teaching must be spiritual not social apart from the repetition of "peace" slogans acceptable to the regime, and even the churches' charitable activities must be handicapped or forbidden. Of course conditions varied from country to country, region to region, and period to period, but this was the prevailing Communist line. On the other hand, if religious groups refused to have dealings with the state, they had to go underground. Yet the governments did not turn out to be completely successful in this intimidation. Even in Romania and Bulgaria, where the dominant Orthodox Churches tamely supported the regimes, Christian worship continued to suggest a non-Marxist view of life. And behind the astonishingly non-violent revolutions of 1989 were the Catholic Church of Poland, the Protestants of East Germany, and the Catholic and Reformed Churches of Hungary and Czechoslovakia. In Czechoslovakia Christians were active in the Charter 77 movement which kept the flame of freedom burning under a particularly harsh regime and half a million signatures on a petition for religious freedom signalled the coming revolution. Pope John Paul II's return to his native land in 1979 led directly to the rise of the Solidarity movement in Poland, Catholic priests sustained its struggle and Catholic intellectuals led the new government which it formed in 1989. In East Germany Protestant churches somewhat nervously housed "peace groups" including protest meetings against the Communist regime, and after its overthrow dialogues ("round tables") between reformed Communists and other groups often used churches to begin the "new thinking". In Leipzig, where the homes of protest were historic churches associated with Luther and Bach, prayers preceded demonstrations, and an army of hundreds of thousands of Germans marched armed with candles and flowers. Many observers agree that the astonishingly peaceful character of these revolutions, apart from Romania, was influenced decisively by the churches. And in Romania the costly revolution against the worst tyranny in Eastern Europe, an uprising which had to use counter-violence, began when a Protestant pastor, Laszlo Tokes, was arrested and beaten up for protesting. When the news of the tyrant's flight reached a crowd of 200,000 gathered in Opera Square, Timisoara, for a Christmas service, the chant arose: "God exists!"

In the Soviet Union the search for an alternative to Stalinism (and perhaps also to Marxist-Leninism) has been sustained by the surviving strength of the Russian Orthodox Church (with almost fifty million members) and other religious traditions, including the Catholicism which inspired Lithuania's declaration of independence in 1990. The systematic pressure of an atheist Marxism over seventy years, including the great persecutions of 1918–43 and 1959–64, has of course eroded the status of Christianity. It has often been said that religious faith is hostile or irrelevant to modern realities, God not having been discovered by any spaceship; and it would certainly be unrealistic to underestimate the effects of the sustained project by the victorious Communists to banish religion to the margins of society and to the museums, excluding believers from higher education and responsible jobs, and prohibiting all religious education except of children by their own parents. Yet many of the Party's critics are known to be religious believers, the churches and religious bodies have a far longer record than the dissidents' groups as communities not based on the official philosophy, and beyond either the articulate dissidents or the religious bodies have stretched the vast numbers who have been (perhaps vaguely) aware that in the old days the religious traditions fed a spiritual life which Marxism has not been able either to give or to take away. While many churches and mosques remained undemolished (even the Kremlin retained its ecclesiastical appearance) the memory of religion could not be erased. While the novels of Dostoevsky and Tolstoy remained as classics, and writers such as Pasternak and Solzhenitsyn were known to speak the truth about Soviet society, the Christian elements in the living heritage could not be denied. And it was widely known that many Christians were prepared to accept exclusion from the privileges of a Communist society, treatment in "psychiatric hospitals", exile to remote places, imprisonment in labour camps and death by ill-treatment or shooting rather than deny their beliefs and their consciences. In the whole history of Christianity no churches have produced more martyrs than the churches of the Soviet Union in the twentieth century – and no churches have been able to watch a larger harvest to support Tertullian's saying: "the blood of Christians is seed".

In his 1987 book on *Perestroika* Mikhail Gorbachev wrote: "Today our main job is to lift the individual spiritually, respecting his inner world and giving him moral strength" (p.30). By 1989 he was confirming the report that he had been baptized (and named after an archangel) as an infant, was visiting the Pope and was promising as imminent a new law guaranteeing religious freedom. Already there had been some official participation in the celebration of a thousand years of Russian Christianity, large numbers of churches had been reopened and used with enthusiasm, and the religious instruction of children and religious meetings in homes had been permitted. The religious beliefs which were once thought to attract only the elderly and the ignorant now interest many students and young professionals. The intelligentsia is more religious than it was for most of the nineteenth century. When in some republics the Islamic Revolution arouses more enthusiasm than what remains of Communism, and when in others the Christian Church shows a moral strength greater than the Party's as it pours memories and hopes into nationalist protests against control by Moscow, what has happened? Is it a resurrection of religion, to defy the secular centralization that seemed to have crucified its critics? It would be foolish to pretend that the religious bodies command the loyalty of the managerial class in the Soviet Union or are certain of a popular triumph, but the signs are that Christianity and Islam are beginning to see Communism wither away. When Khruschev denounced the memory of Stalin in his great speech in 1956, three years after that tyrant's death, what he was saying – although he never publicly admitted it – was that the ideology which had made Stalin possible was dead. But the tyranny had been so complete that it took thirty years to see that the death had occurred. When Gorbachev promised a freely elected Parliament and the rule of law in another great speech, in 1988, what he was saying – although he did not admit it until 1990 – was that a united Communist Party's "leading role" could no longer be guaranteed by law – or by Communism's travesty of law.

So it can, I believe, be demonstrated that the Christian religion has been influential both in the evolution of the European Community and in the transformation of Eastern Europe. It can also be demonstrated that the European churches have been willing to cross frontiers, and even the Iron Curtain itself, while it was a terrible reality, in order to affirm the unity of the baptized.

For the most part this willingness has been shown simply in prayers for each other. Ordinary Christians do not go to international church meetings. But the willingness has resulted in efforts to maintain and deepen common organizations. Protestant, Orthodox and Anglican churches have taken part in the strong life and work of the World Council of Churches since 1948, and of the Conference of European Churches formed in 1959; both bodies have their headquarters in Geneva. In the 1960s a number of lay Christians working in the institutions of the EC set up an ecumenical "association" (later "commission") for "church and society" in Brussels, which has consistently emphasized the Community's duty to be open to Eastern Europe and the poor in other continents. An office in Strasbourg was opened in 1986. In East Germany the Protestants did not form their own Federation of Evangelical Churches before 1969. Before then they had been administratively united with the West German Protestants, and even then German Protestants of east and west persistently refused to get out of touch spiritually, thus preparing for the many reunions of the 1990s. The Kirchentag, the great rally of the German Protestant laity, proclaimed a form of the faith – biblical, boldly personal but also passionate about questions of justice and peace – that criticized the secular ideologies of both Communism and capitalism. Parishes in the two Germanies were twinned in a bond of prayer. Gifts were made wherever possible – from the west, gifts of money; from the east, examples in Christian discipleship under adversity. The Roman Catholic Church in Europe has consistently defended its communion with the Pope and its guidance by the Vatican. A council of representatives of its conference of bishops in Europe has met regularly. At times Catholics have had to resist very strong pressures to cut such links. The Communist regime in Czechoslovakia, for example, attempted to set up a National Catholic Church in the 1950s and, when that attempt failed, sponsored a pro-government movement to cause disruption in the Church (the *Pacem in Terris* movement). These moves had precedents: the Czechoslovak Hussite Church broke away from Rome in 1921, taking the name of the national hero, John Hus, burnt at the stake as a heretic in 1415. The Orthodox Churches of Europe are united much more loosely than is the Roman Catholic Church but are very much aware of the tradition which they have in common. Their bishops and theologians maintain contact under the ill-defined seniority of the Patriarch of Constantinople.

In May 1989 the Conference of European Churches and the (Roman Catholic) Council of European Bishops' Conference jointly sponsored the first European Ecumenical Assembly in Basel. It was called the most representative gathering of European Christians that had taken place in the whole of history, and the claim seems accurate. The presidents were the Metropolitan of Leningrad and the Cardinal Archbishop of Milan. Inevitably the main value of this meeting was the sheer coming together. Controversial problems about the future of Europe could not be solved, or even explored deeply in public, but the meeting produced a strongly felt discussion of "justice and peace" and the environmental cause on a global scale, with a new emphasis on the work of the Holy Spirit, renewing an old creation in a time of new hope. The final document, prepared after long consultations and adopted with near-unanimity by almost five hundred delegates, was remarkable evidence of a consensus that Christianity was powerfully and urgently relevant to the problems of the continent and the world. It showed Christians looking far beyond the problems of local church life. It briefly expounded a number of themes (which I am trying to develop independently in this book); and more importantly, it inspired Christian leaders from Eastern Europe to proclaim these themes during their countries' liberation from Communism, so much nearer than anyone then in Basel dared to hope.

The life of the spirit

So far I have concentrated on the contribution of Christians with a creative influence in the public life of the continent. What of Christians who are not needed as standard-bearers for democracy and other popular causes? What of churches which are not crowded as platforms for political protests? It cannot be denied that in a Europe now marked by pluralism committed Christians and regular churchgoers often feel depressed – and, in the context of history, surprised – to find themselves in a minority. But it is also clear that Christianity still matters in the spiritual life of Europe. Its influence on recent political developments would have been impossible, had it not possessed a base in the practices of the faithful and in the affections of the public. That is obviously true of Greece, Bulgaria, Romania, Poland, Lithuania, Austria, Italy, Spain, Portugal and Ireland, where the old links between Church and State have been loosened without destroying the Orthodox or Catholic traditions of the bulk of the people, including religious "practice" in large numbers. But Christian influence is strong in Germany, the Benelux countries and Switzerland, with their mixture of Catholic and Protestant. And it is strong to a lesser extent in countries where churchgoing is less popular. I offer brief comments on three of these situations often said to be secular.

In France the separation of Church and State has been conspicuous since the Church was formally disestablished in 1905 by politicians who thought it right to complete the work of the great Revolution. The alliance of throne and altar in the *ancien régime* had been so close, and both monarchism and clericalism had become so conservative, that this *laique* reaction was an almost inevitable part of the eventual triumph of democracy. The exclusion of religion from the whole of the state's educational system since 1881 has resulted in the formation of an intellectual world – existentialist, structuralist, technical or whatever – which virtually excludes belief in God. At another intellectual level the working class has been shown by many analyses to be largely alienated from organized religion although the statistics vary from region to region. This history contributed to a drop in ordinations in the Catholic Church from more than a thousand a year in the 1950s to fewer than a hundred in 1990. In the same period the percentage of children being baptized fell from about ninety to about fifty. In response to such challenges there has been a profound division between Catholics so traditionalist as to condemn the Second Vatican Council, and Catholics so radical as to be extreme in the eyes of many Protestants. But the Catholic Church has not capitulated, has not been completely torn apart, and has sponsored some gallant missionary work. It is estimated that about thirteen per cent of the population attend Mass at least once a month and that about eighty per cent regard themselves as Catholics. And as the Church has come to accept the

Republic so public opinion seems to have shifted, during and since the First World War, towards admiration for at least the moral standards of Christianity and towards sympathy with the clergy. In 1984 Socialist politicians proposed to withdraw the remaining state aid from church schools. There was an outcry and the proposal was dropped. The intellectual vitality of French Catholicism – the religion of Péguy, Claudel, Bernanos, Maritain, Mauriac and the most influential theologians of the Second Vatican Council – has sadly diminished, but one explanation is that most Catholic intellectuals no longer feel themselves to be a France within a France, whatever may be the controversial vigour of the "reaffirmation" of their religion by traditionalists. The less spectacular spiritual life of the Catholic laity, expressed in Bible study or a "charismatic" prayer group or concern for world problems, has deepened, perhaps because there are fewer priests to be dictatorial. The Protestant minority has decreased in numbers (or at least in the numbers of regular churchgoers) but has maintained a high educational standard and with it a distinguished contribution to the intellectual and political life of France.

In Britain, as almost all my readers are surely well aware, the religious situation is more complex than in France. Largely because the Roman Catholic Church is weaker, weekly church attendance is a bit lower. But about a fifth of the population tells pollsters that it goes to church at least once a month; it may be an exaggeration but it is interesting. More people go to church than to football matches; many more than to political meetings. A vaguer "diffused" or "folk" religion, probably unorthodox, shows up in the funerals (of which some eighty-five per cent are religious) and in the polls where God, Jesus and prayer get the votes of the majority. People mostly support, or acquiesce in, acts of worship and religious instruction in the state schools under legislation which was strengthened in the 1980s. Religious programmes on TV and radio appeal to large audiences. A smaller but still substantial public buys religious books, and theology is far more vigorous in Britain than in France. The Church of England and the Church of Scotland remain established as National Churches and there is no public demand that things should be otherwise. And more significant still is the interest taken in the churches as purveyors of spiritual and moral values into a harsher age. This largely makes the churches a conservative influence. A Church of England report on *Changing Britain* (1987) quoted as the conclusion of a study of public opinion: "the British see themselves as a relatively unchurched, nationalistic, optimistic, satisfied, conservative and moralistic people" (p.12). But the churches are by no means always conservative. During the first ten years of Margaret Thatcher's Premiership, 1979-89, the spokesmen of the churches often seemed to be forming a kind of Alternative Opposition to a government believed to be lacking in community-mindedness and compassion. The hostility of some supporters of Thatcherism towards church leaders, in reply to these criticisms, was a tribute to the churches' influence. It is also a fact that the party conferences of the Conservatives begin with a Christian act of worship. The fact is typical of a complicated situation.

In Scandinavia the true situation can only be described in paradoxes. Atheism is often expressed with conviction and frankness, but the overwhelming majority informs pollsters that it identifies itself in membership of the National Churches, which officially adhere to the Lutheran form of Protestantism. The clergy are salaried out of a tax which few decline to pay. In Sweden in 1972 a commission which had been sitting since 1958 proposed the separation of Church and State. The idea was welcomed by most of the clergy, but the laity have taken no action. Regular churchgoing is very low but most adolescents agree to undergo courses of instruction leading to the service of confirmation. Traditional sexual morality is widely rejected (one child in every two born in Sweden has unmarried parents), and serious films and novels put a tough-minded integrity far above any conventionally Christian view of life – yet politicians are expected to be untainted by self-seeking and ardently involved in current good causes, taxpayers are expected to be happy to support an elaborate Welfare State, and the individual's spiritual journey is taken with great seriousness, a serious compassion being the tone expected of any serious writer. The realities vary, Denmark being the most secular country and Norway the least, but the general picture is of a Scandinavia not completely divorced from its Christian past.

Is it possible to say briefly what has been the Christian contribution to the life of the spirit in Europe? Obviously there have been many differences from place to place, from time to time, from church to church, and an observer of European religion (as of European politics) might well conclude that an entrenched argumentativeness is the most striking feature: Europe's Christians quarrel. But some other features are part of the character of almost the whole of this spiritual tradition.

One feature is the high humanism of the belief that the individual is capable of the spiritual development recommended by the spiritual teachers. Admittedly much of the European literature of spirituality has been addressed primarily to monks, nuns, clergy and the leisured middle classes – as was inevitable, because these were the people who might read such books. But the tradition has affirmed that in principle every individual, however humble, is if humble enough capable of becoming an "athlete of God", full of the divine Spirit and thus able to contemplate God, even to be in some sense a partaker of the divine nature. The tradition has said that the alternative is to be perpetually restless. It has also affirmed that the whole world is shot through with the grandeur of God and it has encouraged worship of the Creator through the celebration of the beauty of the creation by art and music. It has affirmed that God invites his children to use the world as a garden and to supplement his bounty by the creation of their own wealth out of abundant raw materials. At its best this tradition has also encouraged philosophy, the pilgrimage of the mind to truth and wisdom, and the scientific study of nature as the work of God: this is the tradition of Aquinas and Newton. And it has produced a positive estimate of history as well as of nature – for if God has disclosed himself in some history, then all history has some meaning: this is the tradition which has dated all years with reference to the coming of Christ.

It has, however, never been said by the Christian teachers of Europe that material wealth is essential to spiritual progress. On the contrary, the emphasis has been on detachment from material possessions and ambitions. The fact that much of the spiritual literature was directed to people vowed to lifelong poverty, chastity and obedience in religious communities has to some extent made the literature élitist. On the other hand, it has made it clear that a good income is not necessary for a good Christian. This teaching can involve a bold identification with the poor and a celebration of poverty as an opportunity for closeness to God, as in the Franciscan tradition. The one essential has been seen as reliance on the "grace" of God mediated through the Saviour, Christ. This reliance has been most profound in those parts of the tradition most influenced by Paul and Augustine – for example, in the Lutheran proclamation that the Christian is "justified" (reckoned righteous) not if he has many merits of his own but if he has faith in Christ. But across the whole of the Christian tradition in Europe is found an insistence on the centrality of frequent thought about Christ himself – as in the constantly repeated Jesus Prayer in the Eastern Orthodox tradition ("Lord Jesus Christ, Son of God, have mercy on me, a sinner"). This concentration on Christ develops an identification with him in his own human experience, supremely in his suffering on the cross. It can be said that there is no form of human suffering that has not been shared with Christ in prayer. But always Christ has been seen as triumphant in suffering. This Easter light has shed some light of hope on the sufferings of countless Europeans.

The Christian's relationship to Christ has often been felt as a relationship to a king or a judge, but the main theme in European piety has been the friendship of Christ, attracting, forgiving and sustaining. The response has been one of a devotion expressed in a person-to-person love and imitation. It has involved for many – including many of the laity, amid the pressures of family life and daily work – a serious quest for perfection, encouraged by the heroism of the acknowledged saints and in its turn encouraging what can be called Puritanism. But it has also involved an acceptance of the human inevitability of sin, calling for repentance but also for patience, for rebuke but also for the sinner's inclusion. One of the reasons for being interested in saints has been a fellow feeling with their human struggles.

The relationship to Christ has led Christian thinkers to explore what is meant when God is revealed as love. For those advanced in the art of prayer or the science of theology this has meant a willingness to continue to love God even when, in the "dark night of the soul" or the "cloud of unknowing", the transcendence of God over all that can be thought or imagined is known painfully, and even when conventional forms of public worship and private prayer cannot satisfy, perhaps because the mystery of evil is for a time overwhelming. But for simpler Christians the parent-like love of God can be enjoyed simply through practices such as devotion to Mary the mother of Jesus – and the honouring of Mary as the "Mother of God" has had an effect beyond calculation on the position of other women. (Like almost every other bit of history before the rise of the pioneers of feminism in the nineteenth century, the Christian Church has been largely "patriarchal" – but it has never entirely forgotten the supreme Pauline vision that "in Christ there is neither male nor female" and in practice it has often affirmed the dignity of women.) For Christian women and men, response to the love of God has been made not in abstract thought but in the performance of everyday duties with some delight. And the vision of common life and work as a place for love and joy, full of the presence of God, has transformed drudgery.

All of the Christian attitudes which I have mentioned so briefly can be found in the New Testament. Some can be found in other religions. But all have been intensified in the life of the spirit as lived in Europe. And all have influenced European views of the human condition.

Scepticism and its limits

I add a few reflections about the alternatives to Christianity in the Europe of the 1990s. I do not wish to be entirely negative about them, one reason being that in the setting of Europe these movements of life and thought all have a Christian background and include Christian elements. I also have considerable sympathy with their revolts against Christianity, or at least against its corruption. Scepticism is in many ways attractive to Europeans including myself. In comparison with most Americans (for example) most Europeans seem to be disillusioned and proud of it. They tend to be humanists in the sense that they tend to measure religion, like all other subjects proposed for their attention, by the criterion of human welfare. Does it, or does it not, make for a happier and more fulfilled life for men, women and children? And because their allegiance goes to the "party of humanity" most Europeans are sceptical about the record of religious institutions which seem less than humane. They also tend to be sceptics in the sense that they tend to rely on their own intelligence applied to people and things they can see and touch (and possibly manipulate). They tend to value religion, if they value it at all, as something which lies within human experience and seems sufficiently reasonable. And so Europeans tend to be sceptical about the right of a religious institution to propound dogmas which deal with mysteries beyond the reach of a human mind. These attitudes are transmitted within family life, of course, and in the chat of friends. But they are also transmitted by formal education, where the emphasis is on the young person's own development (rather than conformity to a set pattern) and intelligence (rather than acceptance of an official ideology). If their education has included some knowledge of history, Europeans know that they are the heirs of the Renaissance and the Enlightenment. President Gorbachev, who has shown himself to be a true European by allowing criticism, likes to mention the Renaissance and the Enlightenment when he praises the heritage of "our common European home". And many Christians would agree with him.

Religion, then, needs scepticism: it may be the salt of the earth but it needs criticism to save it from its own corruption. Europe's history is full of warnings about what happens when religion denies this. The sceptical question "Does it benefit humanity?" rebukes many of the evils which a corrupt religion has persuaded human beings to inflict on one another. The sceptical question "What do I know?" destroys a lot of nonsense, including religious nonsense, which has darkened the human mind. In Europe's history the asking of these questions by enlighteners such as Montaigne, Hume, Voltaire, or Kant, or in a later period Freud, Russell or Camus, was as useful as it was brave. To forget their questions now, as some fundamentalists advise us, is to prefer the dark to enlightenment. But religious bigotry or dogmatism is not the only darkness to be seen in European history. There is a darkness which comes when scepticism has put out the light of belief in human dignity – a belief which the best religion has upheld in Europe's past and which almost all religion upholds in Europe's present. Much of Christian (as of Jewish or Muslim) social thought can be called a commentary on Psalm 8:

> What is Man that you should be mindful of him:
> or the son of man that you should care for him?
> Yet you have made him little less than a god:
> and have crowned him with glory and honour.
> You have made him the master of your handiwork:
> and have put all things in subjection beneath his feet.

When religion has been dethroned, it is often said that no religious basis is needed in order to assert human dignity; that there is no need to talk about "virtue" any longer; that all that is required is that people having a proper self-respect should behave with justice, justice being what all reasonable people think right. And if all goes well such a position may well be more humane than a religious tradition which is used to defend the power of the powerful. But the theory that justice can safely rely on common sense turns out to be vulnerable when experience shows that, in the world as it is, the powerful tend to interpret "justice" in a way which distributes most of the world's goods to them. If they no longer need to twist religion they will twist common sense; and whether or not the underprivileged think them reasonable, history is likely to go their way, at least in the short term. The conclusion comes that might is right, so that rightfully men have power over women, whites over blacks, bosses over workers, governments over peoples.... The Anglo-American philosopher Alasdair MacIntyre analysed contemporary Western society in these sad terms in his two books *After Virtue* (1981) and *Whose Justice, Whose Rationality?* (1986).

In the modern history of Europe, where human rights have been brutally suppressed and tamely surrendered, we see that scepticism, no less than religious fanaticism, can put out the light. Human dignity cannot be defended as obviously reasonable when *homo sapiens* is seen cynically as producing and consuming *homo economicus* and no more, as a wage-earning "factor of production" and no more, as a conscript soldier and no more, as the slave of passions, as the creature of circumstances, or simply as a fool easily duped by the advertisers and victimized by the strong men who seize control in a society with a low opinion of itself. In history it does not take long for defeatism about human nature to become self-fulfilling.

Scepticism has often been counteracted in the modern world by the philosophy of human rights, which can be said to be the agreed value system in a society which then practises pluralism. That philosophy animated the American and French Revolutions. After the defeat of Nazism it was hoped that it would be acknowledged by all, so that the Universal Declaration of Human Rights formed the spiritual basis of the United Nations (in 1948). When Communism showed its inhuman face, the Council of Europe adopted the European Convention for the Protection of Human Rights and Fundamental Freedoms (in 1950). When Communism wished to reclaim respectability, the Helsinki Final Act reaffirmed these rights and freedoms, at least approximately (in 1975). One trouble, however, has been that only the European Convention has produced a Commission of Human Rights which can only be petitioned by those who consider themselves to be the victims of wrong decisions by public authorities, and a Court of Human Rights which can deliver judgements almost certain to be upheld in national courts. In the late 1980s the Commission was registering well over a thousand applications every year. Under the other declarations, it has been left to the nations to criticize each other for alleged breaches of the Conventions, without recourse to any court of law.

Another trouble about the philosophy of human rights is that it is dangerously evasive about the question "What is the basis of these rights?" The Declaration of the Rights of Man and of the Citizen in 1789 excluded "women, at least in present circumstances, children, foreigners and those who contribute nothing to the common weal" (in the words of Sieyès). It also excluded what came to be called "social rights" (as illustrated by the European Social Charter of 1989). On what basis, it may be asked, were *any* rights included? On what basis were the Rights of Man affirmed in the 1770s by Americans who did not end slavery before the 1860s?

Christianity can be understood as an answer to this question. Like Islam it inherited from Judaism the conviction that every child, woman and man has been created by the one God, and solely by being human is an image of that God – of the divine power, rationality and love. It added its own message that when God wished to do something more marvellous than the creation of the universe he expressed his supreme characteristic, love, by becoming human. According to the Christian Gospel the miraculous tongue in the human mouth, obedient to the demands of the miraculous computer in the human skull, spoke the divine word and human hands were nailed divinely to the cross of love. And this double vision of Man made in the image of God, and of God made Man for our salvation, has inspired many centuries of Christian humanism.

The Renaissance of the fifteenth and sixteenth centuries was a glorious affirmation of human dignity, but it has not been understood when it has been interpreted as a mere prelude to the modern secularization of Europe. In many respects it was in fact continuous with the Middle Ages, as everyone ought to have known all along in view of the prominence of patronage by the Papacy and of religious pictures in any representative gallery.

The Renaissance brought renewal, enrichment and adornment to some élites in Christendom, rather than any fundamental shift in beliefs and values. It increased both beauty and knowledge by providing easier access to the architecture and literature of Ancient Greece and Rome, but this supplement was seldom seen as any challenge to Christianity, any more than the honoured presence of Virgil in Dante's visions had disturbed medieval orthodoxy. On the contrary, part of the excitement arose because it was newly possible for scholars such as Erasmus to go with a simple devotion to "the fountains" – the Hebrew and Greek of the Bible. The surroundings, the dress and the music of princes and merchants were made more sumptuous, but more of the same glamour was brought to churchmen and their churches. There was an open pleasure in the wealth created by the beginnings of modern capitalism, but almost always the wealth was used in ways which the Middle Ages would have understood. There was a delight in the human body and in the detailed sights of nature, but almost always this was supported by a complete acceptance and celebration of the Christian belief that *Adam* (Man) and the world around him had been created by God – as when Michelangelo showed God's finger touching Adam's in the Sistine Chapel.

The élites touched by the Enlightenment of the seventeenth and eighteenth centuries were much larger than the élites of the Renaissance, and the departure from the Middle Ages was much more radical, but here too the new movement of life and thought was linked firmly to Christianity. The Enlightenment has been misunderstood when the explicit and systematic atheism of Holbach has been said to be typical, or when Hume's joke about the "miracle of theism" or Gibbon's taunt about "religion and barbarism" or Heine's preference for "Hellenes not Hebrews" has been said to indicate a general determination to abandon the whole Christian heritage. In fact the Enlightenment, influenced by thinkers such as Descartes, Spinoza, Newton and Locke, usually preserved a firm belief in God the Creator and a strong moral code which would not have displeased St Paul. Voltaire attacked *l'infame*, the Roman Catholic Church, for its dogmatism based on the literal interpretation of myths and its cruel intolerance, not for the belief that Man was God's creature. As in the Renaissance, figures from classical antiquity such as Plato or Cicero were brought in to enrich and adorn, to civilize – not to spread paganism or atheism. There was much more appreciation of science and technology than in the Renaissance, but there was still very little sense that the mind and spirit of Man belonged to an animal or a slave. On the contrary, the Enlightenment may be justly criticized for a naïve optimism about the capacities of Godlike Man. The future seemed limitless once Man would dare to be wise, knowing his immortality and his freedom, responding to the commands of his conscience as a lord under the starry heavens. This was not yet the best of all possible worlds, but enlightened humanity could, it was hoped, eventually make it that. It was a mistake better than the despair which overwhelmed many Europeans in a later age, when no one could call the continent enlightened.

I have entered briefly into the history of the Renaissance and the Enlightenment because I want to stress the healthy difference made when scepticism did not deny that human rights are established by God's creation. A difference has also been made to the workings of the economy by religion teaching morality. There has been controversy among historians about the exact nature of this difference. Scholars such as Max Weber and R.H. Tawney emphasized the role of Protestantism in stimulating the rise of capitalism, for example. They pointed out that Protestantism did not condemn the making of profit by lending money, as the medieval Catholic Church had done in accordance with the Hebrew Scriptures. More positively Protestantism praised hard work and thrift, which enable people to save and invest. But other scholars have pointed out that modern capitalism started in Catholic cities – in Italy and Germany, Bruges and Antwerp – before Protestants took the lead in the Netherlands and England. And they have shown that like Catholic priests Protestant theologians and preachers very seldom gave any direct encouragement to capitalism: they preferred warnings about the moral dangers of wealth and especially about any neglect of the poor. Calvin's Geneva was no Paradise for businessmen. The Calvinist Dutch were embarrassed by their riches. It seems reasonable to conclude that Europe's modern economies owed much to their setting in a continent which was officially Christian. They were encouraged to prosper while also warned that material prosperity had its great dangers. That is not an exciting conclusion to the historians' controversy, but it fits the facts.

Adam Smith, who more than anyone else supplied theoretical foundation for the early stages of industrial capitalism in the eighteenth century, constantly stressed that if there is to be fair competition in the market on terms generally acceptable, it must be on the basis of a morality which the market does not create. He showed that the "invisible hand" of the price-mechanism of the market was the hand which fed people once the stage was passed when those living close to the soil ate only what they themselves produced. But he had no illusions about the human nature of merchants, whose habits in gaining privileges from governments in order to exploit consumers he denounced vigorously. He wrote on "moral sentiments" as well as "political economy". He taught that people could safely be trusted to pursue their own self-interest without undue harm to the community, not only because of the restrictions imposed by the laws of an uncorrupt state, but also because they were "subject to the restraint derived from morals, customs and education".

What that has implied for a Europe deeply influenced by Christianity may perhaps be expressed by saying that economic development depends on individuals having enough confidence in themselves, and enough sense of their own potentiality, to be willing to exert themselves ambitiously. But it also depends on people having enough confidence in their neighbours to be willing to serve them and to make deals with them, trusting them to be honest. It depends on stable and loving families which turn out citizens able to compete in the market. It depends, too, on uncorrupt governments which establish and enforce the rules of the game. And it depends on the successful having enough human compassion in them to help the disadvantaged and the unfortunate, so making the game more or less acceptable to those who do not profit personally by it. All these virtues are encouraged by almost all the ethical systems in the world but the encouragement is reinforced by almost all the world's religions – and in the history of Europe such morality has been taught by the Church and the Bible.

Communism and consumerism

Can religion teaching morality now be replaced by "Socialism" as defined by Communists? Or can it now be replaced by the consumerist drive which the free market automatically generates?

In the early 1990s it is surprising but true that one need not say much about Communism. It is a creed which traditionally has had no room for belief in God but also no room for scepticism about its claim to be building Paradise on earth.

The fact that there was scope for Communism is a European and a Christian tragedy. The origins lie among the European revolutions of 1848 and in the intellectual ferment as the Europe of the royal dynasties entered modernity. Karl Marx's intellectual system was a gospel for this new age (as was appreciated in the best book on Marxism by an English theologian, Nicholas Lash's *A Matter of Hope*, 1981). In this it resembled the all-embracing system of a great German philosopher, Hegel, who was a sort of Christian (and as a schoolboy Marx seems to have been devout). Indeed, although it stood Hegel's "idealism" extolling "Spirit" on its head, Marxist "historical materialism" was a philosophy akin to a religion, and it has been given many of its opportunities in situations where religion has seemed powerless (in China, for example). It has claimed to interpret human experience and history as a whole; it has claimed also to be able to change the world; it has pressed this claim through the enthusiasm of a dedicated, and if need be self-sacrificing, élite; it has preached morality (of a kind) and has extolled the innocent optimism of youth; it has embodied its message in sacred scriptures, with a promise of a radically new and infinitely better society to follow the conflicts of the present age. And like religion, Marxism could be corrupted. The ugly side of Christian faith is plain in the history of Europe: its alliance with power and privilege, its own intolerance, its suppression of thought believed to be contrary to its doctrines, its aloofness from the real sufferings of real people. Marx's own formative experiences were membership of a circle of young intellectuals rebelling against the censorship imposed by the alliance of Church and State in Prussia, and then observation of the sufferings of the working class in England under ruthless industrialization. But if we look at the history of Communist faith, we find the poison of the people.

For a time it seemed as if Communism might be hailed as salvation by a Europe which wanted to be saved. Marx and Engels preached the faith that this was the only solution to the problems of early industrialization in Western Europe, and after their deaths it could seem to be the answer to slumps and wars as capitalism developed. Lenin and Stalin believed – and ruthlessly insisted that others should believe – that this was the only way to modernize the peasant societies of Eastern Europe. In the late 1940s and early 1950s countries which were later to rest snugly in the bosom of the prospering EC often seemed to be moving towards this answer to their problems, for Communism appeared to be the strongest force on the Left. This was true of Greece, Italy and France, and the Social Democrats of West Germany were closer to Marxism than to capitalism. The Marxist influence on the Socialists of Spain lasted for another twenty years. Many Europeans applauded when Mao raised high his guiding light for Asia, when Castro preached his gospel to Latin America, and when Marxism inspired anti-colonial movements in Africa and elsewhere. The laws of history seemed to have been revealed, and with them the inevitable, and if only people would accept the costs of their liberation one day all would be well. But that day has never come. In the Marxist lands humanity has been made to pay a terrible price – for what? The reality has been in many countries some improvement in living conditions in comparison with the years when only landlords and capitalists flourished. But in comparison with the records of non-communist Europe it can be seen that these peoples could have made more progress under systems more adapted to the realities of economics and of human nature.

Bureaucracy has created in the name of the "dictatorship of the proletariat" the highly privileged "new class" denounced by the Yugoslav dissident, Djilas, or by the Soviet radical, Yeltsin. But it has not managed enough production – not even when it has been free of tyranny, corruption and inefficiency on the scale of Ceausescu's Romania, not even when it has avoided the disasters of Poland. Thought-control by the police has not encouraged enough thought, not even when it has exercised control by methods other than brutal cruelty and blatant lies. There has been a lack of incentives to work and be creative even when there has been no fear of direct punishment. In the end demonstrations and strikes by the actual people in whose name this particular kind of "democracy" had been run have demanded not only more goods in the shops but also more scope for the human quest for what is good. The cries for "freedom" and for genuine "democracy" arose from Berlin to Beijing and surrounded the Kremlin. They could not be drowned by propaganda or gunfire and they signified more than "better fed than red".

It can be seen in retrospect that in Europe the Communist illusion was condemned when Tito broke with Stalin in 1948. It died in Western Europe in 1959 when the Social Democrats of West Germany finally abandoned Marxism in their Bad Godesburg conference: West Germany saw Marxism's birth and death. The Italian Communist Party embraced a Eurocommunism ready for coalitions, and the French party, which did not, produced a rebel intellectual, Roger Garaudy, who eloquently expounded the need to value Christians and collaborate with them. In Eastern Europe the death of Communism was for long concealed by the absence of freedom and the presence of more than half a million Soviet troops, but in 1989 remarkably few pressures by the people were enough to switch on the light of reality and to expose the death. As the new Polish Finance Minister said: "We have to put an end, once and for all, to a situation in which the government pretends to pay for everything and the workers pretend to work" (*Guardian*, 18th December).

It does not follow that it is correct to claim that "Socialism is dead" in every sense as the 1990s begin. Gorbachev's *perestroika* has been presented as no more than a new phase in "the construction of Socialism" and is unlikely to develop into Socialism's total deconstruction. Elsewhere in Europe "Socialism" lives as a determination to accept and operate an economy based on the free market but also to tilt the balance of power by state expenditure in favour of "social justice" meaning in favour of the workers, the peasants, the unemployed, the sick and the old. In 1990 many governments in the European Community are "Socialist" in that sense, and the new governments in Eastern Europe seem unlikely to be different. But "Socialism", meaning Marxist-Leninist (or Stalinist or post-Stalinist) Communism as a half-religious creed offering a comprehensive alternative and opposition to Christianity, controlling the mind as well as the market, stinks with the stench of death. The decisive evidence for this comes not in dialogues between Christians and Communists – dialogues which have occasionally made progress when conditions favoured them, as in the Prague Spring of 1968 before Soviet tanks crashed into the conversation. The evidence comes in dialogues between orthodoxy and realism within the minds of leading Communists – Yugoslavia's Tito, Italy's Togliatti, Czechoslovakia's Dubcek, Hungary's Kadar, Poland's Jaruzelski, East Germany's Krenz, Romania's Iliescu, the Soviet Union's Gorbachev....In such minds a rigid Communism ceased to bear fruit because it had no roots in the realities of the economy and of public opinion. Such realities were acknowledged only gradually because the admission must create a new revolution, one made by the people. But the surrender came – and Erich Honecker, who had ruled East Germany, became an old man, utterly disgraced and riddled with cancer, who was given shelter in the home of a village pastor. Uwe Holmer's hospitality was a moment of *Christian* triumph.

The long-term alternative to Communism does not seem to be alcoholism, despite the situation in the Soviet Union. Nor does it seem to be consumerism, despite the glittering attractions of the shops in West Berlin. To be sure, all Europe now feels itself entitled to see desirable goods on sale and within the reach of the currency in people's pockets. It believes that such goods must and can be produced in abundance by efficient technology and scientific agriculture, by modern management and distribution, without wrecking the environment and without cutting back fatally on long-term investments. But few Europeans deeply believe that consumer goods guarantee human happiness, because human nature is well known to be a phenomenon which needs more than the world of consumerism to feed it. The decisive evidence for this comes not in sermons by preachers, not even in the teaching of a Pope (although John Paul II has been the most influential of all Europe's critics of post-war consumerism). It comes in the reality of public opinion in the countries where consumer goods are most abundant. As an example the suicide rate in Sweden is evidence. So is drug addiction among the prosperous Dutch. But other evidence is German.

Within a quarter of a century after World War Two West Germany became the richest nation in Europe outside Scandinavia. It supports many charities and its taxpayers have been paying far more per head than any other nation to maintain the EC. They appear to be willing to subsidize Eastern Europe also in the 1990s. But this is the nation where consumerism is the main climate of opinion and where the rejection of consumerism is the most passionate – not only among the terrorists who have occasionally murdered prominent businessmen and not only among the pacifists whose ideals can be called escapist. The rise of the Green Party has given a political expression among adults to the defence of nature against industry – a defence which draws on the German Romantic tradition but also on many down-to-earth anxieties which can quote science. More subtly and much more surprisingly, considerable numbers of adults reject the artificiality of the social conventions which have for long kept industrial production and the business world operating smoothly. And still more significant is the fact that West Germany has had the lowest birth rate in the world. Before the flow of refugees from East Germany resumed in 1989, its population had declined since the mid-1970s and was set to fall by a third in the period 1990–2030. West Germans have tended to prefer spending on the "standard of living" to spending on children, it seems.

Apparently a society which concentrates on consumer goods with an enormous success has made family life often seem the unaffordable luxury. That attitude can be defended: it may be in keeping with the world's need to limit its population. But in West Germany it has accompanied a lack of pride in the nation, shown up in many opinion polls. That can be explained because Germany's recent history is partly evil and largely tragic. Yet the lack of pride in the past has been linked with a lack of confidence in the future. Here, it seems, is the basic reason why the instinct to enjoy children, to bring them up and to hand on achievements to them, has been crowded out to such an extent. Amazing and highly praiseworthy economic achievements have not healed the wounds in the German spirit and have therefore not been thought worth handing on to a larger new generation. At the same time, the falling birthrate in East Germany offered a commentary on the propaganda of Communism. Unless these trends are reversed the population of a reunited Germany in the year 2025 is expected to be only sixty-seven million, ten million fewer than in the two Germanies of the 1980s, when the superficial affluence of consumerism confronted the profound depression of life under Communism.

A new sound on Dover beach?

I have stressed the inadequacies of the secular alternatives to Christianity in the modern European experience. I hope I have not done so in order to make cheap propaganda for Christianity. The truth is tragic: Europe has been on the defensive, but so has European Christianity. Europe has been burdened by guilt – guilt about the social injustice in regimes where the privileged exploited the poor; guilt about the exploitation of other continents by European empires; guilt about the wars which devastated this continent, and involved much of the world, when empires clashed; guilt about scepticism as a pathetically negative response to the crisis of a society; guilt about the damage done by the secular gods to which the continent turned during and after these disasters. For Europe it has been a time of achievements – but mainly of disgrace. A long catalogue of expressions of European pessimism might be assembled if that obvious truth needed to be proved. But European Christianity has also been burdened by guilt. It failed to make an adequate response to the challenges posed by these tragedies. In response to social injustice, it was too often acquiescent; in response to war, too often merely patriotic; in response to colonialism, too often blindly racist; in response to scepticism, too often arrogantly dogmatic; in response to Communism, too often frightened; in response to consumerism, too often indulgent. For European Christianity it has been a time of contributions, sometimes heroic – but mainly of failure and statistical decline.

This sad time for Europe and for European Christianity entered a new phase when the wars began with the Prussian invasion of France in 1870. Three years before that, Matthew Arnold published his poem "Dover Beach". Its climax, written some years previously, showed how at the deepest level of his personality he had responded to his prophetic sense that disaster was coming – and to the loss of his assured religious faith which had been preached by his father (Thomas Arnold, Headmaster of Rugby School). He had retreated (at least in this mood) into a private world, a world where any religion had become an escape from public realities.

> Ah, love, let us be true
> To one another! for the world, which seems
> To lie before us like a land of dreams,
> So various, so beautiful, so new,
> Hath really neither joy, nor love, nor light,
> Nor certitude, nor peace, nor help for pain,
> And we are here as on a darkling plain
> Swept with confused alarms of struggle and flight,
> Where ignorant armies clash by night.

After writing that announcement of European despair, he added lines which have become equally famous through their image of the retreating tide of European faith. Now he sees through the window the calm, moonlit Channel which puts water between two states of Europe:

> ...on the French coast the light
> Gleams and is gone, the cliffs of England stand,
> Glimmering and vast, out in the tranquil bay.

But as he listens at the open window he hears the "grating roar of pebbles which the waves draw back and fling". It is the sound of the tide ebbing on Dover beach and he reflects:

> The Sea of Faith
> Was once, too, at the full, and the round earth's shore
> Lay like the folds of a bright girdle furl'd.
> But now I only hear
> Its melancholy, long withdrawing roar,
> Retreating, to the breath
> Of the night-wind, down the vast edges drear
> And naked shingles of the world.

In the 1990s it is possible that the increasing union of the states of Europe will have no basis that is in any sense Christian or religious; that the sea of faith which once encircled and covered this continent will withdraw further and further with consequences still more melancholy for Christianity; that, so to speak, Dover beach will be left finally empty. Perhaps the town of Dover, a traditional end of the Channel crossing since Julius Caesar landed hereabouts, will also be emptied by the success of the Channel Tunnel. Perhaps services will no longer be held in the little church in the castle at the top of the white cliffs – a church incorporating Roman bricks. But I want to ask whether a defeatist mood among European Christians is necessary. If one listens in the new Europe, a Europe where despair no longer seems sensible, is it possible to hear a turning of the tide of faith, a new sound on Dover beach?

First let me try to say something about how a Europe forgivable by the world, and supportable by the Christian conscience, might develop. That means trying to come to terms with Europe's colonial past – and then some reflection about Europe's future now that the rival, warring empires are being replaced by the European Union. Finally I shall submit a few thoughts about Christianity's own future in the new Europe, believing that this future can be better than anything in the past.

5

After the Empires

What Columbus discovered

1992, the year when the European Community is supposed to be discovered as a single market and an embryonic union, will also bring many commemorations of the European discovery of America. The voyage which took thirty-two days in 1492 is now officially called "The Encounter of Two Worlds". After it all the continents were dragged into many encounters which made talk about one world more realistic – for Columbus inaugurated European colonialism.

This was a phenomenon unique in the world's history. It was unique in its great extent: in 1914 eighty-four per cent of the world's land surface was either inhabited by the Europeans or under their colonial control. And it was unique in its impact. Profits made out of it lit the fuse that exploded in Europe's own massive economic development, and the fall-out from that commercial and industrial explosion showered down on all the peoples of the world. Gradually Europe united the continents in a single economic and cultural history, so that when these military empires ended quite suddenly within the thirty years 1944–74 (with an epilogue about the Soviet empire), the very protests about European dominance had to use European ideas about human rights. Today Europeans cannot form anything like a full image of themselves unless they form some estimate of what these empires, military or commercial, did to their own continent and to the rest of the world. It is instructive to take a voyage into history – including the history of Columbus himself.

He belonged to the Europe of the Middle Ages. National frontiers had not yet hardened. Although a son of Genoa, he wrote in Castilian Spanish spelt in the Portuguese style because he had left Italy to be a sailor in Mediterranean and Atlantic waters, with first Portuguese and then Spanish employers. He was also medieval in that he relied on the combination of knowledge and faith which the Middle Ages had achieved. To us it is a very curious medley, but it was enough to drive him across the ocean. In his mind lay the navigational knowledge, most of it originating with the Arabs, which had been adequate for the Mediterranean and for the exploration of the African coast and its offshore islands in the Atlantic. This was combined with the knowledge and guesswork of the geographers of the Greek and Roman world, and with the information that seemed to be conveyed by the infallible Bible. Also in the mixture was a sincerely devout Catholic faith. His letters all began *Jesus cum Maria sit nobis in via*. "Jesus with Mary be with us in the way!" These simple and conventional words reveal the ultimate source of the confidence with which he acted on the information he thought he had. But another part of the mixture in his mind was an economic incentive.

Like the explorers of the African route to eastern riches who had secured Portuguese patronage, Columbus was looking for material wealth, chiefly gold, as well as for pagan souls to be saved. There was a market for new routes, intensified when Diaz rounded the Cape of Good Hope in 1488, and his voyage was a business proposition competing with those Portuguese enterprises which were to extend to Brazil in 1500. Needing capital prepared to take risks, he was backed both by the state and by a group of private investors. He was personally motivated by the hope of profit, for he was promised that he would become Admiral and Viceroy of any lands to be discovered together with a slice of the proceeds of their exploitation. He was fortunate because what were to be known as the trade winds carried him westwards from the Atlantic islands which had already been discovered and colonized – the Canaries and the Azores. But he was also fortunate in that he did not exactly know the risks he was running. His ambition was to reach the riches of Cathay (much as Europeans of the present day dream of equalling the wealth of Japan). He did not know the distance. All the experts, from Aristotle downwards, had underestimated it grossly. He kept his log of the voyage secret, lest his increasingly alarmed estimate of the sea miles covered should dismay the crew (who, however, calculated for themselves a smaller distance which turned out to be more accurate). He had reason to be afraid as the voyage dragged on: had there been nothing but salt water between Europe and Asia the sailors in those three tiny ships would certainly have died of thirst. (Not for the last time, Americans rescued Europeans.) He took the risks, however, and although no large quantity of American gold appeared until the discovery in Brazil at the end of the seventeenth century, he discovered something more important.

He discovered a continent where wealth could be created by work. The beauty of the Bahamas was such that he reported back to Spain that he was on the borders of a trouble-free Paradise. In fact the development of America was to need work – much of it the work of races who were to be wickedly exploited. The creator of wealth was not El Dorado, the legendary gold-painted ruler of Manoa, but a man at work in the field or the factory, bathed in sweat. And the wealth made in America was to benefit Europe only in so far as Europeans were also prepared to work, arduously, shrewdly and creatively.

In one other way this story is relevant to Europe towards the end of the twentieth century. For Columbus took risks and accepted suffering in a vulnerable faith.

It was the tradition of the old Europe that people should be compelled to embrace the official orthodoxy by the combined power of Church and State, shown most notoriously when heretics were handed over by the clergy of the Inquisition to be burned. It was another tradition, although less officially formulated, that non-Europeans who were non-Christians were in effect non-persons who could be exploited and enslaved without a qualm of conscience. Racism taking the name of "Christian" was such that it was a marvel that non-Europeans were thought human enough to be baptized and to become the mothers of the large numbers of children who were to begin Latin America's racial mixture. It was even more of a marvel that some of the Spanish clergy, most famously Bartoleme de las Casas, defended the human rights of the "natives" against the colonists, and persuaded the Spanish Crown to include some protection in the legislation (which was often ignored). These evils in the European "Christian" tradition were to justify the ruthless decimation of the native populations of Central and South America and of the "Red Indians" to the north: baptized or not, bedded or not, "natives" could be left to die. These evils were even to justify the slave trade across the Atlantic, transporting perhaps nine or perhaps eleven million of terrified human beings when labour was needed in the sugar plantations of Brazil and the "West Indies", in the cotton fields of the north and in the growing of Europe's favourite drug, tobacco.

We can, if we wish, find some excuses for these evils. The arrogance and cruelty which repeatedly shock any modern student of imperial history were the ways in which Europeans often treated other Europeans when in a position of power and privilege: what was said about "natives" was also said about European servants and peasants. And arrogance and cruelty seemed to be essential, for there was a war on. The Christian Europe of the Dark and Middle Ages was surrounded by enemies, whether pagan or Muslim, and very soon after their births the nations of Europe were at enmity with each other, fighting it out around the world when opportunity offered. It is understandable that it was thought essential to maintain and defend the identities of such societies by affirming their religious identities, and nowhere is this easier to understand than in the history of Spain. The reconquest of Spain from the Moors was seen as a long battle between Catholicism and Islam, with the Jews offering an uncertain allegiance. The very year of the first Columbus voyage saw the recapture of Granada by the army of the Catholic Monarchs and the expulsion of the Jews from the now more-or-less unified Spain. It seemed to follow inevitably that Catholicism – Catholicism as defined by the Inquisition – should inspire the exploits of the *conquistadores* in Central and South America and the disciplining of the pagans. It also seemed proper that the Spanish Crown should appoint all the bishops in the empire, being itself the authority that ought to decide the empire's morals. (The Papacy allowed the same system in the Portuguese empire.) But all these excuses for the militancy of Christian arrogance die on the lips when we reflect that men such as Columbus thought they were taking the way of "Jesus and Mary".

More worthy of imitation in our time is the willingness of Columbus and his companions to be vulnerable. That was in fact how Christianity was to reach and touch people's hearts and minds around the world. Spanish missionaries were to be vulnerable as they planted churches in a great chain from California and Texas to Peru; Portuguese missionaries as they left Goa for India and Macao for China and Japan; French Jesuits as they lit camp fires by the Great Lakes of Canada. Protestants were to be vulnerable to the hardships of the American Frontier and the fevers of tropical Africa. Christian women were to be vulnerable as they nursed or taught. This vulnerable faith was going to remain infectious when the empires had all been dismantled.

Columbus and his companions had a faith which included many illusions doomed to disappointment, and their courage was only human. He faced a near-mutiny during his most famous voyage. He died an embittered man and would have been sadder had he known that the "Indies" he had discovered were to be named after Amerigo Vespucci. But as they stumbled into a new world in their seamen's clothes, these men had at least been brave enough to leave security on the other side of the ocean. No miracle had saved predecessors such as the sailors from Genoa who had disappeared in the Atlantic in 1291. It may be felt that Christopher ("Christ-bearer") Columbus was not completely unworthy to plant in new soil the sign of a poor man crucified.

In this chapter I cannot offer a full balance sheet showing the losses and gains to the world in Europe's military or commercial or religious expansionism that followed the voyage of 1492. My guess is that no human being will ever be able to make such a judgement justly. What I offer is a little attempt to move towards an assessment more truthful than colonialist or anti-colonialist propaganda – an assessment which sees the Europeans' motives as mixed, their evil as diabolic and their total impact as partly good. For today's Europeans that means repentance, but not a complete condemnation of all that Europe has done.

The expansion of Europe

Soon after the Second World War representatives of the Protestant churches of Germany bravely accused themselves in the Stuttgart Declaration. They confessed that even when they had not collaborated in the crimes of Nazism, they had mostly kept silence. Since then many Europeans have become convinced that a similar admission of guilt about the crimes of colonialism, perpetrated by many nations, has become essential. They feel implicated in an evil system – whether because they are in some way responsible for the sins of their fathers, or because they themselves still enjoy the profits of those sins. And many more Europeans who do not feel personally guilty ask whether in the cupboard where the continent's memories are stored there may be a thousand million skeletons.

In 1989 a document called *The Road to Damascus*, denouncing colonialism and calling for the conversion of rich Christians, was signed by theologians and church leaders from El Salvador, Nicaragua, Guatemala, Korea, Namibia and South Africa. It was published by three agencies – the Catholic Institute for International Relations and Christian Aid in London and the Center of Concern in Washington DC. It deserves continuing attention because it suggests what kind of confession of sin by Europeans would be thought right by many Christians and others in the Two-Thirds World. So I shall quote it extensively.

> Except in the case of Korea which was colonized by Japan, the European nations that colonized our countries pride themselves on being Christian. Conquest and evangelization, colonization and the building of churches advanced together. The cross blessed the sword which was responsible for the shedding of our people's blood. The sword imposed the faith and protected the churches, sharing power and wealth with them.
>
> As a result of "discovery and conquest", millions of people have been killed; indigenous populations have been eliminated; entire civilizations and cultures have been destroyed. Millions have been enslaved, uprooted from their native land, deculturized and deprived of their wealth and resources. Women and children have been victims of additional and distinct oppression. Natural resources have been exploited and abused to such an extent that they cannot be replenished....
>
> Today, most Third World countries are no longer colonies, but we are still dominated by one or more imperial power – the United States, Japan and Western Europe. Their

web of economic control includes an unfair international trade system, multinational companies that monopolize strategic sections of our economy, economic policies dictated by leading banks and governments together with the International Monetary Fund and the World Bank. Even technology is used as a tool for domination. The staggering size of the Third World debt is only one dramatic sign of our subordination to imperialism.

In some of our countries imperialism violates national sovereignty by establishing military bases with nuclear weapons that endanger our people's lives. Various methods of political intervention subvert our independence, usually with the co-operation of local rulers. Our educational system, mass media, religious and cultural institutions reproduce a subservient colonial mentality; this is reinforced by Western habits of consumption....

The effects of imperialism upon the Third World form a litany of woes: our children die of malnutrition and disease, there are no jobs for those who want to work, families break up to pursue employment abroad, peasants and indigenous communities are displaced from their land, most urban dwellers have to live in unsanitary slums, many women have to sell their bodies, too many die without having lived a life that human persons deserve. We also suffer because of the plunder of our natural resources, and then we ourselves are being blamed for it.

That, it seems to me, is largely the truth – truth which ought to be burned into consciences. But it is not the whole truth about the recent contribution of companies based in the United States, Japan and Western Europe to the poverty or development of other lands. It may be misleading to call this connection "imperialism". Latin America, for example, was never in a North American or Japanese empire, has been politically independent of Western Europe for almost two centuries, and deserves a closer analysis of its problems. And the completely negative verdict of *The Road to Damascus* was not the whole truth about the story of the expansion of Europe into Africa, Asia and the islands of the Pacific in the age of colonialism. These stern judges failed to ask two questions. Why was Europe able to conquer so much of the world? What was the condition of the world before Europe expanded?

The voyage of Columbus was a treasure hunt not an invasion, for medieval Europeans did not dream that it would be their future to reshape the world. A few of them hoped for converts to their religion, but medieval Christendom was self-absorbed (as the Protestant Reformation was to be) and the honest truth was that they most wanted to trade. They wanted gold because they were short of coins. They wanted spices such as pepper because that helped them to eat their meat, deteriorating because animals had to be slaughtered at the beginning of winter. They wanted silks because the best clothing that Europe could make was heavy cloth. Unfortunately the countries which possessed these luxuries did not want what the Europeans had to sell; not before the eighteenth century did Europe export more than it imported.

The Islamic countries and India were superior civilizations, at least in the lifestyle of their élites, and in the thirteenth century Marco Polo describing the splendour of Kubla Khan was like a poor child marvelling at a shop window. The hordes of peasants were worse off than most peasants were in Europe, but Asian élites could afford to laugh at the early European traders. (The later dominance of European shipping in Asian trade came when the ships carried Asian goods mostly purchased with American silver.) So medieval and earlier Europe was far from being a menace to the rest of the world. It was during the Dark Ages overrun by wave after wave of invasions from the steppes of Asia, the last being the migrations of the Magyars and Tartars, and it was during the Middle Ages unable to bring its crusades against Islam to any permanent victory. Only in 1480 did the Russians begin to take Europe back into Asia as they crossed the Urals and embarked on the centuries-slow journey of colonization that was to end on the shore of the Pacific, to be checked at the beginning of the twentieth century by the awakened power of Japan. Most of the Russians remained in the slave-like condition of serfdom until the 1860s, and all over Eastern Europe severe famines were experienced until the eighteenth century.

But the peoples of Western Europe were growing restless. A recent authority, G.V. Scammel, concludes that

> no single or simple reason explains what set in motion and sustained the staggering sequence of European exploration, conquest and colonization which commenced around 1400, although the whole gamut of human motives from economic necessity to idealistic fervour has at various times, and in various combinations, been invoked.... The triumphs of the Europeans and the establishment of their first oceanic empires have been explained, like the onset of their imperial urges, according to the predilections of the times (*The First Imperial Age*, 1989, pp. 51, 71).

One stimulus, it may be agreed, was the envy of the rest of Europe which knew that the spectacular wealth of Venice had been founded on trade with the East. Venice's rival Genoa had alos profited from trading ports in the Black Sea. When Constantinople fell to the Ottoman Turks in 1453 the Black Sea was barred to European traders and, when the Ottoman conquest of the Levant followed, the eastern half of the Mediterranean became an Islamic lake, with Venice doomed to its destiny as a centre of tourism. In response to such challenges, and to their own mysterious restlessness, the Europeans were compelled to develop their assets which had already been used by Portugal in the exploration of the African coast – although Portugal was one of the poorest areas in Western Europe, with a population of under two million.

One European asset was the climate, which was healthy enough to encourage a substantial population as the basis of economic development (an advantage over the Islamic countries). It seems that the population of Europe in 1500 was about a hundred million, about double the population of Africa. But Europeans knew that they could not provide for unlimited children, and their custom of postponing procreation until spouses could set up an independent household reflected this realism. Until they could save enough to marry, most Europeans worked as servants, a custom which did something to increase their knowledge. After the plagues and famines of the fourteenth century the European population did not outstrip its agriculture until about 1760, when industrialization began to come to the rescue.

Having no great abundance of cheap labour to work the fields, Europeans knew that they had to develop technology: their need was greater than the slave-supported Roman empire's. They developed the watermill, the heavy plough drawn by the shod horse, the three-field system to preserve fertility (with only one field maximally productive at one time). And they knew that they had to trade. Their way to wealth was the road and the sea – for example the Baltic, a highway for trade in grain, timber and furs exchanged for manufactures. Their trade created cities which became rich enough to purchase "liberties" and to resist taxation. These cities in Italy, Flanders, North Germany and elsewhere became the birthplaces of capitalism. Capitalism needed many devices – accountancy, insurance, a banking system with bills of exchange – but it also needed factors which may be called cultural or even moral: literacy, numeracy, rationality, a sense of time, trust in fellow merchants, energy enough to take risks. And the rewards of trading capitalism encouraged the development of the instrument that, more than any other, made Europe's imperial expansion possible. This was the ship. Beginning in thirteenth-century coastal voyages, the ship's development ended in the multi-masted sailing ship navigated with the aid of a compass. When equipped with the cannons developed in the fifteenth century in order to batter down castles, such a ship was lethal. The Arabs were for long better sailors, but in the battle of Diu (1509) the Portuguese gained control of the Indian Ocean because their ships were strong enough to carry their cannons around the Cape. Such ships could command all the seas of the world – and they could protect what became the global commerce of European capitalism.

In time this development, aptly called the European miracle, seemed no more than natural. Adam Smith, who magisterially analysed the economy created by this miracle, is reported to have observed to a friend that "little else is required to carry a state to the highest degree of opulence from the lowest barbarism, but peace, easy taxes and a tolerable administration of justice; all the rest being brought about by the natural order of things." But that remark does not sufficiently take account of the uniqueness of the development in early modern Europe. The contrast with other civilizations is very striking. The Chinese empire, for example, fostered commerce and its inventions included paper money as well as gunpowder. But it was highly centralized, the delegates of its emperor being civil servants who were salaried out of taxes and moved about frequently – and after about 1330 rulers saw no need to develop inventions into technology on a large scale for there was no shortage of peasants. Nor did they see any need of commerce outside their own vast domains. Foreign trade had already been banned for sixty years when after 1430 the Ming emperors decreed the end of all foreign voyages, despite the previous achievements of Chinese sailors. The art of building large ships was forgotten. The most characteristic monument of imperial China was to be the Great Wall keeping barbarians out. In India no large bureaucracy could be established, but Mughal emperors (1526–1707) and local rulers grew rich by confiscatory taxation. Merchants, thus prevented from making productive investments, were far from enjoying the prestige which they were beginning to acquire in Europe. The Hindu system was a caste system, where occupations were hereditary. Priests and warriors were at the top of the pile because their good deeds in previous incarnations had earned them that supremacy. So far from sailors receiving patronage, Hindus who crossed "the waters" were subject to excommunication from their castes.

These factors do much to explain why Europe found itself ruling the seas for the sake of Asian trade or the mining of silver in Peru or the great catches of cod off the coast of Newfoundland. But they do not account for the conquest of vast territories. The clue here is provided in a sentence by John Hall, one of the many scholars who have recently debated the causes of European expansionism: "The complete formula of the European dynamic is that competition between strong states inside a larger culture encouraged the triumph of capitalism" (in *Europe and the Rise of Capitalism* which he edited with Jean Baechler and Michael Mann, 1988, p. 35).

That sentence points to the division of Europe into peoples never completely unified and quite often coalescing into nation states more stable than India's principalities. Geography encouraged the formation of such states along the Atlantic coast – Spain, Portugal, France, the Netherlands and England. These nations fought each other within Europe and became rivals for the profits of trade overseas. That rivalry was a further stimulus to adventure and investment, for fear that others would get there first. It was also a stimulus to the military occupation of territory, for fear that others would occupy it first. Frequently the history of colonization, specially in Asia, begins with the local ruler being hospitable to some Europeans, in the belief that he could use the new force against his own rivals. Then other Europeans arrive, make their own alliances and begin to trade. A band of adventurers or a trading company (the British or Dutch East India Company, for example) has to be allowed to employ an army (usually of mercenaries) and to administer a territory, in order to exclude rivals. And as complaints against maladministration by this company mount, the government of the mother country has to assume responsibility with what the Dutch in Indonesia called an "ethical" policy. A colony has happened. In African terms, that was how the enterprise of Cecil Rhodes became Rhodesia.

But the competition between these colonizing nations took place within a shared culture, which in religious terms was Christian. Before the expansion of Europe across the seas this framework had helped Europeans to understand each other and to trade, as well as to fight, with each other. Now it meant that advantages secured by one nation in expeditions overseas led rapidly to imitation. Above all, it meant that all these European nations were united by the belief that their culture, including its Christian element, was superior to all others in the world. Even as the Christians shot each other to pieces they were certain that they were better than all the others, for all other religions were idolatry or devil-worship. From this fixed, scarcely argued-for, belief that the Europeans were now God's chosen people was drawn the conclusion that the rival nations had a moral right to acquire as much of the rest of the world as they could manage. The relationship of Spain and Portugal illustrates all these tendencies. At first rivals, they were more or less reconciled when their rights to colonize the Americas were allocated by their Treaty of Tordesillas (1494), blessed by a Spanish Pope who claimed from God the right to allocate all earthly power. Later the arrangements were revised. Finally in 1580–1640 the much larger size of Spain enabled it to absorb Portuagal and its empire. In the colonization of a new world, the Spaniards and the Portuguese were both rivals and collaborators. A later example of these tendencies is provided by the relationship of Britain and France, whose *entente cordiale* of 1904 was primarily an agreement to curb their own colonial rivalry and to exclude Germany from empire-building.

Competition, often including piracy or declared war, led to the Dutch takeover of Asian trade and trading centres from the Portuguese. Until the nineteenth century the British were not strong enough to make much of an impact on South America, but they took over the territory around the well-stocked seas and the great rivers of North America from the French and earlier colonists. Rivalry also led to the British victories over the French and their allies in India, with the result that after the disintegration of the Mughal empire Britain ruled India with an always small army and often by "indirect" rule in the principalities. The British had gone there to trade, fanning out from Madras, Bombay and Calcutta, and if one thing is certain about their *Raj* it is that it was very seldom intended or predicted before Clive's victory in Bengal in 1757. Commercial considerations alone, without that intensity of rivalry between the nations, would probably not have stimulated the expense of treasure and lives involved in the battles by sea and land up to the end of the eighteenth century.

In the last quarter of the nineteenth century the Europeans' international rivalry entered a new phase, colonizing a quarter of the globe. The scramble for Africa was motivated by fear that another colonial power would add extra territory to its empire, much more than any purely commercial calculation. Propagandists for the new imperialism offered hopes which were almost all as illusory as the hopes of Columbus; for example, Germans were promised "another India" in Central Africa. Somewhat more realistically some businesses were relieved to have secure sources of raw materials and secure markets for their products – secure because governed. And many individuals, then as in the earlier stages of imperialism, found a better life abroad than at home. But economic historians tend to agree that the only country which made a large profit out of Africa was Belgium, whose king established the most brutal of all the colonial regimes, to exploit the rubber and the mines along the Congo river. It was Joseph Conrad's "heart of darkness".

When the European powers divided the map of Africa between them (as in the Berlin Conference of 1884-5), national pride counted for more than commerce. Much in that story bears out the definition offered by a great economist, Joseph Schumpeter: "Imperialism is the objectless disposition on the part of a state to unlimited forcible expansion." To say that is not to deny that there were economic objectives – for example, the acquisition of Africa's palm oil to lubricate Europe's machines and to make soap for Europe's workers. But history does not support Lenin's general theory, advanced in his *Imperialism the Highest Stage of Capitalism* (1917), that the whole scramble for Africa was the result of the contraction of Europe's markets and anxiety about raw materials during the great recession of 1875-95. The truth seems to be that the great recession was cured not by imperialism but by cheaper prices – of food through American and Australian production and of industrial goods through the modernization of Europe's own factories.

The imperial expansion of France from the Riviera to the Congo made economic sense at first, for it began in the 1830s with the occupation of Algeria where French colonists, the *pieds noirs*, could settle. But as it expanded over the deserts and into the tropics it became an empire which enthused the Army (because of glory) and the Church (because of missions) much more than the business world. After 1871 it was prized as emotional compensation for the loss of Alsace and Lorraine to Germany. British expansionism along the Cape-to-Cairo route was heavily influenced by anxiety about these French ambitions. At the same time a competitive "scramble for Asia" was beginning. In Indo-China the French acquired a compensation for their loss of India and for the Dutch grip on Indonesia. The Americans entered the imperialists' competition with the acquisition of the Philippines from Spain. Had the twentieth century continued this story, China might well have been carved up like Africa by these colonizing rivals.

German imperialism, although a great source of anxiety to its rivals, was fed by national pride rather than by sober calculations about an empire which received only two per cent of German investments overseas and which, when it disappeared during World War One, included no more than fifteen million people. The British empire was a far more considerable and profitable affair and its markets increased in importance to Britain as British factories found it difficult to make goods which other industrial nations wished to buy. In the 1950s almost half of British exports went to the empire or Commonwealth. But much of the economic value of the empire at the height of its glory was provided by India or by the stepping stones from England to India and to the "Far East". And even India was the prestigious "jewel in the crown" – not a mere investment to be justified by maximizing profits. It produced wealth, but it also, and increasingly, necessitated expenditure and caused troubles. The British were not being completely hypocritical when "the Indian Mutiny" at the end of the 1850s had brought home to them the fact that their presence as mere traders was finally over and that their days as rulers were numbered. They often said that their remaining task was to act as "guardians" before the inevitable independence had to be recognized (of course, paying themselves for this work). In 1914, of the forty-six per cent of British investments overseas which went anywhere in the empire, most went to South Africa, Australia and Canada. Of the total investments overseas, about twenty per cent went to the USA, about twenty per cent to South America, and about five per cent to Continental Europe. A purely economic analysis suggests that the most profitable investments were made outside the colonies which were to belong to the "Third" world. They were made in places where expenditure was not needed on military occupation and civilian administration, and where a wide range of British goods found a large number of consumers able to pay for them. A similar calculation of French interests in 1914 ends by pointing to investment in the development of the Russian empire as far more profitable than Africa. And the French knew it then. Less than ten per cent of their foreign investments were in their empire.

The charges made against European colonialism in *The Road to Damascus* were all based on history. But history also shows that the Europeans did not usually conquer by massacres (the extermination of the natives of Tasmania being a notorious exception to this rule). What caused the disappearance of the Caribs and the decline of the native population in Latin America was partly demoralization and hard labour under the new regime, but largely diseases brought over from Europe. Cortes, commanding just over four hundred men, had not massacred the Aztec empire which he conquered. What caused the cultural decline of non-European value systems was partly the deliberate policy and propaganda of the colonial power, most systematic in France's *mission civilisatrice*. But a fatalistic feeling had more effect. Europeans had the prestige because they had the power through better organization and better technology, particularly in the ship and the gun. Here, for the Two-Thirds World, was an immense uprooting tragedy, and humanity should weep over it. But it was not caused simply by bullets.

The authors of *The Road to Damascus* came from countries where the consequences of colonialism were (and in the 1990s remain) at their worst. They spoke out of many particular tragedies. But they did not give the whole picture. Along with great suffering, the Europeans brought benefits to other peoples. Some of these peoples had been primitive in ways which no fantasy about the "noble savage", no romantic view of the "primitive" or "ethnic", can conceal. Theirs was an unrecorded history because there was no ability to keep any record apart from oral folklore – and the history, had it been recorded, would have been a tale mainly of poverty, disease, terror-filled superstition, cruel intolerance and a tribalism frequently at war with other tribes. Europeans are rightly condemned for the iniquity of their slave trade – but most of the slaves seem to have been delivered into their hands by African chiefs. Before the Europeans went to Africa there was no modern medicine or education or justice, no wheel or plough, no maize, potato, cocoa, cotton or tobacco (all these crops had been developed in America). Europeans were wrong to generalize about African barbarism: they should have paid more attention to the Mali and Songhay empires in the west, to Benin in what is now Nigeria, to the Bantu kingdom around the Congo and to the cohesiveness of tribal life elsewhere. But many customs in the old tribal life are condemned by modern Africans as barbaric, female circumcision being an example. Pre-Columban America could boast elaborate social systems, developed by the "Red Indians" but supremely by the Aztec and Inca empires to the south. But before the Europeans went to America tribalism was often as inhuman as in Africa; the Caribs, for example, were cannibals. Not more than ten million people found sustenance in the whole of North America, and the empires in the centre and the south rested on the exploitation of subject tribes who therefore often welcomed the European conquerors. Those empires, deservedly famous for many achievements, lacked the wheel (or at least its general use), the horse, the ox, the pig, the sheep, sugar, wheat and any simple system of writing. India had a civilization far older than Europe's. It might, or might not, have flourished if left to itself. But as a matter of history the Europeans who went to it made it possible for India to be today a more or less unified nation and a democracy with an independent system of justice and a large sector of modern industries and services, the development of which began under the British *Raj* (admittedly after World War One) and was regretted by Gandhi.

Modernization inflicted much damage on Europe's empires – as it did on Europe. Age-old crafts declined as European manufactures arrived. Agriculture on which the population had traditionally subsisted was changed in a number of countries by "monoculture", the concentration on one crop for export, threatening the population's own food supply and running the risk that world market prices would fall. Sugar, cotton, peanuts, rice, cocoa, tea, coffee, rubber and tin were some of these dangerous products. And it was a fact that these arrangements, which left the bulk of the populations in poverty, were initiated or encouraged by the colonial powers in order to benefit their own manufacturers and consumers. The new trade was between Africa (for example) and Europe, not within Africa. But another fact was the increase in the "native" populations assisted by the introduction of European methods and standards of medicine and hygiene. Without the economic development brought about by the colonial connection – limited as that development was – it is very doubtful whether these increased numbers could have survived. It was in the colonial era that the world's population problem began to be the biggest of all its problems: the growth between 1830 and 1930 was approximately from one billion to two billion.

The sins of European colonialism certainly deserve anger, shame and repentance. But a totally just verdict on this complex phenomenon, were that to be possible for mortals, would probably not be simple condemnation. The modernization which the profits of colonialism made possible in Europe spread to North America, to Japan and to the rest of the world, including the colonial world. The colonies suffered through this connection, but countries which largely escaped it – imperial China, Thailand, Afghanistan, Ethiopia – did not prove any theory that it was only colonization that prevented modernization. And to be thoroughly just, an all-wise judge would have to ponder the question what the world would have looked like without Europe's ideas – which were used in order to protest against European dominance. The very idea that humanity is entitled to unlimited material progress is European. So is the idea that the individual should assert himself in order to claim his rights. So is the idea of a democracy recognizing the rights of oppositions and minorities. Modern maps of Latin America, Africa and Asia reflect the nationalism which was learned from European conquerors, not caused by the earlier history of those continents. Historians of India agree that the rejection of foreign rule could not be achieved until the foreign idea of the nation had been absorbed and propagated by the foreign idea of the political party. The Marxist attack on imperialism was named after a German who wrote books in London, and the overthrow of apartheid was led by an African whose Christian name was Nelson.

Until an all-wise judge pronounces, some words from a German history of *The Dissolution of the Colonial Empires* (translated into English in 1989) seem fair. Franz Ansprenger wrote:

> The colonial domination by European nations and their imperialism constitutes an unhappy chapter in human history, not only because of the bloodshed it involved (a price common, unhappily, to every chapter of human history) but rather because of the conditions of poverty, and, worst of all, the immorality, with which Europe oppressed the rest of humanity during those centuries, and which we have grown accustomed to glossing over by speaking of "underdevelopment". The positive core of imperialism, however, was and is the drawing together of humanity into a global society. The question is whether this global society will be capable of assuming a more humane face (p.304).

The way to wealth

It was hard to part with empires. The British clung to India until 1947, and with even more stupidity the Dutch fought to keep Indonesia until 1949, and the French to keep Vietnam until 1954 and Algeria until 1962. The battles to retain Portugal's African empire ("Christian Civilization") lasted until 1974. Gradually, however, the European peoples have learned that their way to wealth does not involve "imperialism" if that word be defined as the permanent, armed occupation and control of the territories of other peoples. The wealth (Gross Domestic Product) of the nations in the European Community rose more in the short period 1950-80 than in the whole of 1800-1950. Then Europe almost caught up with Japan – which in the 1860s had begun to imitate the Europeans whom it had attempted to exclude. Disastrously Japan imitated Europe's colonialism. When cured of that folly by great suffering and humiliation, Japan imitated Europe's export drive. It then learned that, in order to grow rich, it need never have attempted to conquer Asia. Within Europe Germany also learned, at a very great cost to other peoples and to itself. It never did secure an empire either in Europe or overseas. But after their total defeat the West Germans rose to unprecedented heights of prosperity by their export drive. To be first in the world, a country has only to sell the world something which the world wants: and perhaps in the 1980s and 1990s the Soviet Union has been learning this lesson as it has dismantled what may be the last of history's land empires. The decision which liberated Eastern Europe was that occupation and intervention by the Red Army could no longer be afforded. The benefits to the overstretched imperial power did not now outweigh the costs.

For long Western Europe was mesmerized by the doctrine of mercantilism, although in practice Europeans often flouted it for their private gain. Mercantilism meant that a nation's wealth was to be measured by three standards – the amount of gold or silver, the amount of territory, and the number of men who could be paid by the gold and silver to control the territory as soldiers or sailors. If a nation had colonies, the function of those parts of its territory was to provide raw materials which the "mother country" could transport in its own ships to its own merchants, thus adding to its own wealth. Any goods exported from the colonies and not wanted in the "mother country" were to be penalized by heavy customs duties.

This system had obvious advantages to the mother country, as *The Road to Damascus* pointed out with force. It was the system which over a long period prevented (for example) the development of an Indian textile industry able to compete with the factories of Lancashire. Together with the surplus derived from the improvement of agriculture in the eighteenth century, the profits of this system provided much of the finance which developed British inventions. From the 1770s or thereabouts England became the world's first industrial nation, "the workshop of the world", and it remained the leading industrial nation until the 1870s. As late as 1900 about a third of the world's manufacturing exports was British. So were almost two-thirds of the world's merchant shipping. Consequently Britain sustained a fourfold increase in population between 1801 and 1911. But in the end the system worked to the disadvantage of the mother country. It meant that Britain felt obliged to frustrate the developing trade and shipping of its American colonies – one of the main grievances behind their war of independence in the 1770s. Thus almost the whole of the first British empire was lost. That did not end the acquisition of new colonies, but it did end the illusion that colonies could be milked easily and endlessly. Accordingly it became the general opinion in Britain that colonies were, in Disraeli's phrase, "millstones hung around the neck". The Royal Navy was so supreme after Nelson's victory that colonies which offered harbours (preferably on the way to India) could be picked up easily, and virtually all the salt water in the world could be treated as British territory, but it was realized that fresh conquests of land were not needed extensively and that the Navy was best employed in the protection of international free trade, greatly to Britain's advantage. Later, attitudes changed. Victorian "imperialism" (a word which acquired its modern meaning in 1881) began to wave flags, encouraged by Disraeli's acclamation of the Queen as Empress of India. In 1896 a Canadian politician referred to "these somewhat troublesome days when the great Mother Empire stands splendidly isolated in Europe". It now seemed that the empire was an inexhaustible resource and market which (it began to be added) deserved "protection" from the menace of free trade which would benefit foreigners. Actually, however, in the shaping of the future, competition with other industrial nations in high technology or mass production was to be more significant; and there Britain, lazy in its imperial security, began to be outclassed. In the last quarter of the nineteenth century its imports of manufactures from "the Continent" and the USA more than doubled, and many of these goods which (so to speak) belonged to the twentieth century had an ominous country of origin: Germany.

Being without any sizable empire overseas, Germany had the incentive to develop modern industries and to modernize old ones, relying on its better educational and training systems. Life remained harsh for many workers and peasants: to that, the influence of Marxism on Germany is sufficient testimony. But this economic advance helped the German population to rise from about thirty-five million in 1840 to sixty-three million in 1910, giving it the advantage over France (which grew in the same period from thirty-five to only 41.5 million). Tragically, however, this growth led the German ruling class to believe that a territorial empire was both necessary and possible – first in Europe, then overseas. Such ambitions of a Germany now allied to the Habsburgs' Austro-Hungarian empire aroused the fears of France, Russia and Britain, who allied and thus encircled Central Europe. In response the German General Staff planned to knock out France through Belgium before Russia and the British empire could mobilize and before the Austro-Hungarian empire was broken up by the forces of nationalism. The date became 1914.

The defeat of Germany and its allies in 1918 was followed by the disastrous Treaty of Versailles, imposing economic "reparations" which made it impossible for the Germans to rebuild their economy in time to withstand the effects of the Wall Street crash in 1929 – thus creating the conditions for the rise of Nazism. (In the 1940s the victorious allies very nearly repeated the mistake when their demand for unconditional surrender, which probably prolonged the war, was followed by talk about permanently depriving Germany of industries and military forces.) But the folly of Hitler was worse. It was to imagine that the recovery of Germany demanded the conquest of its neighbours in order to provide *Lebensraum*, "living space", the Third Reich as a new empire. What Germany needed in fact was what was developed by the Christian Democrats under Adenauer and Erhard in the 1950s – a determination to earn a better future by work. Essential features of the post-war German "miracle" were wages which were at first realistically low and were then negotiated annually with a minimum of strikes; high investment in new technology by banks and other financial institutions; the acceptance of innovation by trade unions which did not compete with each other; regular consultation between management and workers (although "co-determination" was not accepted by the Christian Democrats before the 1970s); social security which grew with national income and was accompanied by the total rejection of budget deficits and therefore of inflationary public borrowing; and an export drive which for many years was helped by a devalued currency. To this formula the Social Democrats added in the 1970s the necessary policy of influencing Eastern Europe, not by refusing to recognize any government which had dealings with East Germany, but by strengthening every possible kind of link. With such policies West Germany outstripped countries such as Britain (and France) which were still living in the imperial past. When the British market was fully opened to it within the EC, West Germany's exports to Britain rose fivefold in the period 1976-86.

Even as late as the 1930s it was possible for some of the British to imagine a development of the empire somewhat similar to the development which later occurred in the European Community. The "white dominions" were then virtually sovereign nations; the colonies had not yet achieved independence (although a League against Imperialism had been formed in Brussels in 1927); it was possible for the advocates of "imperial preferences" to envisage an economic union of the quarter of the globe still covered red, even if the dream of an "imperial federation" propagated at the beginning of the century had to be abandoned. But these ideas were all dreams. The dominions and India needed their own international trade (particularly with the USA) and protection against British exports; the British had no intention of living under any higher authority; distances would always handicap imperial trade; in the 1940s the USA was to refuse post-war help to Britain unless "imperial preferences" were scrapped in the interests of US trade. Imperial dreams lingered, and they cost Britain dearly when the European Community was being formed as a permanently fruitful market. Nevertheless, despite Britain's *relative* economic decline, if we ask when in all history up to the end of the 1980s Britain had the largest population earning in the largest number of jobs and enjoying the highest living standards, with the widest distribution of homes and shares, we do not find the answer in any period of the empire on which the sun never set. We find it, of course, in the 1980s, when Britain began to learn the lessons which a harsher history had taught to Germany and Japan.

The British empire was not the only one which in the end led its mother country to wander from the way to wealth. The Spanish empire did not shrink on the map until early in the nineteenth century. But by then it had brought disaster to Spain.

After the disappointment of Columbus the conquerors of the new world found the prize he had been looking for – silver, for a time mined abundantly in Mexico and high up in the Andes. But the prize turned to dust. As E.L. Jones commented in *The European Miracle* (1987, p. viii), for the miracle of economic progress to work there had to be a commercial and industrial energy only needing to be awakened.

> On the face of it, a case can be made out for seeing the acceleration of European growth as the effect of the bounty of overseas resources brought by the discoveries. However, what looks more to the point is the existence of economies that could make good use of what was discovered: a native European rather than an imperialist peculiarity.

And this ability to turn an empire into modernity was not present everywhere in Europe. It was lacking in Portugal. The consequent contrast between the poverty of the Portuguese and the wealth of the Dutch (no more numerous, and latecomers to empire-building) is dramatic. The ability to use the new wealth creatively was also lacking in Spain.

Instead of using the American bonanza to modernize their own country, the Spaniards developed the attitude that only the Church, the empire, the army and an idle landlordism provided honourable careers. American silver could buy anything, so Spain's own agriculture and industries were neglected. Labour was despised, and slaves were imported to perform it. The image of Spain became the castle dominating poorly cultivated fields.

The Spanish ruling house, the Habsburgs, used much of the new wealth to pay for their territorial ambitions in Europe. Great quantities of silver went to defend the vast empire which

Charles V had acquired through dynastic marriages, although in his memoirs the emperor never stooped to mention America. Long and very costly wars were fought against the Turks until 1581, against the Dutch until 1648, and against the French until 1659. By the time the flow of American silver stopped during the seventeenth century, it had become clear that it would leave two legacies. One was the extension of Spanish rule over part of Italy. Another was an inflation which, combined with a general diversion to militarism and imperialism away from commerce, wrecked the Spanish economy. The net result was that Italy and Spain declined together. The inflow of silver helped prices to rise fourfold in the sixteenth century. All the structure of a traditional society was battered by this inflation, and the only nations to escape relatively unhurt from the crisis were those such as the Netherlands, England and (to some extent) France which had begun to use the new money to modernize. It has been reckoned that nine-tenths of the American silver found its way to these three countries, who were Spain's competitors and enemies. Increasingly the Dutch and the French handled the trade with the Spanish empire, and when Latin America had thrown off colonialism the British stood ready. Antwerp grew richer than Lisbon, Amsterdam than Seville, London than anywhere else in the end. It can be suggested that instead of crossing the ocean Columbus might have been more of a benefactor to Spain had he urged the improvement of the irrigation of the country's own parched fields.

As it was, the thorough modernization of Spain and Portugal had still not been achieved when the celebration of the long voyage of Columbus was being planned almost five hundred years later. And the thorough rejection of colonialism and racism in the European conscience had to wait until the story of the empires could be seen in retrospect. Today Western Europe is the scene of a very large migration from ex-colonies and other nations in the Two-Thirds world, dramatically reversing the imperial trend. About seventeen million immigrants or "guest workers" or their descendants have black or brown skins which make them permanently conspicuous as symbols of Europe's new relationship with the other continents.

Of course it is necessary not to exaggerate the strength of the attitudes which signalled Europe's knowledge that the age of the empires was over. A great deal of nostalgia for imperial glories has lingered, specially in Britain. A great deal of racism has been expressed towards the new immigrants, most openly in France. There has been a refusal to grant the "guest workers" civil rights, social security or the right to own a business, especially in West Germany. The immigrants were recruited to do jobs which Europeans either could or would not do as their own prosperity rose to more-than-imperial heights during the post-war recovery, and hostility to the newcomers increased when competition for employment and housing increased in the 1970s. But few of the newcomers were expelled; most of their neighbours gradually accepted their customs; many symptoms of the racism that damaged them were made crimes by new national laws; their cause was joined by many whites. The newcomers showed that they thought their present situation preferable to the prospects which would have been theirs had they left Europe, both by staying in their adopted countries and by wanting relatives and friends to join them; and their numbers increased by natural fertility even when the legal limits on immigration were tightened as governments sought to reduce tensions. In however reluctant and confused a style, Europe has shared with these new millions in its midst some of the fruits of a development which could not have taken place without the profits of colonialism. In the way that the history of the world works, it was perhaps as near as could be expected to an apology for the sins of the empires; and if the acceptance of these new Europeans can be deepened, that may be some compensation for the evils involved in the expansion of Europe's "miracle" to change the destiny of every human being on earth.

In a world which may come to forgive this miracle which created misery along with wealth, what will be the shape of Europe?

6

Towards the Union

Voices of 1986

IN 1986 Sir Michael Butler published his reflections on *Europe: More than a Continent*. He had been heavily involved in EC problems for many years as a British Foreign Office official, and had been British Permanent Representative to the Community in Brussels during the six years 1979-85. Looking back on many negotiations, he wrote:

> European integration is, in its everyday life, primarily about solving detailed, complicated and usually technical problems by consensus in a political framework which makes it extremely difficult for governments to do other than agree in the end. That is what makes it so interesting and so unique (p.169).

But he dismissed the big questions about the future of Europe.

> No one is arguing that the ultimate destination of the journey the member states are making together should now be defined. Most ministers and officials have long since tacitly agreed that it would be useless and divisive to try to spell out a constitutional aim. A Federation? A directly elected President of a European executive? A Confederation (whatever that may be)? It is best to leave these questions aside (p.165).

In 1986 another book by an English expert on European affairs appeared. Sir Christopher Tugendhat, formerly a Conservative MP, was a member of the EC Commission for eight years, 1977-85. In *Making Sense of Europe* - it is interesting that such a title was thought necessary – he looked back on many difficulties, many agreements and much progress, usually slow. But he, too, was sceptical about the value of discussing any ultimate aim for the EC. Rhetoric about federal union was, he insisted, unrealistic and misleading. He wrote:

> The hope that common policies commonly financed would one day form the arches that would link together the various national economies and make possible the long and difficult process of fitting national economies together into a coherent and mutually compatible whole has had to be abandoned (p.48).

However, at about the time of the publication of these two books precisely that hope was revived by a new reality – the agreement of all the governments in the EC to create a single market by the end of 1992. Questions about the future shape of the European union as a coherent and mutually compatible whole then became topical and urgently debatable. "Union" is an ambiguous word and has therefore been suitable for many communiqués from political summits which meant less than they said. But after 1986 the discussion of what union ought to mean was no longer the monopoly of a few enthusiasts or alarmed theorists. Controversies flared up as the approach of union was seen to threaten the independence of national governments and parliaments. Standardization and (short of that) "harmonization" altered the scenery of daily life and work. People had to change their routines, learn new languages and even find new jobs as the European dimension in business became inescapable. Anxieties competed with hopes as immense risks were weighed against the prospect of a peaceful prosperity greater than anything known in any national history. Union was seen to be a process not rhetorical but economic, monetary and political. And of course many millions of Europeans asked: Where will it end?

Jean Monnet's plan

The idea which ended up as the European Community gathered strength after the two World Wars. After the first war the great hope was that the League of Nations would end war and teach the nations, newly assured by President Wilson of their right to be self-governing, to collaborate in the tasks of peace. But influenced by the example of Wilson's own Senate which vetoed American membership, the nations refused to collaborate effectively; and those nations which were in due course rebuked for aggression simply walked out of a league they despised. A similar, but chastened, hope accompanied the later foundation of the United Nations Organization, to be followed by further disillusionment. Many Europeans who reflected drew two main lessons from their very costly experience. One was that Europe must boldly construct its own future, although within the setting of the United Nations. The second was that the co-operation of European nations must create strong common institutions which would gradually change the scarred face of Europe. Something more than a debating society was needed and something more than nationalism was the goal.

We have noted that the reconstruction of Europe after 1945 was led by a trio of definitely Christian politicians, Robert Schuman, Konrad Adenauer and Alcide de Gaspari. But much of the intellectual stimulus came from two men who never said much about religion and who never held high office in national governments – two men with different philosophies and strategies, Jean Monnet and Alterio Spinelli. The influence which such men exerted, in and out of government, contradicts the theory which has been too often propounded by Europeans in the twentieth century – that nothing can be done.

Monnet was an internationally-minded French businessman

and civil servant. His background was cosmopolitan. Born in Cognac in 1888, he worked for a time as a salesman marketing brandy in other countries, and his commitment to internationalism was deepened when he was one of the organizers of allied co-operation in both World Wars and Deputy Secretary General of the League of Nations, 1920-23. After 1945 he made a great contribution to French recovery as the brain behind *le plan*, the policy sponsored by de Gaulle of stimulating and co-ordinating economic modernization and growth through the voluntary collaboration of leaders of government, business and trade unions. This plan brought France prosperity despite the instability of successive governments of the Fourth Republic. But Monnet's horizon (unlike de Gaulle's) was wider. In June 1940, drawing on earlier federalist dreams, he had put forward the idea of a Franco-British union, which Churchill in his turn proposed to France as a gesture while that nation was being conquered. Ten years later he refused to support Adenauer's idea of a Franco-German union: it was premature. However, he became the chief architect and the first President of the High Authority of the European Coal and Steel Community, formed in 1952 and operational in 1953.

As the grand title of the committee over which he presided hinted, this was the centre piece of a plan for Europe. At first it had been hoped that all the victors in the Second World War, as fellow members of the United Nations, would applaud as the European nations chose to live together in freedom and peace. But the dream died with Roosevelt. When the intentions of Stalin became brutally clear, it also became clear that Western Europe must rearm and that it was impossible to keep West Germany disarmed. Because the local population overwhelmingly objected, it was also impossible to pursue the plan of detaching from that nation the Ruhr and Saarland now being rebuilt from ruins. Yet no Frenchman could ignore the danger that a rearmed Germany might be tempted to begin a Third World War if the Soviet Union did not do so first. It had become imperative to internationalize the control of coal and steel, the most basic of the industries which Germans would need to prepare for war. The West German government under Adenauer, anxious to bury for ever the image of German militarism, agreed. So did Italy and the Benelux countries, which had their own reasons for concern about the Soviet Union and Germany. And many in these countries shared Monnet's hope that the Coal and Steel Community would lead to practical co-operation and to more in many other fields. At the press conference in Paris called to launch the new venture, Monnet's friend Robert Schuman called it "the first step towards European Federation". Monnet nursed this hope until he retired in old age in 1975 from another of his creations, the Action Committee for the United States of Europe. But neither Schuman nor Monnet defined the nature of the union which was their ultimate goal.

In his *Memoirs* (translated into English in 1978) Monnet recorded a distaste for "general ideas". Never a university student and seldom a reader of books, he was always an *homme d'affaires* – or, as political theorists have classified him, a "functionalist". He scorned emotional appeals to the public, preferring to make practical suggestions to the few in government or in circles close to governments. He was always an élitist, a man who murmured in the corridors of power; yet without ambition for office or publicity. He would repeat the saying of the American journalist Dwight Morrow, that there are two categories of men: those who want to be someone and those who want to do something. And he also repeated his own saying: "Before anything else, have a dining room." It was his hope that when offered realistic suggestions about how to respond to specific challenges, preferably over a good lunch, enough intelligent and influential people would take action. Each crisis would give them an opportunity to "build Europe" if they took Monnet's advice. "I have always believed that Europe would be built through crises," he wrote, "and that it would be the sum of their solutions" (p. 417). He had a great faith that people would discover what they had in common and that shared institutions would preserve and expand their discoveries. Institutions, he believed, are wiser than individuals. That was his road to union as a *solidarité de fait*.

Up to a point he was proved right, for the Coal and Steel Community was only one among a number of responses by governments to the twin challenges of an expansionist Soviet Union and a rearmed Germany. In 1947–51 Marshall Aid from the USA poured in to save Western Europe from ruin, despair and Communism, and the Organization for European Economic Co-operation had to be set up to co-ordinate the distribution of this bounty. When the American nuclear umbrella had to be cast over nations threatened by the Soviet coup in Czechoslovakia and the blockade of West Berlin, the North Atlantic Treaty Organization was formed in 1948. In the same year a 750-strong Congress of Europe was held in The Hague. There Churchill offered an orator's inspiration alongside Spain's Salvador de Madariaga; France's Paul Ramadier offered a veteran's leadership alongside Adenauer. The College of Europe in Bruges perpetuates that great affirmation of Europe's identity, made within three years of the ending of the Europeans' civil war. The Council of Europe was founded in Strasbourg in 1949 to affirm Europe's democratic and humanist values, and next year it produced the European Convention on Human Rights. "Uniting Europe", its first Secretary General declared with what he reckoned was caution, "may take twenty years."

The French government grew increasingly alarmed as Communists invaded South Korea. It did not wish to rely on the Americans to co-ordinate Western Europe's defences, now including a large West German element. A European Defence Community was therefore proposed, with forces wearing a single uniform, under a joint command. Since the joint command would need political orders, a European Political

Community was also envisaged, with a European Executive responsible to a European Parliament. The United States of Europe seemed to be achievable because it would be the only effective answer to Stalin.

But Monnet, and those who thought and planned and hoped like him, had underestimated the strength of nationalism. Britain held aloof from all these projects apart from Marshall Aid, NATO and the Council of Europe. Australia and New Zealand seemed nearer than "Europe" – and in 1950 the National Executive of the Labour Party actually said as much. There was no serious debate even about the possibility of joining. Less predictably, French leadership was withdrawn when the National Assembly refused to ratify the government's proposal for a European Defence Community in 1954, and the accompanying plan for a Political Community was shelved. For the next six years or so most experts in Britain thought that all schemes for a European union would suffer a similar fate and were not worth the sustained attention of busy politicians and civil servants. In other countries attitudes were almost equally discouraging. In the USA J.F. Kennedy listened eagerly to Monnet's ideas about partnership with a United States of Europe, and initiated the talks which were to cut the tariffs and increase the trade internationally (GATT) – but he was assassinated in 1963. The much older de Gaulle became President of France in 1958 and mused aloud in press conferences on the sacredness of national independence. In 1963 he vetoed the British application to "go into Europe", seeing Britain as the American "Trojan horse" sent to deceive and dominate. Four years later he again exercised his veto. For a time it looked as if he might take France out of the economic structure of the growing unity of "Europe", and in 1966 France did withdraw from the military structure of NATO. All that could be achieved was the West European Union, primarily in order to monitor West German rearmament and in particular to supervise the ban of West German manufacture of atomic, bacteriological and chemical weapons. The WEU, despite its name, was to be definitely an alliance, with no supranational authority such as the Coal and Steel Community's. As the anxiety about West German intentions decreased (thanks in part to the success of the Coal and Steel Community), and as fear of Soviet expansion beyond Czechoslovakia grew less (thanks in part to the success of NATO), the nations of Western Europe might feel safe in remaining just that – nations, allied with strictly limited aims. This explains why when some nations eventually agreed on wider economic co-operation, the atmosphere was an ambiguous mixture of some federalism with much nationalism.

The European Economic Community reflected in its origins both "the European idea" and a reluctance to make the organization more than intergovernmental. It was proposed at a conference in Messina in Sicily in 1955 and was planned by a committee chaired by Paul-Henri Spaak of Belgium, the Belgian Socialist leader. The Coal and Steel Community was available as a model, with a Council of Ministers representing the governments, a "Common Assembly" representing national parliamentarians but with far less power, and an executive Commission. France needed help for its farmers, its peasants and its nuclear hopes; West Germany needed large and assured markets for its expanding industries; Italy and the Benelux countries had their own reasons to take initiatives once the right signals were received from the bigger two. But the next thirty years made it plain that the purposes and powers of the Community were limited despite some continuing federalist rhetoric. The crunch came when in 1965 the Commission (still under its formidable first President, Walter Hallstein) proposed that the expanding Common Agricultural Policy should be financed by the Community's "own resources" under the supervision of a Council of Ministers which would take decisions by majority votes and under the ultimate control of the European Parliament. These resources were to be a guaranteed slice of the customs duties and Value Added Tax levied by all the national governments. An affronted de Gaulle refused to take part in the Community's affairs for seven months – so drastic was the change in French official attitudes since Schuman's grand talk of a European Federation. When the quarrel was patched up by the Luxembourg Compromise in 1966, recognizing the right of national governments to veto proposals contrary to their "vital" national interests, the arrangement was rightly called an agreement to disagree. In practice no major decisions could be taken without unanimity.

Alterio Spinelli's vision

Eventually Jean Monnet's plan got on the road again. The Coal and Steel and Economic Communities (sharing a single Commission from 1967) proved indispensable in the growth of the economies of their member states. Not even de Gaulle could safely withdraw from them as they developed their own momentum – and they lasted longer than de Gaulle's power to delay their political consequences. But the developing union owed something to Monnet's great rival in the intellectual leadership: Alterio Spinelli, the most charismatic of all the many Italians who have advocated the unity of Europe. He criticized Monnet's belief that all that was needed essentially was a dialogue "between Eurocrats who proposed and governments who disposed". He offered something more, something to touch the hearts of peoples through their national parliaments. He offered the vision of a Parliament to be the source of political authority in a united Europe.

Spinelli, in early years a Communist, had been imprisoned by Mussolini on the island of Ventotene near Naples. During sixteen years of brooding he exchanged Marxism for a vision of equal grandeur – a Europe in which governments such as Mussolini's would be impossible because the main strength of social life would lie in the smaller regions, and there would be a European federal government controlled by a European Parliament. Simultaneously this vision was appealing to many scattered in the Resistance across Europe. The exiled governments gathered in London were attracted; the Polish leader Sikorski proposed a federal union with Czechoslovakia, for example. Even Britain had some eloquent federalists for whom nationalism was discredited by the approach, and the horrors, of war, and echoes of their thoughts reached Ventotene.

After the war Spinelli was able to spread his vision as an Italian statesman, as the Secretary General of the European Federalist Movement, as a member of the European Commission 1970–76 and as a member of the European Parliament 1976–86. Gathering some Parliamentary colleagues for regular dinners in the Crocodile (the best restaurant in Strasbourg), this veteran inspired the initiative which led to the Parliament's Draft Treaty for European Union in 1984. Essentially what was proposed was that the Parliament should be empowered to ask the Commission to propose legislation which it could then amend. There was to be a council composed of ministers specially appointed by the national governments and this was to be virtually a second chamber, a senate, in the legislature although such terms were avoided as being too provocative. This council was to appoint the President of the Commission (as before) who was to appoint his colleagues (an innovation). The heads of the national governments were relegated to a "European Council" with vaguer powers, and on the Council of Ministers national vetoes were to be abolished gradually. It was clearly intended that these strengthened institutions of the Community should deal with political as well as economic affairs.

Spinelli was convinced that Monnet had begun to build Europe "badly" because he failed to appeal to the peoples – if necessary, over the heads of the governments – to abandon nationalism and to obtain instead the democratic control of power in a federated Europe. His *European Adventure* (translated into English in 1972) announced that "institutional reform of the Community and progress towards political union are one and the same thing" (p.16), in basic agreement with Monnet – but his was the approach of a politician, not a civil servant; a populist, not an élitist. He was willing to be somewhat cautious or devious: the word "federal" did not appear in his draft treaty. But he was sure that the peoples, if appealed to through their existing parliaments, if allowed to elect a central parliament with power, would share his own preference for prosperity in union. And there he was wrong. As the reception of the draft treaty showed, the peoples of the EC's member states remained more interested in their own nations, and more confident about their national institutions, than Spinelli imagined. What he contributed was a vision which was before its time. This is not uncommon in the history of prophets.

The road to union

As things turned out, progress was achieved not because the peoples demanded that more power should be given to the European Parliament but because the French and West German governments became convinced that the advantages outweighed the disadvantages in another idea – that decisions reached by the majority must create a single market, which in its turn must create economic and monetary union. Inevitably there were many hesitations when the parliaments and publics of France and West Germany were informed of this idea. But the governments were able to commit their nations. Willy Brandt, for example, the Socialist who was either Foreign Minister or Chancellor of West Germany 1966-74, had had a Norwegian mother and had been during his early years an exile from Hitler's Germany in Sweden, forming there a picture of the continent as a whole. When he came to power, his concentration on *Ostpolitik* seeking an understanding with Eastern Europe was accompanied by a growing enthusiasm for the integration of Western Europe, partly because he became convinced that only the success of the Economic Community in the west would create a force undeniably superior to Communism in the east. The road to German reunification seemed to lie through Brussels. After his fall from power he chaired a memorable commission on the relations between developed and other nations. And successive French Presidents were men who saw an opportunity for France under a new kind of monarchy to exercise a new kind of leadership in Europe.

In 1969, with de Gaulle safely in retirement, the project of "Europe" could be relaunched by the agreement of the French and German governments under Pompidou and Brandt. The project continued as the economic climate worsened. It became safe and even fashionable to look forward to "economic union". In 1975 the European Council was established to replace the occasional "summits" as a regular meeting place for all heads of government. The Commission had survived de Gaulle's displeasure. It contributed to the discussion before the Tindemans Report of 1975 (which was more cautious) by looking forward to its own absorption into a European government including ministers nominated by national governments. It wanted "an executive body with political authority under the supervision of a Parliament to which it would be responsible".

This came close to Spinelli's vision. As one step towards that goal, direct elections to the European Parliament were first held in 1979, twenty-two years after the Treaty of Rome had made provision for them. Its new democratic basis encouraged the Parliament to take the Commission to the Court of Justice because it had not yet proposed a transport policy and to reject the budgets proposed by the Commission in 1981 and 1984 as being too conservative. These moves had little long-lasting effect since the national governments would not release funds to allow for bigger budgets. Nor were they keen to abdicate their powers when the Draft Treaty on European Union was submitted to them. Even a 1981 proposal from the Foreign Ministers of West Germany and Italy (Genscher and Colombo) along lines close to the Draft Treaty's did little more than to keep the pot boiling or simmering. But under growing pressure the governments did agree on a "Solemn Declaration on European Union" in 1983 and on the Single European Act in 1985, allowing most questions to be decided by majority voting in the Council of Ministers, weighting the votes to reflect the varying importance of their nations but excluding only a few subjects thought to be vital to national interests. In legislation the Commission was still to make proposals to the Council alone, but the Parliament was to be allowed to amend most of the Council's legislative decisions unless the Council reaffirmed them unanimously.

There were strong political reasons why the national leaders became willing to fix 1992 as the year of the single market leading to economic and monetary union. The Franco-German alliance which had been decisive at previous stages had entered a new phase. The French President, François Mitterand, had been pro-European since the times when he had attended the 1948 Congress of Europe and had been a candidate for the Presidency against de Gaulle. He learned from the failure of the more thoroughly Socialist policy of his earlier years in power (1981–83) that it was now impossible to establish a society out of keeping with the rest of the EC. It was also impossible for one nation to "go for growth" alone, for inflation accelerated and the balance of payments became adverse: Britain's experience became France's. He had come to prefer a role which came as near as any national figure could come to being the *de facto* President of Europe, presiding over a combination of democracy with a modern prosperity. Here he was in harmony with Jacques Delors, the French Socialist with a Catholic background who as President of the Commission came near to being the Prime Minister of Europe. The two represented a clear development in the complicated story of French Socialism's attitude to the EC. Now the Community was seen to be needed for the technological modernization on which social progress depended – and it was seen to be perfectly capable of adding a "social dimension" which would give powerful protection to workers' rights.

The German Chancellor, Helmut Kohl, belonged to the Christian Democrat tradition which at the EC level had become explicitly federalist; its name in the European Parliament was the European People's Party. As a national statesman he adhered to Adenauer's policy of anchoring West Germany firmly to Western Europe, and he saw the prosperity which this policy had helped; the anchor, originally of steel, was now golden. And now he (like Adenauer) could feel almost all of West Germany behind him as he let out the anchor further. The new Socialist leader (Vogel) urged him to make faster progress to the European Union, since he had the advantage of "a national consensus in matters concerning Europe". The reluctance of Margaret Thatcher either to see Britain too involved in "Europe" or to be isolated through the use of the veto added to the opportunity which such statesmen seized as their chance to make history. In keeping with the developing character of the EC, they received decisive help from two non-Marxist Socialists. One was Bettino Craxi, the Italian Republic's first Socialist Prime Minister, who presided over the crucial summit in Milan in June 1985. At the head of a five-party and short-lived coalition, he believed in a more united EC as "a model of civilization, of collaboration, of stability, of peace" – a model, moreover, which helped Socialists to win the Left over from their rivals, the Communists. Another important figure was Felipe Gonzalez, Spain's first Socialist Prime Minister, who saw the integration of the new democracy into the European Union as the strongest possible guarantee against a return either to Fascism or to his own Marxist past.

But there were also solid reasons in economics for the new commitment of so many governments to the idea of union. After 1973-74 the nations belonging to the EC had been plunged into recession and unemployment; not even West Germany had been unaffected. The main oil-producing states, taking advantage of the fact that oil resources were finite, had quadrupled their prices, and nuclear power had turned out to be an expensive and dangerous alternative to oil. This disaster over energy prices had coincided with the decline of many of Western Europe's old industries. High technology was replacing old methods, and other rich countries were more willing to invest in it and to accept its introduction. Cheap labour was needed for successful competition where "high tech" was not necessary and poorer countries, for example those on the edge of Asia, provided workers willing to accept low wages, to the EC's disadvantage. The Albert and Ball Report of 1983 showed that in 1960-73 economic growth in the EC had averaged 4.6 per cent per annum, but in 1973-80 a mere 2.3 per cent. However, by the mid-1980s energy prices had fallen again because oil producers needed to sell their only important product – and because in Europe alternatives and savings meant less dependence on that product. Simultaneously the old industries presented less of a problem: largely, they had been either closed down or modernized. So the possibility existed of economic growth being resumed on something like the scale which had made the 1960s seem an economic miracle. Why development" by not selling the products in large and therefore profitable markets? It spent on research and development twice as much as Japan and it could draw on the brains of some 3,600 institutions of higher education. And why, when the USA had managed to increase its jobs by about fifty per cent since 1970, should the EC be unable to use the energies of about seventeen million citizens officially registered as unemployed? This was about thirteen per cent of its work force – a proportion due to sink in the next few years, but only to about ten per cent. Why should forty million people in the EC still be living below the poverty line? The answer seemed to be that a single market was needed, with more than 320 million customers and a position in international trade unequalled in the world.

Opportunely, the Cecchini Report commissioned by the EC predicted that if a single market could be constructed, abolishing all barriers to the free movement of goods, services, people and capital within the Community, it could "within the space of a few years put between four and seven percentage points on the Community's domestic product". If the governments would agree to the removal of border controls and customs, divergent technical standards and regulations, conflicting business laws and the restriction to nationals of competitions for contracts for public works, the peoples – not only the Germans or the French – would grow richer by being able to sell more widely and to buy, borrow, transport and insure more cheaply. And "inflation, traditionally growth's ugly sister, will be cooled down by the drop in prices provoked by open markets". This drop was expected to average at least six per cent. Unemployment would also fall. Moreover, "a dynamic European market, trading with the world on a footing of revamped competitivity, will provide a much-needed shot in the arm for other markets and economies in less buoyant shape". Meanwhile the "cost of non-Europe" – the cost of its frontiers – was a loss of about £130 billion a year. Lured by such promises, the governments in the EC hesitated but did not finally refuse to co-operate with the Commission in the necessary legislation. In Britain the Conservative government mostly co-operated in practice, although the enthusiasm for "Europe" associated with the fallen leader, Edward Heath, had been largely silenced in the Conservative ranks under Margaret Thatcher, as was demonstrated by the refusal to subsidise a fast rail link to "the Continent". The Labour Party was keener in theory although old attitudes surfaced when the local Labour group sabotaged the proposal to site the European Environment Agency in Cambridge. In Brussels there was a much more useful British contribution.

While President of the Commission Lord Jenkins had kept the idea of union alive, and now as a Commissioner Lord Cockfield began the intricate process of translating that theory into shared standards and agreed and enforced rules. The usual attitude taken in public by politicians in other EC countries was an embrace for "Europe". Over the rules they hesitated.

The European Parliament continued to urge speed in the progress to economic and monetary union, but it was clear that decision-making still rested with the national governments, as Monnet had assumed. The response to the Parliament's Draft Treaty had failed to achieve Spinelli's aim of persuading the national parliaments to downgrade these governments. It had also failed to increase the European Parliament's own power or prestige decisively. Few politicians of the front rank were willing to spend much time in Strasbourg. Contacts between Strasbourg and the national capitals often remained difficult. Public opinion polls and the turnout for Euroelections showed a large and continuing measure of ignorance or apathy, although this varied from country to country. Those who had voted had quite often chosen the candidates of parties (Green or on the extreme Right) which stood much less chance in the more "serious" national elections. Plainly if the single market and any subsequent economic and monetary union were to lead to a political union enjoying popular enthusiasm a new vision of the European future was required as the twentieth century moved to its close.

7

Twelve Stars in the Night

I AM, of course, unable to offer my own new vision of the future. I am not an expert in economics or politics. Even if I had that competence, it would be dangerous to insist on detailed proposals in economics or politics when writing a book which is meant to be definitely Christian. Christianity conveys no instructions about such details, and Christians are perfectly entitled to disagree about them. What I can offer is a short summary of what expert discussion seems to have tended to agree is both politically possible and morally desirable. In an earlier chapter I raised twelve cheers for the main features of the development of the Community up to the end of the 1980s. Now, as I peer into the 1990s and beyond with a telescope provided by others, I think I see the twelve stars of the European flag shining in the night of uncertainty and danger.

This starlight is not clear sunshine. Many things could go wrong. But what I see is in contrast with what a distinguished historian, James Joll, saw when he concluded a survey of *Europe since 1870* in 1983: the scene then seemed almost totally dark.

> At the start of the 1980s, fears of nuclear war and fears of economic decline and a rapidly changing and volatile situation in Europe meant that the prophets who for decades had been predicting the end of Western civilization seemed to be coming into their own again.... The basis for optimism is not easy to find.... Let us hope that there will still be historians left a hundred years from now to assess whether the epoch since 1870 was just the end of an era or the beginning of a new one (pp.489, 491).

In 1990, problem after problem is illuminated by the reality of the European Community – a hopeful reality.

1. If the EC is to be a community of peace, it must face the question which confronts every society not containing a majority of pacifists – how to deter potential aggression by maintaining military forces at a level which is the minimum consistent with security. So it cannot for ever escape the revival of the question raised by the plan for the European Defence Community in the 1950s. Indeed, the question is already topical in the 1990s, when the spectacular reduction of the Soviet threat has transformed the needs of the rest of Europe for security.

There is simple logic in the proposition that nations which trust each other sufficiently to have a single market leading to economic and monetary union ought to be able to trust each other sufficiently to have a single defence force. There is sensible economics in the reminder that a great deal of money has been wasted on the development of weapons, aircraft and ships by nations independently of each other. And there is military wisdom in the argument that this fragmentation of European effort has meant the fragmentation of European security. One result has been that the defence of Europe's divided west has depended on American willingness to sustain NATO as an alliance. American resources have even been essential to Britain's "independent" nuclear deterrents, Polaris and Trident. Another result has been that some parts of Europe's defence have not contributed to the security of fellow Europeans – for example, France's *force de frappe*, a massive nuclear "warning shot" planned to be fired all at once. This has been more genuinely independent than Britain's deterrents, but it has been no asset to West Germany, Italy or Spain. Many expert commentators on military affairs have for many years urged that more resources should be pooled within NATO.

The collapse of the European Defence Community was of no

great significance for the next forty years or so because in fear of Soviet expansionism the USA poured resources and men into NATO, an alliance which was already in place when the EDC failed. In particular the USA offered its own nuclear shield to deter any thought of aggression against Western Europe. Part of the strength of NATO was the willingness of the USA to consult its allies in an organization whose Secretary General was by tradition a European. The contrast was great with the firm (and on occasion ruthless) Soviet control of the Warsaw Pact, an organization which was only superficially a mirror to NATO. But NATO always had two points at which it was vulnerable when it confronted the Warsaw Pact.

One was its difficulty in persuading the rest of the world that its purpose was authentically and exclusively defensive. Because it was dominated by one of the two superpowers fighting the cold war, it was open to the charge that it was designed to bring pressure on the Soviet Union, whether or not that pressure involved any intention of beginning any military action. Many groups within Western Europe therefore opposed rearmament in NATO, and in particular campaigned against successive developments in NATO's nuclear weaponry, strategic, cruise or battlefield. NATO's position was justified by its governments as being defensive, but in order to deter aggression credibly Americans and Europeans had to be trained to use these arms against the Soviet Union and the rest of the Warsaw Pact, probably with the first use of battlefield nuclear weapons. Proclaiming its own love of peace, the Soviet Union constantly argued that NATO was aggressive in purpose; that the Warsaw Pact was a defensive alliance formed after NATO; and that any training of Warsaw Pact forces to advance into Western Europe was merely insurance. The Warsaw Pact, it was said, needed the capacity to strike first in a crisis brought about by "NATO imperialism". The presence of hundreds of thousands of American troops and some four thousand "tactical" nuclear weapons on German soil, whatever its real motive, was inevitably perceived as a threat. The minimum security required by the Soviet Union was the withdrawal of all foreign troops and nuclear weapons from both Germanies – and at one stage Stalin offered Adenauer this deal, which was rejected because of the obvious possibility that it might ease the advance of the Red Army. In the 1990s Soviet feelings about NATO will not disappear although a united Germany's membership is accepted.

The second major defect, or vulnerable point, in NATO has been its reliance on the willingness of the USA to be involved in Western Europe's defence should a crisis occur. During the many years when the Soviet Union was perceived as actively threatening the USA itself, it made sense to expect the Americans to value Western Europe as a useful base in a worldwide chain established to "contain Soviet aggression", as a fence might be built around a dangerous dog. But the policy was always very expensive. This fact became more and more noticeable as the deficit in the US budget increased together with the reluctance of the US public to pay taxes – and as the EC became the trading rival and almost the economic equal of the USA, the more able to pay for its growth because it did not need to pay fully for its own defence. And the policy always contradicted the previously traditional US preference for isolation from the world's troubles. Most Americans belong to families which crossed the Atlantic precisely in order to escape from Europe, and despite frequent reassurances to NATO at the official level the natural instinct of the public has been to "bring the boys back home" and get them out of uniform. As the Soviet threat has seemed to diminish (largely because the Soviet Union has had much more massive economic problems), the "decoupling" of Europe from America has become more attractive to Americans as well as to the anti-American elements which have never disappeared in Europe. Paradoxically, Soviet weakness seems to be achieving what was the aim of Soviet bullying in the age of the cold war. At least, the willingness of the USA to be so expensively and dangerously entangled in a Europe growing richer at its expense has become openly questionable. It was in fact always doubtful whether, in the ultimate nightmare, the USA would have been willing to invite its own nuclear destruction by using nuclear weapons under its control to defend Western Europe – although for many years NATO's credibility as defence against superior Soviet non-nuclear forces depended on this question not being pressed.

It is another genuine question, whether the EC would be the right replacement for NATO should the Americans demand that the Europeans should shoulder the bulk of the responsibility for their own defence – or should the Europeans make their own decision because they had recovered their self-confidence. As the 1990s begin the arguments against have prevailed repeatedly. Some have come out of neutralism. A neutral nation, Ireland, was admitted to full membership in 1973 and another, Austria, applied in 1989. Neutral Sweden and Finland may well apply during the 1990s, as may Eastern European countries. A reunited Germany cannot station near its eastern frontier forces perceived by the Soviet Union as a threat. In other EC countries vocal movements (including many Christians) want to have as little as possible to do with militarism and military alliances and in particular want to see the whole of Europe, or at least the whole of Central Europe, as a nuclear-free zone. And some arguments against the EC becoming a defence community have arisen out of nationalism. Many patriots in many countries, but specially in de Gaulle's France and Thatcher's Britain, have been extremely reluctant to surrender national control over the economy and defence – although Britain has not applied this argument to its membership of NATO under American hegemony. Many would feel that if the transfer of sovereignty in these two areas became unavoidable it would be safer to make the transfer to two authorities, not one. Otherwise the fear would be that a European government (it might be whispered: under German control, less palatable than American) would make nonsense of all past victories won in defence of national freedom.

But such arguments are looking increasingly weak. The arguments of neutralism are losing their force in a Europe where it is beginning to seem realistic to develop military security at a fairly low level of military expenditure, and for purposes which are (and are seen to be) purely defensive. Any military alliance between the EC and the USA could realistically claim to be purely defensive if it merely provided a promise of American retaliation (for what such a promise would be worth) in the event of Soviet aggression. In the new climate security could, it seems, be maintained without a single foreign soldier in Eastern Europe or East Germany. From Finland to Yugoslavia there could be a demilitarized *cordon sanitaire*, to reassure the Soviet Union. No country would be invited to join a heavily armed anti-Soviet alliance, potentially aggressive, if it were to be invited to adhere to an EC with a military dimension of that strictly limited nature. Such considerations suggest that unless a country is totally pacifist, without any means of military self-defence (which is a position rejected by every European country including Switzerland), it seems logical to revise neutralism in the new Europe.

The arguments of nationalism, already weak in the sphere of economics, are becoming less realistic in the military field. Any defence force depends on the economy which sustains it; NATO depends in the last analysis on the American economy. Any European army, navy or air force would ultimately depend on the economic strength of the European Community or Union. Moreover, any defence force which is not a complete waste of money needs a coherent strategy under a decisive command. It exists to deal with emergencies, and in any emergency orders would have to come from an established authority. (In the last analysis NATO is commanded by the American President.) To create in Europe two political authorities, one for economics and much else and one for defence, would be to create a double-headed monster of a kind that has not appeared anywhere in history. It would be a recipe for confusion.

Should the EC as a defence community possess nuclear weapons? The long, and rightly emotional, debate about "the Bomb" was stimulated by proposals for unilateral disarmament countered by "realism". At last it is in a new phase. Fortunately it seems possible to hope that "battlefield" or "tactical" weapons will not be necessary either to repel or to deter a Soviet invasion of West Germany, because the possibility of such an invasion is now virtually nil. Ever since these weapons were developed, they were the most dangerous pieces in the world's nuclear armoury because it was thinkable that they would be used by NATO before the Warsaw Pact felt it necessary to use them – and it was terrifyingly possible that their use would escalate into an exchange of strategic nuclear missiles. A Christian trying to make a moral judgement was in a dilemma: the use of such weapons would obviously be both evil in itself and highly dangerous, yet their possession as a deterrent might be the lesser of two evils since the member states of NATO were unwilling to maintain conscript armies in order to balance what was then thought to be the formidable "conventional" power of the Warsaw Pact. In the 1990s that dilemma seems to be over, with the proviso that if the threat revives this defence can be revived. But the moral dilemma created by the possession of strategic missiles remains. These are weapons which are evil beyond words but which, as deterrents, appear to have helped to maintain the peace during the cold war. Pending an agreed and verified disarmament, their retention as deterrents has therefore been accepted by many church leaders including Popes. My own view is that it would be morally legitimate (although obviously far from morally perfect) if the EC were to retain a small number of nuclear warheads for as long as the Soviet Union does, while completely renouncing the first use of them. These could be either weapons at present British or French.

It seems, therefore, that the challenge to Europe will be to work out a union capable of deterring aggression – with expenditure which will not be very large but entirely its own, and with a military structure grasped by its own elected political leadership. The first discussions of the 1990s have shown that such a development has ceased to be unthinkable, in the interests of the security that makes for peace. In comparison with the history of Europe in the previous hundred years, it would be Paradise. It is no longer necessary to think that there is no realistic alternative to NATO.

2. The dispersal of power in the EC has to be made compatible with efficiency. The two ideas are not totally incompatible, as may be seen by looking at the USA. The consititution of that country is based on two principles: the states exercise those powers which have not been transferred to the federation, and the federal legislature, the executive and the judiciary have separated and limited powers. In American history the states, the Congress, the Presidency and the Supreme Court have very often restricted each other. But the system works because in it there is a sufficient capacity for decisions.

The most obvious defect of the system taken over by the EC from the Coal and Steel Community is that its Parliament cannot legislate. This is glaringly different from the system in every member state, and while it continues the European Parliament will continue to be a body which is not taken with the complete seriousness which it deserves. The democratic logic, well formulated in the Martin Report in 1990, is therefore that the Parliament should share with the Commission the rights to initiate, and to amend or reject, legislation, and should share with national governments the right to appoint the Commission both collectively and individually. Already it shares with the Commission and the Minsters the right to shape the budget. In order to symbolize its increased involvement in the work of government, it agreed in 1990 to hold its full sessions as well as its committee meetings in a new building close to the Council and the Commission in Brussels. No Parliament should appear to be a distant conference. The end of a system which has located these sessions in Strasbourg (and much of the permanent staff in Luxembourg between these sessions) will also substantially symbolize a wish to save the money of taxpayers. No parliament should scrutinize expenditure while being itself a scene of gross extravagance.

The European Council of heads of state or government and the Council of Ministers will always have their places in an EC where the nations matter. In any Community that can be foreseen the nations will continue to undertake those tasks which are not undertaken more effectively by using the central government's real but limited powers: what has often been said is true. For these councils representing national governments to be integrated into a European system reflecting national democracies, it is logical to regard them as together constituting a senate. Alongside the Parliament the councils would be part of a two-chamber legislature whose consent would be necessary to all legislation. If the criticism is offered that this would delay legislation, the answer is that there ought to be far less Community legislation once the single market of 1992 is set up – and in any case every member state already thinks it worthwhile to pay the price of democracy.

The councils making up this senate would have to be appointed by the elected national governments but could be strengthened by much more careful procedures to inform other national politicians about European issues and to include them in discussions; at present customs vary. Informed opinion seems no longer to be attracted to the idea that the Council of Ministers, or a cabinet within it, should consist solely of ministers appointed to specialize in European affairs; the technical problems are too various. But it may well be necessary to review the custom by which the Presidency of the Council of Ministers, with its heavy political and administrative responsibilities, rotates every six months between all the national governments. The smaller of these (with Luxembourg at the extreme) appear ill-equipped to cope with the mounting pressure of business and the probable increase of the Community to include EFTA and Eastern Europe will make the problem worse. The development of the EC may make it seem logical to confine the Presidency to larger countries but to subject them to election by the councils over which they will preside. However, the smaller countries would be bound to resist such a loss of prestige. Increased efficiency would probably not be reckoned adequate compensation. At present the problem is scarcely mentionable.

The Commission has entered the 1990s as a strange mixture of master and servant. It is expected to be the mastermind of "Europe", the guardian of its conscience and its treaties, proposing bold initiatives which will take it into the future. But the Commissioners are appointed by national governments (which have no obligation to consult anyone) although they are then pledged to act in the Community's interest, not the nation's. Consequently the job of a Commissioner has not yet been well defined in the political world, and it can serve as a dustbin for politicans whose removal governments desire for their own reasons. There is logic in the frequent suggestions that the President of the Commission should be a major statesman appointed jointly by the governments through their councils and by the Parliament, and should be able to choose the other Commissioners. By the same token the President and Commissioners should be answerable to these bodies as national ministers are answerable to Parliament.

It has been suggested – for example, by the former French President, Giscard d'Estaing – that an elected and decisive President of Europe is needed if the Community is to participate effectively in world affairs. More modestly, there have been pleas for the Commission to be recognized as the instrument by which a joint foreign policy is planned and executed. As the 1990s open both ideas seem premature and it appears more realistic to hope that a joint approach to the rest of the world will develop from the habit of Foreign Ministers co-operating in their own regular meetings (with a small independent secretariat in Brussels). Such "political co-operation" was recognized as desirable in the Single European Act of 1988. It emerged in the 1970s, when, specially after the accession of Britain, the Community was for the first time seen as a world power, rich and stable, with whom other powers such as the USA, the Soviet Union and China must do business – and with whom the world's poorer countries must attempt to negotiate on less equal terms. By the 1990s there was scarcely a world-shaking event on which the Foreign Ministers of the EC did not try to reach a common position, although they did not always succeed: in 1990 Britain unilaterally lifted sanctions on South Africa, and France bargained arms for hostages with terrorists in Beirut. A development seems to be in progress which will eventually lead to a single foreign policy.

Other institutions of the EC also need to be strengthened for the sake of democratic control – which means that what is decided democratically is done and done honestly. The Court of Justice is likely to have increasing work in order to check evasions of agreed rules by governments. The Court of Auditors must be expanded in order to guard against waste and fraud, and it is logical that it should be supported by its own small, specialist inspectorate, co-operating with national police forces in on-the-spot investigations.

3. The great political argument which will have to be resolved democratically within the EC, but not necessarily by legislation at the Community level, concerns the nature of freedom. No nation in Europe is now willing to sacrifice political freedom to freedom from hunger, perhaps because hunger is less of a threat. Much more surprisingly, by the end of the 1980s every nation in Europe had also grown out of the belief that the state

– or, more accurately, the bureaucracy – could command a regimented prosperity. Freedom in economic activity is seen as the way to grow rich, for a society as well as for the lucky individual. But what will be the remaining functions of governments and civil services in an economy which is market-oriented? It is a question which presents one of Europe's historic opportunities to advance the world's thinking. It calls for fresh thinking, based so far as possible on objective facts, instead of the sterile battle of slogans between "Socialism" meaning state control and "free enterprise" meaning *laissez-faire* capitalism.

The broad answer emerges in Europe that the market is indispensable for wealth-creation. The birth of a prosperous modern nation needs it as much as the birth of a baby needs sex. But it must have its limits set, partly by public opinion and partly by national governments, with some action by the institutions of the EC. One limit is that the market cannot be left to decide entirely what will be the schooling and training of the new generation. As is widely agreed, it is natural and healthy that economic realities such as national budgets and job opportunities should influence education – but it is morally wrong that any child or young or unemployed person should be denied an opportunity in life simply because market forces do not give education or retraining the top priority. Another limit is that the market cannot be left to decide entirely what will be the care of the health of the people. Not all the health care that is possible thanks to advances in medicine and surgery is affordable. But attempts to bring the disciplines of the market place into the hospital or the doctor's consulting room always have to come to terms with what is virtually the consensus in Europe – that more health care is affordable than seems possible if health care is simply regarded as one activity among many which compete for resources. This pressure is going to grow as the population of the EC ages, while knowing that the progress of medicine and surgery means that old age can be prolonged for many more years, and made much more comfortable, than any previous generation thought possible. If the politicians are not to be persuaded by humanitarian considerations, they will remember that old people have votes.

Other limits to the market will become clear as one sphere of European life after another is reconsidered in the light of the European tradition of human dignity. And this development will make increasingly clear what is the European style in politics.

4. The market should not be the master. It must not be allowed to defeat the spirit of a community, rural or urban, regional or national, ethnic or cultural. What seems "rational" to accountants may damage the people, as when excessive standardization blots out the richness of diversity. In Europe today there are many "endangered species" of humanity. So what pressures should be applied by the Community, by nations, by regions and by neighbourhoods, against uniformity? Here again a detailed debate leading to determined action is needed if European life is to keep its flavour. One conclusion seems likely to be that Europe needs a sustained emphasis on the EC as a Community of communities, deliberately encouraging the diversity that still makes sense economically. Up to 1992 the tendency of the EC was the encouragement of standardization, as the mountain of its regulations demonstrated. Most of that tendency was essential to economic efficiency and in the years to come standardization will have to be extended if the EFTA countries and Eastern Europe are to join the EC. But after 1992 much of the emphasis must shift to affirming and celebrating community-in-diversity. Otherwise the full riches of the European idea will be lost.

One of the necessary developments is indicated by the success of the twinning of towns in different parts of Europe. Many other organizations could be twinned, increasing both pleasure and knowledge, as part of the essential transformation of the present Europe of the Elites to a Europe of the Peoples. Such relationships repeatedly affirm the value of diversity. When Europeans visit another town or have contact with another organization, they do not want to find an identical twin. When they return home, they like the feeling that their own customs are best but could be improved.

5. The EC is challenged by the realities that economic giants will be necessary to lead economic progress – but that even these giants will not be able to sponsor all the vitally needed research. There is a growing consensus that the Community must specialize in the control of firms or agencies which after crossing frontiers grown so big that they escape control by national governments. In 1989 it was agreed that the Commission's consent would be necessary to mergers resulting in transnational corporations with annual turnovers of more than five billion ecu. That was a necessary step. Other steps which must be taken to curb the giants will be more difficult. As is widely agreed, they include the control of the quality of transfrontier TV if Europe is not to suffer "cultural pollution" through a bombardment by standardized rubbish thrown out by giants interested only in money.

The economic future of Europe as a collection of "advanced" societies depends largely on the research and development which big businesses can sponsor in association with centres of higher education and government-financed projects. But here the EC is challenged to contribute with something more than regulation. There are fields in which it ought to become a giant itself, as a patron of research. No shortage of funds for commercial or national projects should be allowed to hold up research into energy through nuclear fusion, for example, or the development of the electric motor car. And when the EC does not directly participate in research, co-ordination by it can save much wasteful duplication. It is clear that these tasks in high tech, rather than the Common Agricultural Policy, will be at the centre of the Community's work in the years ahead. Europe's future is white-coated.

6. The darker side of this future will be even greater competition in fields where the old industries of Western Europe, followed in time by those of the USA and Japan, used to be supreme – but where now the advantage lies with cheaper labour. Shipbuilding, now an Asian speciality, illustrates this tendency in a way that is specially poignant after the centuries of European seafaring. And overproduction within Europe has added to the problems. The contraction of the European coal and steel industries, and eventually of the agribusinesses, has been a strange sequel to the optimism in the minds of the founders of the EC. Ahead lie problems of an Eastern Europe moving into the Community, with low wages but also low standards of production.

In the run-down or modernization of old industries in west and east there will be many challenges to the EC to distribute quotas fairly and to help national governments in the compensation and retraining of workers. What "justice" means will have to be worked out in many directives and many payments, but Europeans will have fewer problems if they can meet these inescapable new challenges by co-operation, building on the experience of the Community's past thirty years.

7. This response will be only a part of the continuing struggle to make "social cohesion" a reality, so that Europe is seen to reject the treatment of workers as mere "factors of production" or "hands" doing jobs which machines will one day do better. The philosophy behind the EC's Social Charter challenges trade unions to abandon their posture of confrontation and their restrictive practices. This was shown dramatically in 1989 when the British Labour Party gave up its prolonged defence of the "closed shop" within a few days of the adoption of the Social Charter which discouraged it. But the challenges to the owners

and managers of businesses, and to governments legislating in this sphere, are obviously larger. It is fortunate for Europe that the negative attitude of the Thatcher government in Britain has not been typical.

The Marxist analysis of the worker's "alienation" from his work and from the community had a terrible truth in the conditions of industrialization during the nineteenth century. Marx's collaborator Engels only needed eyes to see in order to see what was wrong in Manchester in the 1840s. Protest against that harshness gave a kind of justification to the claim of Communism to be the party of the workers, but within the twentieth century it has been demonstrated that in a market-oriented economy workers can be paid handsomely and respected as human beings. If they are so paid and so respected, the economy is strengthened by their content and by their purchasing power. Amid economic developments which may be described either as new industrial revolutions or as the coming of a post-industrial society, the EC will have a vital role in setting standards and, where necessary, in legislating against abuses. And to accept the new atmosphere in the workplace will be regarded as a mark not necessarily of "Socialism", or of an enlightened capitalism, but of European civilization. The dignity of the worker has been seen as essential to the dignity of Europe.

8. The EC must be "green" and already it is greener than the US government. As the 1990s begin, the new European Environment Agency will be at the centre of hopes that European humanity will not destroy its own habitat. The time for general "consciousness raising" was necessary but is now largely over. Since the motor car has been such a weapon against the environment (as well as against human lives), it is appropriate that a cleaner future should have begun with practical steps to encourage the catalytic converter and lead-free petrol. The time has come for more intensive research and

debate, and for more effective action, over the whole range of Europe's economic activity. Almost the entire population of the continent knows that and wants to see the emphasis in all spheres, from education to government. But in Eastern Europe the 1990s have inherited an immense legacy of neglect, and in Western Europe, for all the talk, bad old habits die hard. It was ominous that when oil became cheaper in the 1980s Europe slackened in the drives towards energy efficiency in workplaces and homes, and towards the use of renewable sources of energy such as the harnessing of the powers of sun and wind. The call to save nature from pollution or exhaustion is a call for unflagging commitment.

9. The protection of regions not automatically favoured by the new market forces – the regions of industrial decline, rural stagnation or Communist misrule – will be a special concern of the new Europe. This will be the concern not only of the many millions of Europeans who will still live in such regions but of all who know that these regions belong to Europe, with full democratic rights. Whatever may be the pressures on national governments or the Community – from Eastern Europe, for example – it will not be in keeping with the realistic spirit of the new Europe to subsidize declining industries or inefficient farms indefinitely. But it will be thoroughly appropriate to retrain and re-equip the workers and to re-use the land creatively. As in the protection of the environment from pollution, mainly this will be work for regional and national authorities where private investment is inadequate. But it is logical that grants which the combined nations make through the EC should be made and should be labelled as such, for these are signs that the whole Community cares. The trouble is that such grants are too often treated by national governments as reasons to reduce their own contributions.

10. The same principle applies to grants to aid developing nations in other continents. EC grants should be on top of

national grants. It is not realistic to expect national governments to give all their aid through the EC, as is sometimes advocated. One purpose of their grants is to encourage profitable, bilateral trade, and without this incentive the grants would be reduced. And it is healthy to have an alternative to the Brussels bureaucracy. But EC aid, associated as it is with negotiated trading agreements, is one of the better parts of the generally unsatisfactory picture of relationships between the rich North and the Two-Thirds World. Because the EC encourages a dialogue with recipients far more energetically than any donor-government does, it can sponsor more acceptable policies. For example, it can make outright grants, rather than tied or conditional grants which merely soften commercial arrangements profitable to the donor. Its grants are better than loans where the recipient government gambles (usually without much luck) on being able to repay out of future profits and taxes. And its co-ordination can be specially valuable in emergencies where one of the disasters can be administrative chaos.

Far more significant than any likely amount of grants is the future pattern of trade. Most of the expert discussion points to the policy of the international division of labour. The main task of the developing nations as the world's population climbs from a level of just over five billion in 1990 is to prevent the doubling of the population in every generation, for that growth would have to end in famine. The Brundtland Commission predicted a growth to at least eight billion by 2025, and feared a growth by 2075 to fourteen billion, almost certainly an unsustainable figure. A sensible population policy, however, cannot rely mainly on making artificial methods of birth control available, desirable as that is. It must make parents want fewer children and it can achieve this chiefly by making them feel more confident that their children will survive and will be able to support them in old age. This makes it all the more essential that the developing nations should use the techniques now available which can double the yields of agriculture and stockfarming with due respect to the environment. It is also essential that most of that food that could be grown should be kept to feed the local population. But the conclusion emerging from the long discussion about "world hunger" is that in most countries enough food could be grown to feed the mouths likely to be open in the first half of the twenty-first century. However, many in the growing populations will need industrial jobs, so that the development of labour-intensive industries will also be vital. If all this can be achieved – what an "if"! – it ought to be possible to develop increased and mutually advantageous trade with the EC – provided also that European grants are made to key projects in economic development, European prices are kept within reach and European markets are opened.

At the end of the 1980s the EC was the largest importer of farm products in the world (and the second largest exporter). But many Europeans have been eating too much to be healthy, and even if Europe did not worry about slimming it would have an ageing or declining population. If the trends at the end of the 1980s were to be projected into the future, the population of Africa would double every thirty-five years; of Europe, every 185. The logic of the international division of labour is that Europe should import tropical products such as coffee, tea, cocoa, fruits, vegetables and nuts to supplement the food provided by its own farmers, but should concentrate on the manufacture of more sophisticated goods and on the provision of technical and managerial services in exchange for industrial products where the Two-Thirds World has the advantage of cheaper labour costs. Here is no suggestion that Europe should deliberately impoverish itself. Pleas to that effect sometimes heard in Christian quarters are misguided sentimentality. When in the early 1930s Europe did grow poorer, after the Wall Street crash and the consequent withdrawal of American investment from European reconstruction, another result was the impoverishment of countries wanting to trade – and finally, with a dreadful logic, impoverished Germans turned to Hitler. But the realities do suggest that the EC should adjust itself to the needs of the Two-Thirds World whatever the short-term pains. It can afford to do so. It can afford to phase out its own export subsidies; to agree to minimum world prices for the products which the poorer nations can export; to improve access to its markets for these products. And a Europe which was open and generous in that difficult but perfectly possible style would be rewarded on earth as well as in heaven. It could enjoy more of the food that only tropical countries can produce (at present in quantities larger than the market can absorb), fruit being specially compatible with dieting. It could enjoy lower prices for goods manufactured in countries where wages low by European standards are acceptable because the alternative is no wage at all. And if the Two-Thirds World could develop purchasing power instead of asking for loans which pile up the problem of debt, Europe would have a market for its own manufactures and skills incomparably higher and more profitable than any which was created by the discredited and vanished era of colonialism.

Above all, a Europe which was seen to be doing what it could reasonably be expected to do to help the Two-Thirds World could commend to other continents the economic salvation which it has achieved. Obviously the development of the "developing" nations is largely dependent on their own capacities and their own decisions: they can receive help for development, but not development itself. But in their own chosen ways, preserving their own traditions and dignity, always serving the interests of their own peoples, never as the clones of Europe, they need to put first agricultural, and then industrial, productivity at the top of their priorities, as the EC has done (however unwise the methods of the Common Agricultural Policy may have been). To this end, these nations need not the ideology of the Left or the Right but determined, efficient and uncorrupt governments and civil services concentrating on such productivity. They need taxes which are collected. They need stable prices, and in order to avoid cruel punishment by inflation governments as well as individuals have to be realistic in expenditure. They need a wide dispersal of the ownership of land, giving small farmers incentives. They need many schemes for training, low cost credit, storage and distribution, doing what these farmers cannot do for themselves. They need to control the multinational corporations very firmly but to acquire – partly from them – skills in managing private businesses, big or small, that can be run competitively at a profit. From the developing strength of their economies they need to draw strength to subsidize the urban poor, to provide health care, to finance sickness, unemployment and old age benefits. And they need to interpret in their own ways a further hint from Europe. "Food security" can be helped by regional co-operation. Industrial jobs can be created if research, investment and marketing are regionalized. Accordingly a Latin American Common Market began to emerge in the 1980s. The Maghreb Union of North African States is the EC's neighbour. The African Common Market remains talked about. In Asia there is not yet much talk. Aid is a precondition of development in the Two-Thirds World. So is trade. And so is political change, within the poorer nations and in their co-operation.

11. As the 1980s ended probably most Europeans sensed that both the cities and countryside had been bequeathed to the next generation full of problems. The main hope was that the problems had been sufficiently analysed both in rhetoric and statistics. A subsidiary hope was that the financial resources for solutions seemed to be growing, partly because of arms control.

The EC at the end of the 1980s contained 151 cities or towns with more than 100,000 inhabitants. Some of these inhabitants enjoyed living there: jobs were interesting and well-paid, homes and shops were pleasant and pleasantly stocked, leisure was full of delights. Many of the city-dwellers had other opinions. Commuters were weary of the travel, the divided lives, the suburban dreariness. Poorer people, originally drawn to Europe's cities by the prospect of manual work not available in the countryside, now found that their hands were not wanted. Many lived on inadequate social security in disagreeable housing. Many found that family and community life had broken down. The monuments which still stood in many European cities as reminders of a more glamorous past seemed to mock the present realities of urban life.

At the same time the countryside was becoming depopulated. Village schools were closing; country buses were being withdrawn; the poverty might be worse than in the cities because it was hidden. The successful large-scale farmers were being denounced because they were poisoning the earth and ruining the taxpayer, but as competition increased and subsidies decreased even the successful found their incomes dropping. One of the reasons for the economic success of these farmers was that they employed so little labour; in 1990 in France, as in the Community as a whole, just under eight per cent of the workforce was employed on the land, in West Germany under five, in Britain under three. Smaller farmers, with smaller farms and smaller success, seemed to have the alternative of rural or urban unemployment. Three-quarters of the farms in the EC produced only one quarter of its food and half its "agricultural area" was "less favoured land", mainly mountains and hill country.

This depressing picture of urban and rural slums was totally unworthy of Europe and did not deserve to be accepted with fatalism. Much expert discussion showed that the city and the countryside could prosper if their development could be planned by the use of modern administrative methods and sustained by using the new technology. And they could prosper together, respecting each other's identity (with no urban sprawl into the countryside and no pretence that in a town neighbours need not be known). Not only were the inhabitants of cities and towns still dependent on the farmers for food: when their physical necessities had been met, they needed the countryside, with its peace and beauty, for recreation, for tourism and for the second homes of flat-dwellers. (At the end of the 1980s the French had average holidays of five weeks plus ten days a year, and one family in nine had a second home.) And country people needed the urban culture. Not only did they need roads, cars, electricity and TV to end isolation and ignorance: they also needed jobs in the small, modern, prosperous industries, and the craft work which could now be located quite easily in villages (as during all the centuries before nineteenth-century industrialization). The blend of agriculture and industry in villages around Florence (for example) was an attractive work of art, and Switzerland or Sweden could teach the EC how to be both beautiful and rich. Perhaps more significantly for farmers, by 1990 about half their income in the EC came from non-farming sources.

Obviously immense problems have to be overcome before the cracked pavements of litter-strewn inner-city streets, or the neglected tracks of a countryside approaching desertification, can lead to the future which has been glimpsed. Along the way there will be many rows between the Left and the Right in the cities, and between the farmers and their critics. Such rows are inevitable in a democracy, for grants from taxes are needed to support the needy and to train for new jobs in city and country alike, and the guaranteed purchase of agricultural produce will presumably continue, although at lower levels of production. But the 1990s have inherited opportunities as well as the failures of the past. For example, in the EC the farmers accepted the intervention of authorities when they accepted guaranteed prices for a production which was disciplined by set limits even at the height of the expenditure on the Common Agricultural Policy. Now they have no alternative to accepting the control of their work for the common good as the Community and national governments set further limits to production, issue further warnings about environmental damage and encourage the setting aside of more land for non-farming purposes. A symbol of the new rural age has been the extension of woodland, reversing the trend of many centuries.

12. Towards the end of the twentieth century the development of the twelve member states of the EC, or of almost all of them, seems bound to develop into an economic, monetary and political union of the kind which I have outlined very roughly. But there is also coming to birth the union of a wider Europe, which for some years will be capable of being described as a "second tier" of the Community. A more flattering phrase for the future is that these could be member states of the Council of Europe. There Finland became the twenty-third member in 1989.

At that date the relationship between the Community and the Council was illogical. The Parliament of the EC shared the same *palais* in Strasbourg with the Assembly of the Council. The work of the two bodies overlapped. Although the one concentrated on economics and the other on human rights and cultural and technical co-operation, neither did so exclusively. Both the Community and the Council have their own Social Charters. The preambles to their fundamental treaties expressed closely similar ideals, although membership of the Community (especially after the Single European Act) has carried many more commitments than membership of the Council. Another difference between the two bodies may be expressed in a slightly exaggerated form by saying that the Community had all the money and the Council all the ideas.

The logical development would obviously be the merger of the two bodies. Nothing would do more in the improvement of the Community's reputation than to take over the Council's work, which is almost entirely non-controversial once the basic beliefs of European civilization are accepted, but which has never had adequate support in terms of finance, staffing and publicity. Founded always on its Convention of Human Rights and on the legal machinery which condemns violations, the Council has persuaded its members (although not always all its members) to reach other standards also. Its concerns have produced more than a hundred and thirty international agreements. They have ranged from the European Architectural Heritage Year of 1975 to the Convention for the Conservation of Wildlife and Natural Habitats, opened for signatures in 1979, from the Campaign for Urban Renaissance in 1981 to the Campaign for the Countryside in 1987-8, from freedom of conscience and speech to the equality of husbands and wives; from the protection of people seeking asylum in countries not their own to the prohibition of the death penalty and the prevention of the inhumane treatment of prisoners; from the 1964 agreement about the quality of medicaments to the ethical control of research in genetic engineering; from the establishment of a permanent centre for disaster relief to the co-ordination of research into AIDS. Even terrorist suspects have had their rights protected.

This good work will no doubt continue. Indeed, the work of the Commission and Court of Human Rights has so increased that there are delays of up to six years before the final judgement. The answer, if Europe wants justice, is to increase the staff of the Commission and to make the Court sit as frequently as any national court, although with judges fewer than the present twenty-three, of whom seven sit to try all cases except the most problematic.

But a merger between the Community and the Council of Europe will not come quickly – and for a very good reason. As the Council celebrated its fortieth anniversary in 1989 more European nations (led by the Soviet Union) began to be "special observers" or full members. Strasbourg was once again justifying its claim to be the crossroads of Europe. The Council's immediate future seemed to be as a focus of co-operation between European nations. This will include nations whose economies will not be ready for full (or even perhaps for associate) membership of the EC – or whose governments will have no wish to risk involvement in the EC's growth towards political union. One of President Mitterand's ideas is that around the European Union (which presumably would have its headquarters in Brussels) there should be a much looser "European Confederation", presumably meeting in Strasbourg. That may well be a necessary step towards the ultimately inevitable union of Europe.

I now ask: what could be the religion at the heart of Europe?

8

A Single Market in Religion

The world's faiths compete

COMPETITION is an ugly word to use about religions. If the adherents of a religion wish to convert others, they are usually reluctant to begin by thinking of themselves as equal with the others, like athletes at the starting point of a race: they are evangelists, not competitors. Those who do believe that all religions start equal are likely to be horrified by the coarse idea that they should compete. Most believers, however, tend to want to leave other religions well alone. If other religions plainly exist in the same society, it seems best not to criticize. Perhaps people do not feel sufficiently equipped to argue, or sufficiently sure of their own faith, or sufficiently able to advertise their faith by their moral conduct. Perhaps they are ashamed of the record of their own religion. Perhaps they simply think it bad manners to intrude. Certainly they wish to avoid any charge of "proselytism", the making of converts by pressures which the adherents of other faiths would regard as unfair.

Yet this competition happens. All the time when religions are in contact on more or less equal terms they are in competition, however quietly. And competition between the world's major faiths has been a reality in Europe, at least since the 1950s.

It has been created mostly by the presence of communities of immigrants which have become millions-strong, as Muslims, Hindus, Sikhs and others have poured into Europe in search of jobs. Most of them have found little to admire apart from the economic opportunities, which may themselves be disappointing. They have experienced the continuing arrogance of many

Europeans (whether unthinking or crudely aggressive) as racism. While their own uprooting has often made them all the more conscious of the ties of family, they have observed the disintegration or non-existence of family life in Europe. Being mostly poor and ill-educated, they know at first hand about European ignorance, idleness, dishonesty, crime and drug addiction. In a reaction which may well amount to disgust at such decadence, they have proudly practised the religion of their ancestors and left Europe to stew in its own godless juice.

On their side many Europeans have noticed how the religious traditions of these newcomers sustain them in their difficulties. That does not mean that many working-class Europeans seriously consider adopting these traditions, which are "foreign" or "coloured" and may be a cause of acute problems as cultures clash over attitudes to work, ideas of blasphemy and obscenity, the status of women, language, dress, food, noise, smells and so forth. But a world is glimpsed in which other people think that they know the meaning of life thanks to a divine revelation of the ultimate reality – and in which this meaning, accepted socially, dramatized ritually, produces a sense of belonging and therefore both morality and happiness. It is a glimpse of what was best in Europe itself before modernity. To some extent it makes modern Europe think although it is not likely to make modern Europe change.

At a more theoretical level the impact of non-Christian religions is to be seen in almost any serious bookshop in Europe. The world's scriptures are now available in translated paperbacks; the world's spirituality is taught by impressive experts; the art and culture of the world are seen to have been inspired largely by the various religions. In Europe this wealth still has the charm of novelty. Admiration for it is also encouraged by the guilt which many sensitive Europeans feel about their own continent's record – a record of persecution in the past and of modern racism reaching its climax in the extermination of six million Jews; a record of wars here and exploitation in other continents. So Europeans are often prepared to be taught by Judaism or Islam about the power of religion to bind, shape and elevate a society. They are ready to learn about meditation from Hindus or Buddhists. And their hearts and minds are open to many other lessons which they do not wish to learn from the Church of their own history. Some wandering inquirers in this category become converts to faiths which in their eyes are not damned but actually recommended by being "foreign".

Many Europeans with a Christian background are tempted to be bitter in their reaction to this peaceful invasion of their continent – and not only because the newcomers have strange habits and are rivals for jobs. The invasion can bring the threat of religious totalitarianism, as when the British author Salman Rushdie was sentenced to death for ridiculing the Muslim faith of his ancestors. For many centuries, as we have seen, Europe defended itself against Islam, and the upsurge of the fundamentalist, persecuting fanaticism of the Islamic Revolution which has spread out from Iran has revived many old fears – this time, however, in defence of a European creed of toleration and pluralism which is very different from the creed of the medieval crusaders. Now it is a section of Islam (disowned by many Muslims) that conducts the crusade, and Europe replies not with force but with bewilderment that in the 1990s there still are human beings with medieval attitudes. And another difference from European Christianity's past is to be seen in the virtually unanimous agreement of the leaders and teachers of the churches that Islamic-Revolutionary (or other non-Christian) fanaticism must not be matched by a revival of Christian intolerance. If there is a crusade going on in the European churches in the 1990s, it is a battle against a racist contempt for non-Christians who are non-whites. Racism is still a powerfully popular emotion, but it is no longer morally respectable and it is no longer taught in church. The contrast between the antisemitism which infected the German churches before 1945 and the post-war discouragement of hostility to Turkish "guest workers" is very striking. So is the contrast between the former acceptance of colonialism by the churches of the Netherlands and their more recent pressure on the Dutch Reformed churches of South Africa to renounce the sin of apartheid. All over the European churches the cross has been seen to signify something quite different from what the medieval crusaders saw.

It is also striking that a revolution has occurred in European Christian theories about non-Christian religions. The "heathen" are no longer thought to be entirely mistaken, crudely immoral, merely idolatrous or simply devilish, and are no longer consigned automatically to everlasting torments in hell. Instead, Christian thinkers have struggled to find ways of expressing convictions about God's acceptance and love of non-Christians, their goodness and truth, without denying what remains acknowledged as the work of God in the Christian heritage. The Second Vatican Council committed the Roman Catholic Church to a positive view of the non-Christian world, with a generosity which would have astonished many missionaries and their supporters in past generations.

In the 1990s it would be foolish to pretend to be sure that many of the non-Christians who have settled in Europe will settle into Christianity. The new humility of thoughtful Christians does more than their old pride to make spiritual conversions to their faith possible, but it is still easy for non-Christians in Europe to remain unimpressed by the situation which they encounter day by day. They identify Christianity not with religion as they respect it, but with sheer privilege in the class structure or in the international system – a privilege experienced as oppressive. The new tone in Christian thinking about other faiths is welcome to those non-Christians who are aware of it, but that theological revolution is too recent and too confused to have replaced the old image or to deserve complete confidence. At this stage all that should be said, in my own view, is that European Christianity could become more attractive if its humbler attitudes could become more mature and stable, and far better known; if its own spiritual life could be so enriched that it is perceived chiefly as a religion, not as the ideology of imperial Europe; and if the dialogue of the world's religions within Europe could be seen as part of a whole new relationship between Europe and the other continents.

In the nineteenth century, and in the early part of the twentieth, European and other white Christians felt themselves to be morally as well as economically superior to the rest of humanity. The twenty-first century will inherit a radically different situation. Some people once viewed as quaint, most conspicuously the Japanese, have raised their economies to the level of Europe or to a level above Europe's. Amid continuing and deepening poverty around the Two-Thirds World, at least their achievement shows that wealth is not the prerogative of white skins or Christian traditions. And the alleged moral superiority of Europe, including European Christianity, has also collapsed – partly because of Europe's internal wars (a near-suicide) and partly because of the other evils in its history which have been denounced in the worldwide anti-colonial movement and in the later anger of poverty-stricken countries at "imperialist" practices such as charging exorbitant interest on loans for development. Europe has to some extent heard these voices of contempt and anger reaching it across the seas. But it has been much more interested in the domestic danger following its internal wars – its cold war between NATO and the Warsaw Pact. Now as Europe seems to be moving into an age of peace and unity, the drastic reduction of military expenditure could bring a "development dividend" with far greater generosity in the terms of trade and aid. Europe may also be moving into a period when racism reacting to the shock of the first flood of "coloured" immigrants diminishes as the fact of a multi-racial society is accepted more maturely, and even enjoyed, by generations all born within Europe. (I am not trying to suggest that the evil of racism is not a daily reality in 1990. My hope is that it will be reduced by familiarity and shared education – and also by restrictions on future immigration.) Such a transformation of white Europe's position in the world, from conqueror to partner, from reluctant employer to fellow citizen, could alter the way in which the non-Christian majority of the human race looks at Europe's traditional religion. A conversation between the continents unfettered by superiority or inferiority could explore the mystery of God, on the basis of an agreement by all the religions that all alike accept the principles proclaimed by the World Council of Churches as "justice, peace and the integrity of creation". Already signs exist pointing to that spiritual development.

Within Europe, the historic churches have become so discredited because of past errors that many people with a spiritual hunger turn to other food. I know this: I live in London. But these churches are not dead. In their heritage, perhaps buried, there is a rich life of the spirit. It awaits rediscovery. It could change these churches, and their ability to meet the spritual needs of their neighbours, and their position in the eyes of those who look on them from non-Christian backgrounds where at present religion often thrives. It could mean that the true glory of European Christianity lies in the future.

The best route to this spiritual wealth is the road which European Christians can take together, the road which is called ecumenical.

A market for Europe's churches?

Any use of the idea of competition to describe desirable relationships between Christians has to be very careful. St Paul encouraged the Corinthians to compete in the spiritual life like the athletes in the games – but he spoke to them of a heavenly prize and he also spoke about love as supreme. It may be a bit safer to use the idea of the market in a strictly limited way. Dare we say that the spiritual wealth of European Christianity could be rediscovered if there was more exchange between Christians who are now more or less isolated from each other? If a biblical basis is sought, it may be found in St Paul's words to the Corinthians about what they would receive as well as give as they sent money to their fellow Christians in Jerusalem. But even to compare the Christian Church with the exchange going on in a market such as the single market of the European Community may seem blasphemous, or at least shocking. A natural reaction would be: the One, Holy, Catholic and Apostolic Church is meant to be the People of God, the Body of Christ, the Fellowship of the Holy Spirit, the colony of heaven on earth – so how dare you compare it with an arrangement in economics not yet complete as the 1990s begin? There would probably be a strong suspicion that religion is being trivialized. For most Christians in Europe who regard Christianity as more than an ethical code, "true religion" is at least the worship of the one eternal God, the faith that God's active love has been embodied in a unique human life, costly discipleship following in the steps of this Jesus Christ after baptism, joyful dependence on the power of the Holy Spirit, devout participation by faith in the Eucharist, and a life of purity, self-sacrifice, hopefulness and limitless love. That is what has been "believed always, everywhere, by all" (in the words of the fifth-century St Vincent of Lérins, which have often been misused in the pretence that they can apply to some doctrine which many Christians have contradicted). How, then, can religion be understood by comparing it with exchange in the market place which may bring better and cheaper goods to the consumer? Is this a joke?

Up to a point, to speak of "a single market in religion" *is* a joke. I have found it to be a way of speaking about religion which is thought-provoking precisely because it makes an unexpected connection. A good deal of humour does this, and in that sense Jesus of Nazareth was, it seems, a humourist. He made religion fresh by comparing its sacred mysteries with everyday events, from a wedding feast to a burglary, and this was probably one of his habits that offended the more solemn teachers of the religious law. But if it is to illuminate religion a comparison must have a serious point. In many of the parables of Jesus the point was that something about human nature could help the listeners to understand the nature of God: God was like an unjust judge attending to a bothersome widow, or an absent landlord returning for an inspection, or an employer paying the minimum wage, or a friend asked for help at night, or a housewife searching for a lost coin.... Inevitably the theology and organization of the Christian Church have used many models derived from contemporary life – not always so successfully as Jesus of Nazareth. The mystery of the at-one-ment between God and Man has been expressed in terms of the sacrifices offered in a Jewish or pagan temple; in terms of a slave's ransoming; in terms of a Roman law court; in terms of satisfaction for an offence under feudal law; in terms of a moral example given to free persons in a liberal society; in terms of a liberation from economic oppression. The organization of the Church has been influenced by the Jewish synagogue whose life was arranged by "elders"; by the religious or charitable organization led by "overseers" (in Greek *episkopoi*, "bishops"); by the temple with its "priests"; by the city with its governor (more than one governor of a Roman city became its bishop); by the empire with its monarch (the Pope became in a sense the religious emperor of the West); by the school or college with its teacher (the Protestant pastor was primarily a preacher); by the businesses, media, social services and psychiatric consulting rooms of our own time; by modern parliaments. So why not compare religion with a market, in a society which knows all about markets?

In the present comparison between the European single market and the Christian Church, the point is deeply serious. I am trying to say that without achieving, or really wanting, uniformity under a single authority, the EC and the Church have this in common: both seek the growing wealth and union that come through exchange. Economists call this exchange a market. Theologians call it "communion" – in the Greek of the New Testament *koinonia*. For most of Christian history this "communion" has been thought of mainly as the fellowship of a congregation which ought to extend to other Christians, or at least to those other Christians with whom this congregation is "in communion" (such as other Roman Catholics). But it is one of the spiritual advances of the twentieth century that "communion" has been seen to include an enriching exchange of the gifts of the Holy Spirit between individuals and groups not belonging to the same part of the Christian Church. Such an exchange is most intense in meetings which are explicitly "ecumenical" because intended to promote Christian unity. But this enriching exchange is not confined to such meetings. It occurs whenever Christians meet unfamiliar ways of praying, thinking and behaving and know that those are authentically Christian, so that Christian worship and work can be shared. It can be put more poetically by saying with St Paul that when Christians meet other Christians they recognize in them the body of Christ, seeing more fully "the riches of the glory". It can be put more theologically by saying with the letter to the Ephesians that God has planned "to display in the ages to come how immense are the resources of his grace".

Their *koinonia* is a vital part of what Christians can contribute to the new Europe. Christians certainly can contribute a vision of God which leads to a vision of human nature as being Godlike despite all the evil and the frailty. As I have already attempted to say, this Christian humanism is capable of undergirding the philosophy of "human rights" which is generally agreed to be necessary despite all the emphasis on pluralism. And beyond this vision, Christianity offers a vision of nature as God's creation, so that this is a good world despite all that puzzles us in it and despite all the damage which we have done to it. Here is a very strong incentive to respect, and care for, the environment on which humanity depends for its life. But Christianity also has a social dimension and a social message. It says that people, created ultimately by the love of God, are made for love, so that they need communion with each other as much as they need food or drink. Christians in particular need communion – and when they are in communion with God they are given "the fellowship of the Holy Spirit". Therefore their aim and prayer must be that their relationships with each other will be so deep, so loyal and so creative, that the world will say "See how these Christians love one another!" without a sneer. As has been declared in countless pronouncements by church leaders and conferences on the firm basis of the New Testament, the unity of Christians ought to be such that it can inspire all humanity. If it can help Christians to imagine a better unity by comparing the Church with the EC's single market the comparison is, I submit, useful. For what cannot be denied is that the ecumenical movement for Christian unity in Europe needs a fresh look and a new impetus as the 1990s begin.

As things are, the divisions of Christians in Europe are prominent. Just as Europe exported wars to the world, so Europe's Christians have exported quarrels which have produced divisions deeper than any existing within the faiths of Jews, Muslims, Hindus or Buddhists. Most of the divisions between Christian "denominations" to be found in the world originated in Europe. As a consequence Christianity in

Australia, for example, is still shaped by divisions which have crossed many centuries and many miles of sea. Catholic is divided from Orthodox, and Orthodox from Orthodox. Europe has also shipped out the historic divisions of Protestantism which the sunshine of Australia has only partially healed. The religious scene in the USA is so divided by denominations whose historic roots lie in Europe that any other structure has become, for almost all American Christians, inconceivable. Even more divisions are found in rural Africa, where Christians are called Roman or Lutheran, Anglican or Methodist, Presbyterian or Baptist, without any strong awareness that this is very strange. Africa has its "independent" churches not founded by missionaries, and the Pentecostal family of churches has an American, rather than European, birthplace, as is also true of America's Black churches – but nowhere has the religious history of Africa or the Americas escaped the impact of Europe, whether or not it is in reaction against it. Even in India or China Christianity has not yet completely discarded the variously dated fashions of its European clothing; Chinese Catholics, for example, have retained the Latin Mass. Therefore the twenty-first century will begin with most of the world's Christians who are at all aware of life outside their neighbourhoods still acknowledging the special status of Rome, Constantinople, Moscow, Geneva, Canterbury or the German universities, and still being shaped spiritually by the Bishops of Rome or by the saints of Spain or France or by hymns written in English or German or by councils which spoke Greek. In the whole world, the divisions between European Christians are powerfully, sometimes poisonously, relevant to Christian life – the only exceptions to this rule being found in areas where Christianity has not effectively penetrated. So the question arises: if Europeans started these divisions, can Europeans end them?

Often these divisions are maintained on grounds very different from the grounds taken by the rival theologians in the original disputes. Catholic and Orthodox may not be divided basicaly by opinions as to whether the Spirit "proceeds from the Father *and* Son" (the *filioque* clause which the Roman Catholic Church added to the creed); Lutheran, Anglican and Methodist may not be divided by theological loyalties to Martin Luther, Thomas Cranmer and John Wesley; and so forth. The divisions between churches are normally more sociological than theological: they are sustained by nationality, neighbourhood, class, etc. But another reality is the continuing power of old theological quarrels to justify divisions, even if only by supplying dignified and holy labels which can be fixed to ethnic groups and social churches. A divided religion's convenience in sanctifying secular divisions has been clear around the Christian world but it is specially obvious from one end of Europe to another. Sometimes it is notorious. In Northern Ireland in 1990 gangsters are called Catholic or Protestant. In the Ukraine in 1990 Christians dispute (with a history of bitterness and violence) over the possession of churches – for some do, and some do not, prefer to acknowledge a Polish past and with it the spiritual authority of the Pope. So tension arises between the Uniate Church and the Russian Orthodox Church. In between Ulster and the Ukraine other Christian divisions are important, even in politics – divisions between Catholic and Protestant in Germany, for example, or between Catholic, Reformed and Orthodox in the Balkans. The contrast between the Scandinavian and the Mediterranean lifestyles is due to religion as well as to the climate. England feels remote from France because of the Protestant Reformation's success north of the Channel as well as because of the division in language. These divisions often enrich the total life of Europe and of Christianity. Not all are as notorious as the use of religious labels by Ulster's gunmen. But (to say the least) it is not necessary that the Christian religion should be so largely connected with divisions, in view of the urgent emphasis on unity in the Bible and in much of the Christian tradition, teaching that diversity can be maintained without fragmentation. St Paul's question pierces through the quarrelsome history: "Is Christ divided?"

It follows that the future of the divisions in European Christianity must matter to all the world and specially to Europe itself. But how is the right measure of Christian unity, combined with freedom and therefore with diversity, to be achieved?

The modern ecumenical movement is usually said to have begun within Europe, in the conference in Edinburgh in 1910 which saw the damage which disunity inflicted on the work and credibility of Christian missionaries overseas. Europe has been at the centre of many subsequent developments. It seemed inevitable that the headquarters and study centre of the World Council of Churches, formed in 1948, should be located in Switzerland. The movement, at first mainly Protestant, from the first included Anglicans with a Catholic emphasis and attracted Eastern Orthodox participation; the Patriarchate of Constantinople joined the WCC in 1948, that of Moscow in 1961. It was transformed when under mainly European leadership the Roman Catholic Church became more actively and generously ecumenical during and after the Second Vatican Council later in the 1960s, progress being monitored by the Secretariat (now Council) for Unity in Rome. And some of the inspiration came from Europe's tragic history, for Protestants, Orthodox and Roman Catholics were all deeply influenced by their common experience of forming a Christian resistance to the claims of Nazism and Communism. At least they acknowledged each other as fellow Christians, often finding a theological basis for this in their common privilege of Baptism. After the 1960s the Roman Catholics and Eastern Orthodox Churches were in a more friendly relationship (although still not in communion), and no longer taught that Protestants were in every sense outside the Church of Christ. Many historic meetings were hailed as breakthroughs; one was the lifting of the mutual anathemas between the Pope of Rome and the Patriarch of Constantinople in 1965, after hostility which had lasted since 1054. Many beginnings were made in joint prayer, joint study and joint action. Amid mounting excitement it often seemed that Christian renewal would lead to Christian reunion.

Without that European experience of resistance to evil political regimes in the 1940s and 1950s, it is very doubtful whether considerations about the Christian mission outside Europe would have had enough force to transform the attitudes of churches which were European or Eurocentric. Obviously the disunity of Christians can be a handicap when presenting a message said to be the Gospel of peace to the adherents of a religion where disagreements do not lead to such sharp divisions. A Christianity torn apart by internal quarrels does not impress Jews, Muslims, Hindus, or Communists. That has often been lamented, and some unions between churches have been achieved in response to this challenge (for example, in India). But it is a fact that where European or Eurocentric Christianity is respected, its divisions are also often given prestige. Christians whose families come from Europe tend to value the old customs. Christians whose churches were founded by European missionaries tend to honour what the missionaries taught (although many rebel). Therefore Christians outside Europe can be surprisingly complacent about their denominational divisions and it seems likely that the wish which some (not all) of the missionaries and the non-European Christians have expressed for a greater unity would have had very limited influence had it not been reinforced by Europe's own experience of resistance to Hitler and Stalin. When confronting those tyrants and their brutally systematic ideologies, Europe's own Christians discovered that what they had in common was far more important than any division, and many of them wanted to see this spiritual unity embodied in new structures which could be shared.

With these origins partly in the missionary movement and

partly in the European resistance to Hitler and Stalin, the ecumenical movement has emphasized the aim of "visible" or "organic" unity among Christians. That has always been the clear aim of the Roman Catholic and Eastern Orthodox Churches. Before the 1960s that aim was usually expressed by an invitation to return and submit to the unity commanded and founded by Christ and his apostles, and already existing in the Roman Catholic or Eastern Orthodox Church. Then a larger courtesy to "separated brethren" developed. But it was still claimed that the whole Church "subsists in" the Roman Catholic or Eastern Orthodox Church (to use the somewhat ambiguous phrase of the Second Vatican Council), and it was clear that "separated brethren" were still being invited to move towards a full unity in faith and organization. It was also still officially taught that it was wrong to share communion in the Eucharist with other churches ("intercommunion") until further progress to this goal of full unity had been made.

The insistence on a full unity has been shared by most of the representatives of the Protestant and other churches meeting in the World Council of Churches. These churches have for the most part accepted "intercommunion" (in some cases, slowly). But a statement about "the unity we seek" was adopted at the WCC's Assembly in New Delhi in 1961 and has been repeatedly reaffirmed:

> We believe that the unity which is both God's will and his gift to the Church is being made visible as all in each place who are baptized into Jesus Christ and confess him as Lord and Saviour are brought by the Holy Spirit into one fully committed fellowship, holding the one apostolic faith, preaching the one Gospel, breaking the one bread, joining in common prayer, and having a corporate life reaching out in witness and service to all, and who at the same time are united with the whole Christian fellowship in all places and all ages in such like that ministry and members are accepted by

all, and that all can act and speak together as occasion requires for the tasks to which God calls his people.

At Nairobi in 1975 another assembly of the WCC reaffirmed "the goal of visible unity...although it may seem to be only a distant possibility" and added that "local churches which are themselves truly united" should be united with each other by councils.

This was a noble vision of Christian unity and it was propagated by an international fellowship of men and women highly advanced in theological and spiritual knowledge, highly sensitive to contemporary needs and often highly placed in church life. Church leaders of the stature of the two Italian Popes, John XXIII and Paul VI, or the Dutch General Secretary of the WCC, W.A. Visser't Hooft, would be reckoned great in any period of Christian history. What the French priest Paul Couturier called an "invisible monastery" of prayer supported this vision, which has never been disowned by the churches or replaced in their thinking. However, in the 1970s and 1980s it became certain that it would remain a vision for many years to come. In the Two-Thirds World, Christians often felt the need to co-operate for many practical purposes, being a minority in a society full of problems, but there was little interest in schemes for mergers between churches. In countries with a Christian background, in Europe or elsewhere, such schemes became increasingly suspect as too closely resembling mergers between commercial companies. In the life and thought of the WCC the idea of "visible" or "organic" unity between the churches, although never abandoned, no longer provided the central inspiration. It may be said that the disillusionment of those who had hoped for the speedy arrival of such a unity was the religious equivalent of the waning of the hopes surrounding the birth of the United Nations. It also resembles the disappointment which has followed the enthusiasm of the federalist movement for a United States of Europe.

The reality which has wrecked these hopes was, and is, as simple as it is strong. People find their identity and security in a group which is not too large to be loved – and if religion is concerned, they prefer the group to be one that maintains continuity with their past. A reasonably happy and stable family is the best group for these purposes, but a village, town, region, nation or a religious denomination may serve as an extended family. When negotiations for a full unity are opened between churches, fears about a loss of identity and security grow easily. The resistance to any suggested formula or scheme gathers force and is expressed in any of three ways, all equally effective – by a veto exercised by conservative leaders responsive to popular fears; by a blocking of "progress" by a majority or sufficient minority in some council or synod where conservative votes are allowed to count; or by an obstinate refusal to enthuse or co-operate at the local level. Objections to any particular proposal may take the form of criticizing a proposed change or development or fresh emphasis, in doctrine or in organization, but the heart of the opposition is always the feeling that the proposed "fully committed fellowship" would be too large. Many Christians in a particular church do not feel close enough to the members of another church. Without totally condemning other Christians they do not feel sure that they hold the same faith, or want to worship in the same way, or have the same ideas about how to reach out to others. Deep down, they do not feel related in the same spirit to the past or to the present. They do not talk the same language. In a word, they feel *different* – and are not sorry about it. Such feelings will not be ended by any skill in formulating theological diplomatic agreements or in gluing together customs dear to the divided churches. In the Middle Ages, Eastern Orthodox leaders who tried to reach agreements with the Catholic Church of the West found themselves rejected when they got back home; in the Protestant Reformation inaugurated by Luther in 1517, positions on both sides had hardened inflexibly, and as it seemed for ever, by the 1540s; and like the corpses of cattle in a drought, the failures of later reunion efforts litter church history. Not enough people in the churches have wanted such efforts to succeed. And the advocates of unity have damaged their cause by not taking seriously these feelings and asking how they may be met.

The intention of recent advocates of a full, visible or organic unity has been to proceed with the thoroughly conscientious and freely given agreement of the churches. The spirit of the modern ecumenical movement has been in that sense democratic. But the resistance to agreements and mergers has taken forms which may be understood by reflection about fears often expressed in modern democracies – fears that a remote bureaucracy is gaining power over the local community, and fears that when a firm is taken over by a former rival, perhaps with a distant headquarters, it will mean the loss of jobs or at least an unwelcome disturbance. And when reunion with the Roman Catholic Church is proposed, an older fear surfaces. This church can seem to be an absolute monarchy. Indeed, its legal position seems to suggest precisely that, since the Pope, who is assisted by the officials of the Vatican, is only advised by other bishops, who are themselves only advised by priests or laity. Eastern Orthodox or Protestant Christians may mean by "No Popery!" roughly what is meant in politics by the cry "No tyranny!" On the other hand, many Roman Catholics when faced by what seem to be proposals for compromises with other churches have feelings fairly close to the political fear of anarchy.

So in Europe at the beginning of the 1990s the ecumenical movement is in an impasse in so far as its aim is full unity, despite the brave words. At the expertly theological level there is growth in agreement reached by examining the Bible and the Christian tradition together in a calm and scholarly manner. At the local level there is growth in common prayer and co-operation. So certainly the ecumenical movement moves. But in between these levels, the churches stay apart. They profess to want full unity; actually, they usually like things as they are. I want to ask whether a way forward out of this impasse may be found by using the European Community's single market as a model, in order to provide a focus which everyone can understand for suggestions already made by many experts. To compare the Church with the single market which is developing into economic and political union in the EC may help European Christians to see that their own union will grow as, in the life of the spirit, their spiritually enriching "exports" and "imports" grow. Nothing will be imposed by any bureaucracy or monarchy on anyone conscientiously dissenting – because in the life of the spirit nothing can be imposed. Anything new will be agreed because the exchange is known to be – however painful in the short run – in the long run profitable. And one of the things to be agreed will be the formation of institutions with limited responsibilities but real powers, avoiding anarchy and assisting this exchange or communion.

There is a further reason for comparing Christian unity with European unity. The pressure for Christian unity which came from the shared experience of resistance to Hitler and Stalin was accompanied by another pressure, working in a different direction. This was the pressure of the feeling that Christian strength was needed to match the strength of the enemy. For some, as I have noted, this meant strength in unity with other churches. For many, however, it meant strengthening a particular church with a love which asked no question. It was felt that the whole of that church's tradition must be the object of loyalty, otherwise the enemy would take advantage of any uncertainty. This was no time for argument about reforms that might or might not be desirable: there was a war on. That was very largely the mood of Protestantism as it returned to the strong theology of the Reformation, "confessed" Christ against Nazism, and renounced "liberalism" as lacking a backbone. That was the tone of the "neo-orthodox" theology of Karl

Barth. Very similar was the mood of a monolithic Catholicism under Pius XII, when a crusade against Communism seemed to rule out any self-criticism. A solidarity which did not question the Church (at least not in public) strengthened Polish Catholicism under Communist rule, out of which John Paul II came to rebuke the flabby West. And defiance in loyalty to old traditions and mysteries has been the mood of almost the whole of Eastern Orthodoxy, a church of martyrs. But now a new Europe emerges: a Europe of peace, of a more relaxed and tolerant pluralism and (it is hoped) eventually of prosperity for all. As the nations no longer need to maintain vast armies and armaments targeted against each other, so the churches no longer confront an enemy threatening their very existence. It looks like being a time when questions are allowed – and are necessary – for the new danger to all the churches is the feeling, wider than either Nazism or Communism ever was, that they do not honestly seek and speak the truth, the whole truth and nothing but the truth.

Conservative exports and imports

One reason why I am taking Protestantism first is that, when it wrestles with the truth, its internal divisions are so obvious. More or less similar tensions exist within the Catholic tradition but Protestants have been much more free to argue in public and to split up. They protest against each other. They say that the acceptance of Christianity by Europe (for example) is hindered because of the nonsense talked by the other side. In 1988 and 1990 two books, called *Essentials* (in the USA

A Single Market in Religion

Evangelical Essentials) and *Tradition and Truth*, represented my attempts to engage in dialogue with Protestant theologians who were either more "conservative" or more "radical" than I am. Such questions as these are asked:

- Is the Bible "infallible" or "inerrant"?
- What was the attitude of Jesus to the Scriptures?
- What is the authority of the Bible for Christians?
- What interpretation of the cross is taught by the New Testament?
- Can it be communicated as today's Gospel?
- How literally should we interpret the miracle stories of the Bible?
- How does our attitude to miracles affect our understanding of God and salvation?
- Should we expect miracles today?
- What is the authority of the Old Testament in ethics?
- Was Jesus a legislator?
- If the Bible reflects surrounding cultures, how can it guide us in our moral problems?
- Should Christians today mean by the "Kingdom of God" exactly what Jesus meant?
- Are "non-Christians" or "non-believers" perishing?
- How can Christians avoid both "total fixity" and "total fluidity" in evangelism?
- Is the essential difference between the Evangelical and the liberal Christian that the one appeals to Scripture and the other to rationality?

These were some of the questions which I discussed with Dr John Stott, the highly respected conservative Evangelical leader. My critical examination of the work of seven radical theologians in *Tradition and Truth* tackled these immense questions (as a selection):

- Is God only the depth of what is obviously real?

- Is religion only human?
- Does God intervene after creation?
- Was Jesus only a man filled by the Spirit of God?
- What do we know about the man behind the gospels?
- If revelation is culture-bound, is it authoritative?
- Is Jesus of Nazareth the world's only Saviour?

I shall not try to offer now comprehensive reflections on those debates. But I ought to share my conviction that a complete agreement between Christians about the right answers to such questions cannot be reached in the present state of religious knowledge and understanding. These questions concern the truth and are therefore of great importance; often they arouse a deeper interest than does any question about differences between the denominations. The trouble is that any answer excludes people who are by any moral or spiritual test fellow disciples. Some of the questions turn on debatable points of biblical scholarship. Others involve disagreements about the meaning of words (such as "infallible" or "authoritative"). Others spring out of different religious experiences (for example, in response to the death of Jesus). Others reflect different temperaments (optimistic or pessimistic, etc.). Others arise on different educational levels (whether scientific or philosophical). Others result from different exposures to non-Christian religions. And behind these differences are contrasts in intimately personal histories which are actually decisive but seldom mentioned in theological debates. How did a person become a Christian? Did the spiritual pilgrimage involve some unhappy experience of a form of Christianity that was too authoritarian or too vague? What circle of friends does a person now have? Is it too late for that person to be willing to admit a mistake?

I have learned that while it is irritating that Christians cannot agree theologically, in practice the disagreement between "conservative", "liberal" and "radical" can bring benefits if only there is some willingness to learn from Christians in other positions. In other words (words which may cause further offence in relationships where offence is taken very quickly), the disagreement may be profitable if there is some trade in beliefs.

Conservatives have much to export. In Protestantism they stress the authority of the Bible, as in Roman Catholicism or Eastern Orthodoxy they stress the authority of the Church, because that is the source from which they have drunk deep in water which they believe to be the water of ultimate truth and of eternal life. They have found God in that way – not the God who is another name for morality or society, or the God who is a nostalgic memory, but the living God who fascinates. This God is "holy", meaning "different", and he commands those who acknowledge him to be holy. And people who have had this experience, often called "conversion", are willing to accept disciplines which seem silly to outsiders but which are welcomed as being part of love. These may be disciplines of prayer or disciplines of life. They produce characters of steel. The steel may be directed against the official leadership of a church if the leaders are thought to have betrayed orthodoxy as understood by the conservatives. In the history of Eastern Orthodoxy various attempts at reconciliation with Rome have been wrecked by the reaction of traditionalists, and in Russia the still continuing schism of the Old Believers began with protests against modernization in the seventeenth century. The classic example of this phenomenon in contemporary Europe is the ultra-conservative schism founded by Archbishop Marcel Lefebvre, a group which rejects the Second Vatican Council as heretical. It is therefore more Papal than the Pope.

"Liberals" and "radicals" criticize conservatives. Their religion would not exist if it did not have the conservatives to criticize: they are parasites. But they ask questions which, once they arise in reason or conscience, ought to be asked aloud. Is the tradition true? If so, what kind of truth does it contain? Is the moral teaching of a past generation better than contemporary insights? If so, what kind of authority does it now possess? These are the questions which constitute much of the history of Christianity in Europe - or at least in Western Europe. It is because the answers reached after anguish have not been totally unsatisfactory that the religion has continued to convince some people both intelligent and free.

Protestant exports and imports

The essential character of Protestantism is displayed (I have come to see) in a combination of attitudes which together constitute its exports on offer to others in the single market of the Christian Church.

Protestants feed their souls on the Bible and they insist on having a direct access to it, preferably by being able to read it for themselves. The preaching which they most value interprets the Bible. As they read or hear, they ask what the Bible's meaning is for them. They use their own reasoning powers and their own consciences, praying for the guidance of the Holy Spirit. They do not leave the answer to any priest or bishop. It is their belief that the Bible's message is authoritative - is "the Word of God" or "the Gospel" - although they disagree about whether this means the message of the whole of the Bible or the Bible's message interpreted as a whole, as reason and conscience decide which parts have the greater truth and importance.

As Protestants respond to the good news of the Bible they commit themselves to Jesus Christ as their own Lord and Saviour and they find release from the guilt and power of sin. They do not need any priest as a necessary mediator in this forgiveness: they can go to God direct. As liberated people they sing songs of praise, and for the last two hundred years hymn singing has been by far the most popular part of Protestant worship. Within this century, and specially during and since the 1970s, there has been great interest in "Pentecostal" or "charismatic" gifts – the revival of "tongue-speaking" as practised in the New Testament in enthusiastic and ecstatic utterances of faith and joy uninhibited by the conventions of language.

All these Protestant discoveries or rediscoveries have profoundly influenced the Roman Catholic Church, especially during and after the Second Vatican Council. Bible study by the laity has been encouraged. Bible-based worship in the language of the laity has been ordered. The movement of the altar which is the focus (now usually very simple) into the midst of the congregation has been a sign that a barrier between priest and people has been broken. Hymn singing has flourished, using both Catholic and Protestant writers. The charismatic movement has included many Catholics.

After their personal commitment to Christ Protestants make their own decisions about their behaviour, and their liberation includes the liberty to decide what is the right behaviour in conditions not envisaged in the early Christian centuries. The free market of modern capitalism involves "usury", the taking of interest condemned in the Old Testament and by the medieval Church. Protestant businessmen participated in it with few hesitations. Preachers were often more conventional – but not so conventional as Catholic bishops. As capitalism developed lay Protestants could criticize it, perhaps as Socialists – while the Papacy taught that it was impossible to be both a Catholic and a Socialist, and separate Catholic trade unions were organized. When Parliamentary democracy emerged there was another welcome among Protestants – but in the leadership of other churches, another rejection. Protestants did not accept any Papal prohibition against recognizing the "lay" republic of France or the united Kingdom of Italy.

These Protestant attitudes have increasingly been shared by Roman Catholics. Capitalism has been accepted; Catholic trade unions have dwindled except in Poland; and Christian Democracy arising after World War Two was a movement designed to lead Parliamentary politics from the inside, with Protestants as full members and without control by bishops.

Protestants have also made their own decisions when the modern understanding of sexuality has increased together with the ability to limit conception and to abort a foetus; and when the modern understanding of marriage has seen it as love between equal partners who could survive economically (however damaged emotionally) if divorced. Protestants disagree between themselves (sometimes vehemently) about whether any physical expression of homosexual love is allowable for Christians; about whether heterosexual acts should be strictly confined to marriage; about what circumstances (if any) justify the use of contraceptives or the termination of pregnancies; and about what situations (if any) justify a second marriage after a divorce. But the conviction of Protestants is that these decisions should be made not by the clergy (who may lack experience) but by the involved individual after seeking the guidance of the Bible and the Holy Spirit and after listening to fellow Christians.

The pressure of opinion in Protestant Churches may be more or less strongly against some or many of the modern developments, and the Churches may refuse to bless or support personal decisions in their favour; Puritanism has been, and remains, a major force within Protestantism. Most of those Protestants who take modernizing or "liberal" attitudes would definitely not wish to be understood as endorsing all aspects of modern capitalism, modern democratic politics and modern sexual permissiveness. In particular most Protestants continue to see homosexual acts, abortions and divorces as tragedies, whether or not they are morally permitted in certain circumstances. But the Protestant situation is different from (for example) the canon law of the Roman Catholic Church, where an abortion or a marriage after a divorce automatically incurs the penalty of excommunication.

The denial of the clergy's authority to insist on the confessions of sins to them, and to decide ethics in business life, politics and sexuality, has been only the most prominent part of a general Protestant rejection of much of the traditional power of the priesthood. Priests are not seen as possessing magical powers – for example, the power to "make God" by making a physical change in the bread and wine in the Eucharist (an interpretation of the doctrine of "transubstantiation" which Roman Catholic and Eastern Orthodox theologians would also reject). Nor are priests seen as possessing rights over lay consciences in the ethical questions posed by the modern world. Therefore among Protestants (as among the Eastern Orthodox) the clergy are not treated as being aloof from the ordinary run of humanity, exempt from contradiction and as a sign of their superiority expected to refrain from all sexual activity. But the distancing of Protestants from traditional church life can go beyond this. Many Protestant laity see no need to attend frequently the services which the clergy conduct or to pay close attention to the pronouncements of assemblies which the clergy dominate. Some famous Protestant theologians have gone so far as to attack "religion" in the name of "authenticity" (Kierkegaard), "faith" (Barth) or "discipleship" (Bonhoeffer). The "churchgoing" or "religion" being rejected is seen as an activity which makes the laity dependent on the clergy rather than on God, and which encourages the performance of ritual rather than the redirection of life. In particular "religion" is held to have been discredited by its failure to respond worthily to the wars, the social problems and the tyrannies in twentieth-century Europe.

Such attacks on "religion" have often been denounced by the clergy (including some of the Protestant clergy) as being arrogant or at least eccentric; as being fundamentally destructive because disloyal to the Gospel and to its ordained ministers whose authority is derived from Christ. But people who are able to examine the New Testament closely know that does not describe the clergy as a superior caste, does not call any Christian a priest, does not show a Church controlled by bishops, does not limit the willingness of God to forgive the penitent, does not deal with modern conditions in economics and politics, does not consider the condition of homosexuality as understood in modern times, does not legislate against all contraceptives, all abortions, or all divorces, and does not put churchgoing at the top of the Christian's priorities. And in practice attitudes originally Protestant are now shared by many members of the Roman Catholic and Eastern Orthodox Churches. These Christians do emphasize Bible study and do interpret the Bible for themselves; do confess their sins to God, and believe themselves forgiven, without involving a priest (the practice of regular private confession to a priest having declined dramatically since the 1960s); do make up their own minds about business life, politics and many questions of sexual ethics; and as the statistics demonstrate, do attend services less frequently than in the past.

The abandonment of the late medieval view of the priesthood is indicated by the widespread feeling that clergy ought to be allowed to marry. It is also quite widely (although less strongly) felt that it has become unreasonable to exclude women from the priesthood. Particularly in Europe (although also in the English-speaking world), the moral persuasiveness of the Papacy has been very severely damaged by its leadership of the opposition to these modern developments. In the terminology of the market, these Protestant exports have proved acceptable to other Christian minds and consciences. It could be said that here Protestantism has conquered the European market and that no possibility exists that the victory will be reversed.

I am trying to state facts about European Christianity, not to make Protestant propaganda. So far from believing that the future of European Christianity will be predominantly

Protestant in the full sense of that tradition, I have come to see that many spiritual developments in modern Europe endorse the wisdom of Catholicism. Protestantism, so far from being perfect or self-sufficient, needs imports. This cannot be surprising. To name a movement from its protests suggest that it exists only in dialogue with a larger and stronger movement: by definition Protestantism protests against Catholic corruptions, but that does not mean that it is entitled to close its eyes or ears to Catholic holiness or Catholic truth.

I am trying to state what many Protestants now wish to say, not to make Anglican propaganda. I am an Anglican, a member of a church which believes itself to be both Catholic and Reformed and which knows itself to be in need of renewal. As I have tried to state in other books, that membership has shaped my own conviction that Protestantism, however necessary it may be, can be enriched by Catholicism. But I hope I am not being merely Anglican. The conviction that Protestantism needs Catholicism is no Anglican monopoly. It emerges as Christians emerge from Lutheran, Calvinist, Methodist and other traditions to encounter the spiritual wealth of a wider world. I hope that Anglicanism will make a contribution to European Christianity in the coming years, but it is realistic to acknowledge what its custom of worshipping in English when in Europe means. Its presence outside the United Kingdom has been, and must be, primarily as an ethnic Church, predominantly British or American. Sociologically it is not unlike the Orthodox Church which gathers Greeks or Cypriots in England or the USA. The Church of England, although it has recently formed a "diocese of Europe", for many years ministered to its adherents abroad through the Colonial and Continental Church Society, the Society for the Propagation of the Gospel and churches attached to embassies. Anglicanism can contribute (or offer) insights which I am calling "exports", but it cannot set itself up as a model which deserves close imitation throughout the ecumenical movement.

Traditionally in Europe Protestantism, threatened by Catholic reactions which were often military, relied on the support of the state and was in the main willing to accept its control. Luther believed that the Church consisted essentially of congregations where the Word of God was preached and the sacraments were administered. Practically all other arrangements could be left to the Protestant prince. Other Reformers of the sixteenth century entrusted the supreme government of the Church to the local magistrates or to a national monarchy (as in England and Scandinavia). An attempt was made to justify this politically convenient practice by reference to the authority of the Old Testament kings, since it could scarcely be claimed that princes, magistrates or kings were the supreme governors of the Church in the New Testament. I have to confess, as an Anglican, that for many years the nonsensical belief in the "divine right of kings" was *the* distinctive belief of the Church of England. But these Reformation forms of state control over church life have been abandoned almost everywhere in the modern world.

Where the old link between Church and State basically survives despite reforms – as it does in England and most of Scandinavia – it is, on the whole, a handicap to the moral and spiritual influence of the churches, for it associates religion too closely with an elite which may in fact be irreligious. A better example is set by the canon law of the Roman Catholic Church which now forbids the appointment of bishops by national governments (who may, however, be consulted). Much of the change of attitude was brought about by the continuous protests of Protestants in Europe's Free Church tradition, demanding the separation of Church and State. The success of North American religion, freed from any establishment by the state and provoked to be endlessly vigorous and inventive, has been influential. In contrast German Protestants have been ashamed of their general failure to oppose Hitler and of the active support of the Nazi ideology by the so-called "German Christians".

Only in the minority "Confessing Church" was the Lutheran acceptance of the "godly prince" not interpreted as a duty to accept Hitler. But the discrediting of the Protestant Church has also been brought about by a more positive and wider vision of what the Christian Church essentially is – something that slips out of the grasp of any government because it is, as St Paul taught, nothing less than the Body of Christ and a new creation, radiant with the light of Easter. Again and again in twentieth-century Europe the cry has been raised: "Let the Church be the Church!" In East Germany when Communism followed Nazism, Protestants met that challenge and, in the end, earned a truly Christian victory as an evil state crumbled.

Traditionally in Europe Protestantism concentrated on the conversion of the individual to a faith which was held to "justify" the sinner in God's sight and without which the prospects of "salvation" were nil or at best extremely uncertain. An attempt was made to base this bleak theology on the letters of St Paul, since it could not easily be found in the teaching of Jesus. But today most Christians in modern Europe (or elsewhere) find it either inadequate or repulsive. Its individualism denies the God-given reality of human nature. Its emphasis on the terror of the wrath of God denies the supremacy of love in the Gospel, where wrath is the demanding face of love. Its cultivation of emotional decisions to "accept" Christ needs to be set in the far wider context given by the New Testament's pictures of daily discipleship and of baptized church membership. Its own picture of a God who is the Almighty Father but is either unwilling or unable to "save" any but a small minority of his children is now incredible – for most Christians as well as for others. And in fact where either a conservative or a liberal form of Protestantism flourishes in contemporary Europe, the old concentration on the sinner's conversion has been filled out to make a more truly biblical and psychologically healthier message – except for a few pockets of lingering fundamentalism, much less powerful in Europe than in the USA.

Without going back to the compulsory confession of sins to a priest, many Protestants have come to see that for a Christian purely individual self-criticism is no substitute. Even after a full conversion, a Christian is going to remain a sinner until death. Even without intimate contact with a priest or other pastor, every Christian is going to need the candid pressure of some fellow Christians in order to see with unflinching honesty what is sinful, since even the most godly of self-judges is capable of infinite self-deception. And even without the formal assurance of God's pardon on the lips of a priest or other pastor, many a Christian is going to need the help of fellow sinners in order to remove the burden of guilt. We all need home truths and we all need absolution by God and reconciliation to our fellows. So within the life of the Christian Church which in the biblical phrase "binds and looses" sinners there is surely a place for the priest – although a less prominent one than was decreed in 1215, when "confession" to him at least once a year became compulsory for Catholics.

European Protestantism has imported a vision of the Church as a fellowship larger than a congregation of converted individuals or ethically superior intellectuals. Across Europe now, whatever may be the social reality of a particular local church, the Church is known to be in principle wider, to include many classes, nations and races, and to be concerned for the welfare of all humanity and for the protection of humanity's environment. In that sense, to walk into a church is to walk into the world. The message is about the "kingdom" or government of God – a world-embracing perfection which is prophesied whenever art, music or human life is glorious and which is anticipated in the consecration of matter and of society in the use of bread and wine by the faithful gathered in the Eucharist. The proclamation of the Bible's message by the Church therefore ought to be visual and dramatic, contemplative and active – not restricted to the preacher's message to the individual, which may nowadays be conveyed with more professionalism by broadcasting. The Church lifts hearts and captures imaginations by beauty as much as by moral exhortation; by doing things together as much as by awakening personal decisions. That is one reason why its sacraments, when enacted as events in communities, are often more effective than its sermons. And the Church has roots in history going deeper than modern liberal Protestantism or the Reformation of the sixteenth century. It has roots in Catholicism.

Catholic exports and imports

In Europe the resources of the Roman Catholic Church are greater than the resources of Protestantism. This is not only due to the higher birth rate which means that about forty per cent of Europeans are baptized as Catholics. Studies of patterns of church attendance show repeatedly that although there has been a decline almost everywhere lay Catholics tend to be more regular in their "religious duties" than Protestants. In Portugal, Spain, Italy and Austria between twenty and thirty per cent of the population goes to Mass every week; in Ireland, Poland and Lithuania many more do. In France there may be more Muslims than Protestants. In England, where those baptized as Roman Catholics are still a minority, this minority is so much more ready to accept the obligation of churchgoing that its numbers at worship on any normal Sunday approximately equal those of the so-called "national" Church of England. In the Netherlands, where the image since the sixteenth century has been of a securely defiant Protestantism, Catholicism has been moving into the majority, in births as well as church attendance. That has also been true of West Germany, although the tendency which produced a Catholic majority in 1977 has been checked by migration from East Germany. It is even true of Geneva, once the Jerusalem of the Protestant Reformation. The full-time manpower of the Roman Catholic Church has, like the churchgoing of its laity, declined in numbers – but (again, like the laity) it remains formidable. It is formidable spiritually, not least because (with a few exceptions) it has shown its dedication to this work by renouncing marriage. It is formidable statistically, with about 400,000 priests and about 900,000 nuns at work around the world, more than half (in each category) in Europe.

It is clear from these numbers that the main responsibility for the Christian evangelization of Europe rests with the Roman Catholic Church, except in the historic lands of Protestantism and Orthodoxy to the north and east. And for this task, this church has immense spiritual resources. It has been at the centre of the Christian contribution to Europe in past centuries, and anyone prepared to dig in that field will unearth many pearls of spiritual wisdom. That contribution has continued into our own time, as I hope I have shown in this book by alluding to the importance of Christian Democracy (a mainly, though not exclusively, Catholic movement) and Solidarity (Polish and therefore strongly Catholic) and by outlining a tradition of spirituality which means more to Catholics (and Orthodox) than to Protestants.

One of the strengths of Catholicism has been its frank acceptance of the fact that Christianity needs to develop. The whole of Protestantism is of course a development on a very large scale. Liberal and radical Protestants teach what is in many ways a modern religion while conservatives and fundamentalists insist on doctrines which were not so clear in Christianity's first fifteen hundred years. But most Protestants have been shy about admitting this need to develop. They prefer to think of their religion as a recovery of the simple purity of the dawn. Conservative Protestantism is said to be simply "Bible believing", or Jesus the ethical teacher and friendly healer of Galilee is rescued from later superstitions and found to be a liberal in theology and a radical in politics. Eastern Orthodoxy is a development of Christianity, having its centre geographically in Constantinople/Byzantium as the "New Rome" (or in Moscow the "Third Rome") and chronologically in the fourth, fifth and sixth centuries. But Eastern Orthodoxy prefers to think of itself as "the apostolic faith", rejecting both Roman Catholic and Protestant additions to the teaching of the apostles of Jesus. In contrast, the Roman Catholic Church has emphatically affirmed the right of its *magisterium*, meaning in practice its bishops under the Pope, to define dogmas, to order practices and to insist on ethical positions which are not clear either in the Bible or in the Church's early traditions. For long it, too, maintained that it was only repeating what the apostles taught (orally if not in writing). But in the nineteenth century Newman and other theologians argued that doctrines and practices could develop legitimately and healthily, and this argument has been generally accepted in this church. Nowadays most interested outsiders would agree that Christianity's development is a fact in history – and is a necessity if there is to be a spiritual life which is more than a slavish imitation. It is, of course, not so widely agreed that the Papacy has been right to claim that the developments which it favours are compulsory for all.

Some developments in the Roman Catholic Church which have been subject to a blanket condemnation by Protestants and Eastern Orthodox in the past are now seen by many in those churches to contain healthy elements. These Christians would never place themselves under the Vatican's jurisdiction as it has operated for the past thousand years, but the international character of the Papacy is now often seen as a great asset. The Papacy has challenged many attempts by monarchs, local lords and modern politicians to control the Church for their own purposes. It has sponsored many missions extending the boundaries of the Church and has kept the dioceses and their bishops in touch with worldwide life and thought. Recently, in an age when international life has intensified, the Pope has had a prestige unique among the world's leaders. Until the agreement with Mussolini in 1929 it was thought that the independence of the Papacy depended on the possession of its own states in Italy, and Rome was actually ruled by the Pope until 1870. Paul VI was the first Pope to pay visits outside Europe. But John Paul II has made a personal impact on the world by his skilled and tireless use of the media and of mass meetings in many countries, and future popes will no doubt develop this universal ministry, a kingdom infinitely larger than an Italian principality. It has become possible to imagine a Pope for all Christians, presiding over a church with a universality which St Ignatius of Antioch had in mind when, in one of the first uses of the word Catholic (about AD 100), he wrote: "Where Jesus Christ is, there is the Catholic Church".

The Papacy has encouraged devotion to Mary as the mother of Jesus and the "mother" of the Church. The New Testament says little about her life and nothing about her death, and no other historical evidence has survived. Therefore the dogmas about her Immaculate Conception (1854) and Physical Assumption (1950) have often not been taken literally in the terms which the Popes propounded – although both doctrines have long histories in piety, going back in the latter case to the fourth century. The Eastern Orthodox, always reluctant to add firm dogmas to the ancient traditions, have never accepted the Immaculate Conception or insisted on a precise definition of the Assumption. But to think of Mary as unsullied by the world, and now glorious in heaven, is a devotion which has abundantly demonstrated its power to counteract excessively masculine images of God and low images of women, including women's low self-images.

The Papacy has also been associated with doctrines or

practices addressed to the problem of the continuing sinfulness of Christians. The early Church was confused about this problem, and the modern Church has generally rejected medieval developments such as the demand that sins must be confessed to a priest and the offer of "indulgences" remitting "days" of punishment in "purgatory". Many Christians who know themselves to be sinners have more sympathy with some of the Papal teaching. It seems better than any naïve belief that human nature is divided neatly into saints and sinners and can be imagined either as perfect or as beyond salvation immediately after death. It reassures humanity that the Church is not too holy to be open. And Catholics value sacraments whose validity in no way depends on the personal sanctity of the priest.

The capacity of Roman Catholicism to develop healthily was demonstrated in most of the work of two of its councils of bishops. In response to the challenges of Protestantism the Council of Trent (1545–63) reformed a long series of abuses which had entered the Church in the Middle Ages, and launched an extensive programme of more personal spirituality and more systematic education. In response to the challenges of modernity the Second Vatican Council (1962–65) accepted the principle of the freedom to worship according to conscience, recognized Christians outside the Roman Catholic Church as Christians, and blessed wider movements for peace, justice and development in the world. It encouraged a more corporate spirit in the Church, with "collegiality" between the bishops and much more participation by the laity in worship which was to be clearly based on the Bible and in the local language. In all these things it corrected – or at least developed – positions which had seemed right in Trent, and it was assisted by "observers" who were not Roman Catholics. It is to the credit of Europe that some of its bishops, advised by some of its theologians, took the lead in the widespread renewal achieved by both councils. At Vatican II, convened by a Pope who was an Italian saint, the leading Bishops were Cardinals Alfrink, Bea, Doepfner, Frings, Koenig, Liénart and Suenens, and the leading theologians were Chenu, Congar, Daniélou, de Lubac, Küng and Rahner: all were Europeans. A more conservative Pope, John Paul II from Poland, later repeatedly declared that his aim was to see that the decisions taken by the Council were obeyed in the spirit and in the letter. A Synod of Bishops gathered to advise him in Rome in 1985 thoroughly endorsed this aim, which was to a large extent reflected in the revision of the 1917 code of canon law published in 1983.

Cardinal Joseph Ratzinger has summed up the change made by the council and by what was now seen as the long European preparation for it.

> In the age of liberal thought, up to the First World War, the Catholic Church was regarded as a fossilized machine that persistently opposed the achievements of the modern age. In theology the question of Papal primacy was so in the foreground that the Church appeared essentially as a centrally directed institution which one was dogged in defending but which only encountered one externally. What now became visible once more was that the Church is much more, that in faith we all share in living responsibility for it just as it supports us. It had become clear that it is an organic growth that has developed through the centuries and continues today. It had become clear that through it the mystery of the Incarnation remains present and contemporary: Christ marches on through the ages (*Church, Ecumenism and Politics*, 1988, p. 4).

But it now seems to many Protestants and Eastern Orthodox – and, more to the point, to many (and perhaps to most) Roman Catholics – that further spiritual imports are needed by this Church whose councils responded so creatively to past challenges. Probably the new response will need a new council. This may well be the price for persuading Europe and other continents that this church is willing to face realities. The main pressure is likely to come from the Two-Thirds World, where almost three-quarters of the world's Catholics will be living in the year 2000. At the Second Vatican Council the bishops representing those continents were still feeling their way in an assembly where the use of Latin was a symbol of the European domination. Since then few bishops have openly deviated from the wishes of the Pope and his *Curia*, but despite the good will on both sides there have been many signs of a failure by the still predominantly European Vatican to understand the aspirations of Latin America, Africa and Asia (and of Catholics in the USA). However, in Europe also pressure has been building up and the (perhaps half-formed) thoughts of many of the laity have been articulated by theologians. Many European Catholics would doubt whether an eminently conservative churchman such as Cardinal Ratzinger has fully absorbed the implications of his (no doubt sincere) belief that "the Church is not the constructor of truth but is constructed by it and is the place where it is perceived. Truth therefore remains essentially independent of the Church and the Church is ordered towards it as a means" (p.160).

Although the Cardinal went on to refer to "theology *and* the Church's teaching authority as realities that are ordered to each other", he has alarmed many in Europe (as elsewhere) by his treatment of theologians while Prefect of the Sacred Congregation for the Doctrine of Faith in the Vatican since 1981. To mention only two Europeans, the Congregation has declared that Professor Hans Küng of Tübingen should no longer be regarded (or employed) as a Catholic theologian, and has come near to condemning the equally distinguished New Testament scholar Edward Schillebeeckx, because they have criticized some current doctrines. The Congregation was formerly called the Inquisition and its whole style of censorship – continuing when even the Communists have stopped punishing deviants from a rigid party line – seems to many Europeans such an infringement of liberty that the official church which it defends is discredited by it. In 1989 a new oath was required from all clergy and university theologians. They must "adhere with religious obedience of will and intellect to the doctrines which either the Roman pontiff or the college of bishops enunciate", whether or not a particular teaching is claimed to be "definitive". A council with free speech attending mainly to the concerns of the world's coloured poor, but involving theologians free to be critical, seems to be required more profoundly than such an oath if the Church is to be constructed by the truth.

As the 1990s begin, however, it seems very unlikely that in the near future such a council will be allowed or, if allowed, will satisfy the Vatican's critics. It has become the tradition that voting membership of a council should be confined to bishops; by a development which has taken place during the twentieth century, the Pope appoints almost all the Roman Catholic bishops in the world, and a conservative Pope naturally favours conservative bishops whether or not these are wanted by the dioceses concerned. The Pope also appoints all the cardinals who elect his own successor. Those who hope that further changes may be made by a new Pope or a new council may therefore appear to be unrealistic. But it seems worthwhile to state this hope because it would be even more unrealistic to plan for the future of the Roman Catholic Church on the assumption that its official leadership can safely disregard public opinion in that Church.

All the criticisms of official Roman Catholic doctrine which have been mentioned in this chapter find loud echoes in the consciences of many Roman Catholics who are (or who would wish to be) faithful and devout. One echo came when in 1989 163 professional Catholic theologians from Germany, Austria, Switzerland and the Netherlands signed the Cologne Declaration protesting about the silencing of colleagues and the appointment of conservatives as bishops against local wishes. Two hundred French Catholic theologians endorsed this protest. But while theological arguments can go forward and backward without greatly affecting daily church life, at points involving sexuality the moral authority of the conservative bishops is either destroyed or acutely vulnerable in contemporary Europe.

In a situation where most married Roman Catholics think it right to limit their families but to express and strengthen their love for each other physically, their conviction about this matter, to them of very great importance, outweighs the Papal reminder that "the Church, calling people back to the observance of the norms of natural law, as interpreted by her constant doctrine, teaches that each and every marriage act must remain open to the transmission of life" (*Humanae Vitae*, 1968, reaffirmed by *Familiaris Consortio*, 1981). When the growth of the world's population is well known to pose immensely serious dangers, it seems morally offensive for a Pope who claims to teach "in the name and with the power of Christ" to refer loftily to "a certain panic deriving from the studies of ecologists and futurologists" (*Familiaris Consortio*). And the attempt to prohibit contraceptives seems all the more immoral when the alternative in practice is known to produce a large number of abortions, as has been the case in some European countries including Italy and Poland, and the spread of AIDS among "practising" homosexuals. As a result, either the laity will take care to keep out of touch with their pastors on the use of contraception, or the Pope and the bishops will be openly defied by the laity, who may be supported by many priests. The entire relationship of trust between clergy and laity, on which the Roman Catholic Church has been built, must be damaged severely – and the alienation, unless ended, must grow as overpopulation grows, as abortion is abominated as a method of birth control, as improved methods of contraception become more easily available, and as generations of the laity assume that the question has been settled in accordance with their own consciences.

The prohibition of marriage before or after ordination is probably the most important reason why the numbers of the Roman Catholic priesthood in Europe outside Poland are declining. It is known that this prohibition is no more than a custom of the "Latin" Church during its second thousand years, not a theological principle, since it is not the custom of the Eastern Orthodox Church or of the small Uniate Churches which are allowed to retain some Orthodox customs while acknowledging Papal authority; and some exceptions to the rule have been granted by the Papacy to ex-Protestants. It is also known that the rule has not completely stopped sexual liaisons by priests, although this problem is less in Europe than in Africa. For priests bravely faithful to their vow to be celibate, the problem may be one of acute stress or loneliness. The lives of priests who are convinced that God has called them to renounce marriage are greatly admired, and it is assumed that the Church will always hold such priests in honour, but it is also widely felt that pastoral work among families (inevitably a large part of the work of most priests) is not helped by the Papal reminder that "the Church, throughout her history, has always defended the superiority of this charism (virginity or celibacy) to that of marriage, by reason of the wholly singular link which it has with the Kingdom of God" (*Familiaris Consortio*). The usual Christian attitude in our time is that both celibacy and marriage are God's will, his different vocations for different people: as such, they should be honoured equally.

The problem of the statistical decline of the priesthood will grow in Europe as priests ordained in the 1950s (the last decade to produce generally large numbers) retire or die. (It will also grow throughout the English-speaking world, while in the Two-Thirds World the number of priests will be increasingly out of step with the dramatic growth of the population.) And the results of the shortage of priests will affect the whole religious situation in Europe (as elsewhere). The remaining clergy are likely to be more overworked but to be unable to halt the development of Catholicism into a largely lay movement. From a Protestant point of view this would be a desirable development but it would be paradoxical if it were to be the consequence of an insistence on clerical celibacy as superior to lay marriage. And from a Catholic point of view, it seems that to give the maintenance of the custom of celibacy priority over the maintenance of a priesthood large enough to minister effectively to the laity is to make a judgement which is questionable.

Also questionable is the firm stand of the Papacy against the ordination of women to the priesthood. This is less questionable, because here the Papacy is only maintaining the character of the Christian priesthood since it began. But still the question can be raised because in the nineteenth and twentieth centuries the general position of women in society has been transformed. It is therefore questioned whether the Papacy is clinging to an outmoded custom which is depriving the church of valuable service; and the question may be asked sharply since in the Roman Catholic Church few women have been welcomed as leaders apart from the superiors of "religious orders" (nuns) and the women who already do much of the pastoral work in parishes in the USA and elsewhere. For all its devotion to the Blessed Virgin, this church has not begun to come to terms with the moral challenge of feminism.

Whether or not the consciences of bishops assembled in a future council of the Roman Catholic Church allow what may be called further imports from Protestantism, it seems probable that a change will come in what may be called the process of exchange or ecumenical communion. Until the 1960s joint prayer between Roman Catholics and other Christians was officially prohibited or strongly discouraged. The Second Vatican Council declared that "the ecclesiastical communities separated from us lack that fullness of unity with us which should flow from Baptism, and we believe that especially because of the lack of the sacrament of orders they have not preserved the genuine and total reality of the Eucharistic mystery" (*Unitatis Redintegratio*). At the beginning of the 1990s it is still the official position that other Christians should not receive communion at a Roman Catholic Mass. The rule is often broken, partly because dialogues between theologians of the divided churches have recently shown that there is a wide measure of agreement about the nature of the Eucharist and of the priesthood which presides at it, so that it is difficult to maintain that Christians who are not Roman Catholics must believe different things at this point. Here again a dangerous gap exists between what is ordered officially and what is thought and done in practice. Many Christians reckon that the official line against Eucharistic hospitality does not help either the mission in Europe or the development of unity within that mission.

For the Papacy and the bishops appointed by it change would not be easy. But it was not easy to change the practices and ideas of the periods before the Council of Trent and the Second Vatican Council – and change came. And if a change in the style of discipline within the Church does prove acceptable to enough influential consciences, the new teaching will be in line with what has been taught for many years about the right shape of society.

In 1931 Pius XI developed the social teaching given by a previous Pope, Leo XIII, in *Rerum Novarum* forty years before. "It is a fundamental principle of social philosophy, fixed and unchangeable", he wrote, "that one should not withdraw from individuals and commit to the community what they can accomplish by their own enterprise and industry". For this reason the Roman Catholic Church has consistently defended the rights of private property. The merits of this teaching have recently been demonstrated by the collapse of Communism, called "Socialism" in much Papal teaching. In the Second Vatican Council the rights of the individual conscience in religion were also affirmed, and it does not seem farfetched to expect a more generous recognition of the rights of individual Roman Catholics, including theologians, to criticize the teaching of the Vatican. But Pius XI continued: "So too, it is an injustice, and at the same time a grave evil, and a disturbance of right order, to transfer to the larger and higher collectivity functions which can be performed and provided for by lesser and subordinate bodies... The more faithfully this principle of subsidiarity is followed and a hierarchical order prevails among the various organizations, the more excellent will be the authority and efficiency of society, and the happier and more prosperous the condition of the commonwealth" (*Quadragesimo Anno* reaffirmed by *Laborem Exercens*, 1981, and *Sollicitudo Rei Socialis*, 1988).

The principle of "subsidiarity" has been important, at least for Roman Catholics, in the thinking behind the creation and development of the European Community and in various other efforts to strengthen bodies above and below the national government. It has justified participation in trade unions demanding a wage large enough to bring up a family (as Leo XIII advocated, in his time boldly) or counteracting the "international imperialism of money" (which Pius XI denounced) or breaking the monopoly of power in Eastern Europe by the Communist Party (as John Paul II urged). The idea has also been used in proposals for various forms of the ownership or control of businesses by their workers instead of by the state or other shareholders. But despite the general principle that the Church ought to set an example to society, the application of this principle of "solidarity" to the life of the Church has been resisted.

In the Church, it is said, the Pope as successor to St Peter in the bishopric of Rome, advised by the bishops as successors to the other apostles, governs and teaches "by divine law", in some circumstances, infallibly. But increasingly historical knowledge has shown that this idea of the Church cannot be traced back to Christ or his apostles (such as St Paul), and has not been generally received among Christians except among those who have accepted the development of the Papacy under

Leo I (who became Pope in 440) and his successors such as Gregory VII and Innocent III. Such evidence as survives suggests that although Peter and Paul were martyred and buried in Rome, and this was one of the elements in the prestige of the church in the empire's capital, there was no Bishop of Rome – in the royal style – during the first century of that church's life. I ask the reader to tolerate a brief digression about a letter which survives from about AD 96 because it indicates a situation not to be forgotten as the role of the Papacy is discussed in the 1990s. It is a letter from "the church of God in Rome" to "the church of God in Corinth". It rebukes the Corinthians for deposing some "presbyters" who are also called "bishops". It refers to Peter and Paul as it recalls that the apostles founded orderly churches under designated leadership. The tradition as old as AD 170 that this letter was written by Clement seems sound enough, but the author is not named in the earliest texts. He writes to exhort fellow Christians, basing himself on Scripture, but what he does not say is: "I am Peter's successor as Bishop of Rome and therefore I have jurisdiction over you." But about AD 185 Bishop Irenaeus of Lyons praised the maintenance of apostolic traditions by Bishops of Rome.

Other evidence, which is more voluminous, shows that in the age of the "ecumenical" councils of the Church (325–787) the assent of the Bishops of Rome was usually thought necessary to sound doctrine, but this evidence contradicts any idea that the Papacy was the chief teacher and ruler of the whole Church. Not before 1302 did a Pope "declare, state and define that it is absolutely necessary for the salvation of all that they should submit to the Roman Pontiff" (*Unam Sanctam*). The dogma of Papal Infallibility, although widely believed by such Christians over a long period, was not formally decreed until the First Vatican Council met in 1870. That council proclaimed the infallibility "when he defines a doctrine regarding faith or morals to be held by the Universal Church" of Pius IX and his successors. In his famous *Syllabus of Errors* (1864) Pope Pius had "seemed to some to be sounding the death-knell of Catholicism. He hurled anathemas at every thesis of European liberalism. He seemed to condemn democracy, free speech, the free press and virtually every other principle of the liberal order. He seemed to point the Catholic Church in a direction utterly reactionary." (The words are those of a Roman Catholic scholar, Michael Novak, in *Catholic Social Thought and Liberal Institutions*, 1989, pp.19-20.) No new teachings of the Papacy have been officially described as infallible since 1950, but the revision of canon law in 1983 repeated that the Pope as "Vicar of Christ" has "supreme, full, immediate and universal" jurisdiction over the Church. Although the Second Vatican Council placed the Pope within the "college" of bishops theologically, in practice no enforceable limits have been set to his power. Episcopal Conferences have enabled the bishops of a nation or region to speak with a common voice, but their authority has remained unclear.

Many Christians, including many Roman Catholics, specially in Europe, hope that the time will come when it is recognized officially that it is a disturbance of right order when functions which can be performed and provided for by individuals, by local congregations or by synods representing national or regional churches are transferred to a larger and higher collectivity such as the Vatican.

Orthodox exports and imports

The Eastern Orthodox Church has aroused much respect among other Christians in the twentieth century because of its heroic record in the maintenance of a Christian spirituality against all the pressures that could be applied by Communist regimes in the USSR, Romania, Bulgaria, Serbia and elsewhere. In the nineteenth century and earlier it had maintained a similar witness to Christianity against the pressures of Islam in the Ottomon empire, which included Greece and much of the Balkans. It is likely to continue to exert this influence as excommunist (or in the case of Greece, ex-Fascist) countries enter a period when the pressures against Christian spirituality will come from the materialism of consumerism, where (as St Paul observed about life in the Roman empire) the one god really worshipped is the belly. Respect for this survival has been increased when there has been awareness of the past dependence of Eastern Orthodoxy on the Byzantine emperor, who presided at the "ecumenical" councils of the Church. Much of the emperor's prestige and power were taken over by Russian Tsars. The tradition of obedience to emperor or Tsar has helped to make Orthodox bishops reluctant to criticize political authorities far less congenial to them. From 1927 onwards the Russian Orthodox Church, for example, was officially submissive to Communism. In Greece and the Balkans Orthodox Churches moved out of the old Patriarchate of Constantinople into alliance with (and some dependence on) the governments of new nations. Particularly when the state has had a hand in appointments there have been notorious examples of subservience and flattery nauseating to humbler believers who were suffering under persecution or misgovernment. But on the whole other Christians who have been aware of the problems of the Orthodox Church have admired its courage in adapting to the disappearance of its political support – and their respect has grown further as it has been seen that the loyalty of believers to their religious tradition has been secured not by the threats of disciplinary jurisdiction but by the quiet attractiveness of the Church's worship. Orthodoxy has been shaped by its monks (for example, by the *starets* or holy elders in

Russia) far more than by its official legislators; monks rather than bishops have kept it conservative. Since the tenth century, the chief centre of monasticism has been Athos, a mountain in north Greece jutting out into the sea. In contrast with Catholicism's zest for organization, there are no separate "orders" to distinguish Orthodox monks or nuns from each other.

Among the churches of Europe, Orthodoxy is the supreme example of Christianity as communion. Clergy and laity are often bound together by a love which has been strengthened by adversity. It has often been said that in the worship the barriers between earth and heaven are removed, so that the eternal "communion of saints" is entered. It has often been taught that a traditionalism in belief – largely unquestioned – is valuable not for the sake of an intellectual uniformity but because orthodoxy enables the right glory to be given to the revealed God in the power of the Holy Spirit. And this glory leads to the end described by St Athanasius in his startling phrase: "He was made Man so that we might be made God." It might dismay Orthodox believers to find their holy traditions called exports, but many other Christians now know that the spiritual treasures of Orthodoxy can enrich other traditions.

As the twentieth century draws to its close, however, a new age of Orthodoxy is clearly due to begin. The Russian Communist empire has gone the way of the empire of the Ottoman Turks. No longer can modernizing ideas be branded as treachery – or at least they cannot be branded quite as the Living Church movement was said to be a plot sponsored by the Communists. The Church will enjoy religious freedom in the new climate of pluralism, but if it is not content with life in a museum it will face challenges very different from those of the task of survival in recent centuries. Its liturgy (Eucharistic worship), which has adhered with minor modifications to traditions of the eighth century or earlier, may have to be revised for the same reasons that the Roman Catholic Church revised its Mass in the 1960s. Its canon law has never been fully codified and reviewed. It observes Easter on a date fixed by its own ancient method, and in Russian and some other countries the whole calendar of the Orthodox Church is thirteen days behind the Gregorian Calendar used by other Christians. Many other practical arrangements can, if desired, be brought up to date. Church leaders will be free to meet in order to take decisions about these and other questions which could be avoided when it was held that the last of the seven "ecumenical" councils had dispersed in 787 and that no further council could be convened. The Church's international organization will have to be strengthened. It entered the 1990s without having been able to convene the "Pan-Orthodox Synod" which had been in desultory preparation for many years. It has also been unable to end the division of the Orthodox communities outside the traditionally Orthodox countries in the Balkans and Eastern Europe into "jurisdictions" looking to European national churches – a scandal which contradicts the principle that there should be one bishop in one place. If there can be a Patriarch of Alexandria or Antioch, theology suggests that there could be a Patriarch of New York (for example). One of the problems has been rivalry between Constantinople and Moscow, the Patriarch of the former being senior in theology but in charge of much smaller numbers and severely restricted by the Turkish government (which has vetoed appointments). Another problem has been how much (if any) recognition of Papal jurisdiction should accompany the recognition of the Bishop of Rome as "designated to preside in love and honour" over the whole Church (in the words of a Patriarch of Constantinople in 1975).

It seems that if they are to be open to that "whole Church", thoughtful Orthodox Christians, clerical or lay, will have to consider many or all of the questions about Christian doctrine and organization which have occupied the minds of Roman Catholics and Protestants since the time of the Great Schism when East and West divided in 1054. They will not be asked to be false in their own insights but they will have to be in disturbing dialogues with the Middle Ages, the Renaissance, the Reformation, the Counter-Reformation, the Enlightenment, modern science, historical criticism, liberalism, feminism.... There have been theological discussions in the past – with Thomism in the fourteenth century and Counter-Reformation Catholicism in the seventeenth, to mention two examples – but a deeper disturbance seems to be needed now. And the Church's laity will be challenged to contribute more than nationalist cries, or generalized slogans about justice and peace, to the reconstruction of their societies within a more united Europe and elsewhere, so that traditions which may be compared with the Christian Democracy and Christian Socialism of the West will have to be developed.

These tasks are not impossible. Many Russian Christians threw energies and visions into similar tasks of renewal towards the end of the nineteenth century, only to find the religious renaissance cut short or exiled after the Bolshevik seizure of power. Already these tasks have been begun anew in the Orthodox participation in the life and studies of the World Council of Churches, for example, or in some Orthodox thinking in the American environment, or in the acceptance of radical changes producing a more modern relationship with the state in a democratic Greece. But the explosion of energy which is dramatized by the fire and the acclamations in the Orthodox celebration of Easter is needed for the wide renewal which could accompany the new freedom; and the great difficulties which the Orthodox will face in this renewal will be reduced if they can accept from other Christians, when communications improve, not only friendship and loving prayers but also some ideas which may be called imports in a single market.

9

'Come Over and Help Us'

THE Acts of the Apostles may not seem at all relevant to the European Community as it becomes the European Union in a growing unity or association with the other European nations. "European" is not a biblical word. Since the Bible's great dramas of liberation and enlightenment take place in Africa and Asia, in the story of the gift of the Holy Spirit to the Church on the day of Pentecost the only Europeans mentioned are Cretans and visitors to Jerusalem from Rome (Acts 2:10). But the story of St Paul's second missionary journey includes an incident when the pioneering evangelists have been "prevented by the Holy Spirit" from delivering their message in the Roman empire's provinces called Asia and Bithynia, now parts of Turkey. A vision appeared to Paul in the night: "a man of Macedonia was standing beseeching him and saying, 'Come over to Macedonia and help us' " (Acts 16:9). Immediately after this dream, we are told, Paul arranged his passage to Europe. So began a mission which occupies the Acts of the Apostle until Paul, on first seeing the Christians of Rome, "gave thanks to God and took courage" (27:15).

As Christianity enters its third millenium in Europe (with perhaps 2,000 million years to go), Christians are needed to help the new Europe come to birth. But they cannot give the necessary help unless they are prepared to "come over" in spirit, to move courageously from some of their present or recent positions. During much of their recent history their churches have been identified, often exclusively and even militantly, with regions, nations and empires. Now the churches of Europe will have to come to terms with Europe itself. Christians have often been dominated or persecuted.

Now they will be free to serve. Christians have been divided. Now they must enter a developing communion. The Lord of Europe's Christians seems to be asking once again "how is it you cannot interpret this fateful hour?" (Luke 12:56), for the signs of the times seem to be like a budding tree which says that summer is near (Luke 21:30). But as a new Europe is born, European Christianity must be reborn. That prospect alarms all who know and value past history and who are aware of present dangers. But if it has been possible for a President of the Soviet Union to incur immense risks by a policy of *perestroika*, it may not be necessary to think that it would be too dangerous to attempt the restructuring of churches. Gorbachev appealed to the memory of Lenin. "His very image is an undying example of lofty moral strength, all-round spiritual culture and selfless devotion to the cause of the people and of Socialism.... I have long appreciated a remarkable formula advanced by Lenin: Socialism is the living creativity of the masses" (*Perestroika*, pp. 25, 29). Christians have a Lord better than Lenin (whose statues have been pulled down all over Eastern Europe) and Christianity is still, as it has been so often in Europe's past, the living creativity of the divine Spirit. At this turning point, are Europe's Christians to be more frightened than Gorbachev and those who follow his lead? Are they to say that nothing lies ahead except a decay ending in a death?

In St John's gospel (3:4–8) Nicodemus asks Jesus: "How can a man be born when he is old? Can he enter a second time into his mother's womb and be born?" Jesus replies: "The wind blows where it wills, and you hear the sound of it, but you do not know whence it comes or whither it goes. So it is with every one who is born of the Spirit."

For Further Reading

Recent discussion about the European Community in English includes Hugh Arbuthnott and Geoffrey Edwards, *A Common Man's Guide to the Common Market* (Macmillan, 1989); Michael Burgess, *Federalism and European Union* (Routledge, 1989); Sir Michael Butler, *Europe: More than a Continent* (Heinemann, 1986); Paolo Cecchini and others, *The European Challenge* (Wildwood House, 1988); *Europe without Frontiers*, a Socialist symposium edited by Piet Dankert and Ad Kooyman (Cassell, 1988); Marcello de Crecco and Alberto Giovanni's more technical discussion of *A European Central Bank?* (Cambridge University Press, 1989); Kevin Featherstone, *Socialist Parties and European Integration* (Manchester University Press, 1988); Stephen George, *An Awkward Partner: Britain in the EC* (Oxford University Press, 1990); *Europe 2000* edited by Peter Hall (Duckworth, 1978); Michael Heseltine, *The Challenge of Europe: Can Britain Win?* (Weidenfeld and Nicolson, 1989); an Institute of Economic Affairs symposium on *Whose Europe?* (1990); R.E.M. Irving, *The Christian Democratic Parties of Western Europe* (Allen and Unwin, 1987); Roy Jenkins, *European Diary* (Collins, 1989); Robert S. Jordan and Werner J. Feld, *Europe in the Balance* (Faber and Faber, 1986); W.J. Milligan, *The New Nomads* (World Council of Churches, 1984); Jean Monnet, *Memoirs* (Collins, 1978); Altiero Spinelli, *The European Adventure* (Charles Knight, 1972); Paul Teague, *The European Community: The Social Dimension* (Kogan Page, 1989); Christopher Tugendhat, *Making Sense of Europe* (Penguin Books, 1987); Neill Turner, *The Government and Politics of the European Community* (Macmillan, 1989); Nigel Tutt, *Europe on the Fiddle* (Helm, 1989); Helen Wallace, *Widening and Deepening: The European Community and the New European Agenda* (Royal Institute of International Affairs, 1990); Ernst Wistrich, *After 1992: The United States of Europe* (Routledge, 1989). Two reports on Aid from Europe were published by Christian Aid in 1989: *Real Aid:*

What Europe Can Do and Clive Robinson's more general and popular *Hungry Farmers*.

Recent publications of the European Community include Richard Hay, *The European Commission and the Administration of the Community* (1989); Emile Noel, *Working Together* (1988); John Palmer, *1992 and Beyond* (1989). Michael Emerson, Director of Economic and Financial Affairs, tackled *The Economies of 1992* (Oxford University Press, 1988). But the Commission's hopes need to be checked against the realities presented by Nicholas Colchester of *The Economist* and David Buchan of the *Financial Times* in *Relaunching Europe* (Hutchinson, 1990).

The history of European expansionism has recently been assessed by Franz Ansprenger, *The Dissolution of the Colonial Empires* (Routledge, 1989); Jean Beacher, John Hall and Michael Mann, *Europe and the Rise of Capitalism* (Blackwell, 1988); Michael Doyle, *Empires* (Cornell University Press, 1986); E.L. Jones, *The European Miracle* (Cambridge University Press, 1987); Paul Kennedy, *The Rise and Fall of the Great Powers* (Collins, 1989); J.M. Roberts, *The Triumph of the West* (BBC, 1985); G.V. Scamell, *The First Imperial Age* (Unwin Hyman, 1989).

Background reading which has helped me includes J.M. Roberts, *The Pelican History of the World* (Penguin Books, 1988) and the Penguin Books by John Ardagh on *France Today* (1988) and *Germany and the Germans* (1987), by John Haycroft on *Italian Labyrinth* (1985) and by John Hooper on *The Spaniards* (1987). Flora Lewis gave an American view of *Europe: A Tapestry of Nations* (Unwin Hyman, 1988) and Caryl Phillips an anti-racist response to *The European Tribe* (Faber, 1987). Richard Hoggart and Douglas Johnson presented *An Idea of Europe* (Chatto and Windus, 1987) and Denys Hay traced *Europe: The Emergence of an Idea in History* (Edinburgh University Press, 1968). On Eastern Europe before 1990, Timothy Gorton Ash's essays on *The Uses of Adversity* (Granta Books, 1989), and Karen Dawisha, *Eastern Europe, Gorbachev and Reform* (Cambridge University Press, 1988), stood out. So did Henry Ashby Turner, *The Two Germanies since 1945* (Yale University Press, 1987). Abel

Aganbegyan, *The Challenge: The Economics of Perestroika* (Hutchinson, 1988), supplemented Mikhail Gorbachev, *Perestroika: New Thinking for Our Country and the World* (Collins, 1988). Timothy Gorton Ash's *We the People: The Revolution of 89* (Granta Books, 1990) was the best kind of on-the-spot journalism. Reith Lectures by Geoffrey Hoskins were published as *The Awakening of the Soviet Union* (Heinemann, 1990). David Lane offered another study of *Soviet Society under Perestroika* Unwin Hyman, 1990).

Recent books about Christianity in Europe include (as a very small selection) William A. Clebach, *Christianity in European History* (Oxford University Press, 1979); Michael Novak, *Catholic Social Thought and Liberal Institutions* (Transaction Publishers, 1989); *World Christianity: Eastern Europe* edited by Philip Walters (MARC, 1988). Studies by Roman Catholic scholars include J.M.R. Tillard, *The Bishop of Rome* (SPCK, 1983), and Patrick Granfield, *The Limits of the Papacy* (Darton, Longman and Todd, 1987). Peter Nichols inspected *The Pope's Divisions* (Faber, 1981). Timothy (Bishop Kallistos) Ware interpreted *The Orthodox Church* (Penguin Books, 1969) and *The Orthodox Way* (Mowbray, 1982). *The Study of Spirituality* edited by Cheslyn Jones, Geoffrey Wainwright and Edward Yarnold (Oxford University Press, 1986) was an introduction to a treasurehouse. My *The Futures of Christianity* (Hodder and Stoughton, 1987) was an introduction to the world scene.

Recent books in French include Enrique Baron, *Europe 92* (Coutaz, 1989); Pascal Fontaine, *Jean Monnet* (Grancher, 1988); Alain Minc, *La Grande Illusion* (Grasset, 1989). A lighthearted but sharp-eyed account of *Les 12 Tribus d'Europe* has been provided by Stéphane Courchaure and François Marot (Ramsay, 1989). Its exploration of the growing public awareness of the curiosities of other cultures is in contrast with the insistence on divisions which runs through an equally entertaining book by an older journalist, Luigi Barzini, translated as *The Europeans* (Penguin Books, 1984). Essays edited by Juliet Lodge more seriously explored *The European Community and the Challenge of the Future* (Pinter, 1989).

Index

Abortion 80-1, 220-2, 235
Action Française 80
Acts of the Apostles 27, 246
Adenaeur 91, 146, 155-7, 165, 172
Afghanistan 141
Africa 56-7, 123, 136-7, 205
Ageing 180-1, 187
Agriculture 14-15, 57-61, 159, 187-91
Aid 28, 55-7, 185-6
AIDS 193, 235
Airbus 47
Albania 34, 92
Albert and Ball 166
Alcuin 89
Alfrink 232
Algeria 69, 137, 143
American Revolution 108-9
Amsterdam 28, 149
Anglicanism 223-4
Ansprenger 142-3
Antwerp 111, 149
Apartheid 142, 198
Architectural Heritage 193
Aristotle 22, 124
Arnold 120-1
Asia 56, 59, 124
Association with EC 37-8, 66, 83
Assumption of BVM 230
Athanasius 243
Athos 243
Atonement 202, 225
Augustine 83, 103
Australia 158
Azores 123-4
Aztecs 140

Babel 25
Bach 43, 90, 93
Bahamas 124
Balkans 32-3, 242
Baltic 132
Bank of England 62-3
Bantus 140
Baptism 207, 237
Baron 38
Barth 213-14, 221
Basel 97-8
Basques 45-6
Bea 232
Beef 58

Beethoven 26
Beirut 179
Belgium 22, 35-6, 41, 45-6, 72, 99, 136, 146
Benedict 28
Benelux 14-15, 22, 99, 156, 159
Benin 140
Berger 81
Berlaymont 25
Berlin Conference 137
    Wall 70-1, 115, 117
Bernanos 100
Bevin 82-3
Biblical authority 27, 111, 123, 215, 217-18
Birmingham 54
Bismarck 21
Black churches 205
    Forest 53
Bonhoeffer 90, 221
Boniface 88
Botticelli 42
Brandt 163
Brazil 123-4
Bretton Woods 61
Brezhnev 77
Briand 82
British attitudes to EC 15-17, 23, 30-1,
    34-6, 41-2, 48-9, 51-4, 60, 73-4, 82-3,
    158, 168, 179
    Council of Churches 24
    empire 17, 134-6, 147, 150
    life 38, 44, 63-4, 67, 88, 100-1, 111,
    144, 149, 190, 206
Brittany 25
Bruges 11, 28, 43, 111, 157
Brundtland 15, 186
Brussels 25-6, 29, 35-6, 96
Buddhists 197, 204
Budget of EC 21
Bulgaria 32, 68, 72, 98, 242
Bundesbank 64-5
Bush 12
Butler 152
Butt 23
Byzantium 83, 88-9

Calendar 244
California 126
Cambridge 168
Campaigns of CE 193-4
Camus 106

Canada 11, 145
Canaletto 42
Canaries 123-4
Canon law 221, 224, 241
CAP *see* Agriculture
Caribbean 56, 58
Caribs 139, 140
Cars 182, 184
Castro 115
Catalonia 45
Cathedrals 28, 43, 53, 83
Catholic Action 79
    Centre 26
    Institute 128
Catholicism *see* Roman
Ceaucescu 72, 115
Cecchini 167
Celibacy 235
Central European Union 33
Cervantes 43
Changing Britain 101
Charismatics 218
Charles V 149
Chartres 43
Chenu 232
Chernobyl 52
China 86, 92, 115, 124, 133, 141, 205
Christ 103-4, 123, 202, 218-19, 247
Christendom 89-90
Christian Aid 128
    Democrats 16, 45, 79, 91-2, 146, 220, 228, 245
        Social Union 91
    unity 208-14
Church of England 101, 223-4, 227
    Scotland 101
Churchill 82, 155, 157
Cicero 110
Claudel 100
Clement 240
Clergy 221, 231-2, 235-7
Clive 136
Clovis 89
CMEA 69-70
Coal 21, 53-4, 183 *and see* European CSC
Cockfield 168
Co-determination 51
College of Europe 157
Cologne 234
Colombo 164
Colonialism 122-51, 188, 199
Columbus 122-7
Commonwealth 17
Communion 203-4, 237-8, 243
Communione & Liberazione 79
Communism 11, 15, 69-72, 79, 85-6, 93-6, 108, 113-17, 184, 238-9
Communities in EC 40-6, 181-2
Competition 14, 18, 39-42, 66, 134-6, 196
Concordats 80
Concorde 47
Conference of European Churches 96-8
Confession of sins 223, 226, 231-2
Confessing Church 225
Congar 232
Congo 136
Congress of Europe 13, 42, 157
Conrad 136
Conservative Christianity 214-18, 228-9, 243
    Party 24, 63, 101, 168
Constantine 88
Constantinople 83, 88, 131, 205, 208, 242-3
Consumer protection 52
Consumerism 117-19
Contraception 79, 80, 186, 220, 222, 235
Conversion 217, 225
Copenhagen 43
Corsica 46
Cortes 139
Council of Europe 18, 41-2, 52, 68, 157, 192-3
    Ministers 35, 37, 64, 161, 171-8
    Trent 231
Countryside 194 *and see* Rural life
Cracow 43
Cranmer 206
Craxi 165-6
Crete 24, 246
Countryside 189-93
CSCE 33-4
Cyprus 67, 83-4
Cyril 89
Czechoslovakia 32-3, 70, 81, 93, 97, 157, 161

Daniélou 232
Dante 33, 43, 110
da Vinci 42
de Gaulle 19, 155, 160, 163, 173
de Gasperi 91
de las Casas 125
de Lubac 232
de Madariaga 42-3, 157
Deindustrialization 54, 166, 183
Delors 32, 62, 92, 165
Democracy 35, 38, 74-7, 115
Descartes 110
D'Estaing 178
Deutschmark 62, 67
Devaluation 64
Development of Christianity 228-9
    world 55-7, 188-9, 199

Index

Diaz 123
Disaster relief 193
Diu 133
Divorce 79, 80-1, 220-2
Doepfner 232
Dortmund 54
Dostoevsky 43, 90, 94
Dover 120-1
Draft Treaty 35, 161-2
Djilas 115
Drugs 44
Dubcek 117
Dürer 42

Eastern Europe 12, 29-33, 38, 61, 69-73, 81-2, 86, 114, 131, 147
Economic and Social Committee 36
Ecu 35-6, 62
Ecumenical Centre 26, 96
    councils 242, 244
    movement 13, 203-14, 237-8
Edict of Nantes 74
Edinburgh 207
Egypt 69
El Dorado 124
  Greco 90
  Salvador 128
Energy policy 21-2, 185
Engels 184
Enlightenment 90, 110-11, 245
Environment 20, 44, 52-4, 59, 118, 184-5, 193, 204
Epistle to Diognetus 88
Equality 74-6
Erasmus 43, 110
Erhard 146
Essentials 215
Ethiopia 141
Eucharist 237-8
Euratom 47
EUREKA 47
Europa 24
Europe, idea of 12, 21-4, 33-5, 40-4, 66, 87-90, 152-3, 199-200
European Assembly 12, 77
    Coal and Steel Community 18, 91, 155, 159, 183
    Commission 36-7, 49, 64, 159, 160-1, 163-4, 176-9
    Convention on Human Rights 49, 108
    Council 34-5, 161, 163, 176-7
    Court of Auditors 37, 179
        Human Rights 108, 193
        Justice 37, 49, 171
    Cultural Foundation 69
    Defence Community 157-8, 170-1
    Development Bank 55
    Economic Community's origin 159
  and see Treaty of Rome
    Economic Space 67-8
    Environment Agency 184
    Free Trade Association 67-8, 181
    Investment Bank 54
    Monetary System 62-5
    Movement 24-5
    Parliament 29-30, 36-7, 44, 64, 159, 161-4, 168, 176-8
    Political Authority 12
    Space Agency 47
    System of Central Banks 63
Evangelism 11, 195
Exchange Rate Mechanism 62

Familiaris Consortio 235
Featherstone 18
Federal Reserve System 64
Feminism 104, 222, 230, 237
Finland 67, 74, 173-4, 192
Fiji 58
Fisheries 50
Fraternity 75
Fraud 15, 39, 59
Free Church tradition 224
  Trade 90 *and see* Market
Freedom 37-40, 73-8, 179-81
French attitudes to EC 14, 19, 29, 34-6, 56, 60, 162-5
  empire 134-9
  life 22, 31, 41, 45, 64, 80-1, 85, 91, 99-100, 114, 145-6, 149, 150, 159, 179, 190-1, 206, 219, 227
  Revolution 74-7, 108
Freud 106
Friedrich 42
Frings 232

Gandhi 140
Garaudy 126
GATT 158
Geneva 96, 111, 205, 228
Genoa 41, 123, 127, 131
Genscher 164
German attitudes to EC 14, 17-19, 29-32, 34-6, 38, 60, 63, 155-9, 162-5
  empire 136, 138, 143
  life 22, 31, 41, 45, 64, 80-1, 85, 91, 99-100, 114, 145-6, 149, 150, 159, 179, 190-1, 206, 219, 227
Gibbon 110
Glasgow 28
Glasnost 77

Goa 126
God 78, 84, 102-3, 216-17, 225-6, 247
Goethe 43
Gonzalez 166
Gorbachev 12, 53, 72, 84, 95-6, 106, 116-17, 247
Goya 42
Granada 126
Greece 19-21, 32, 35, 38, 41-2, 55, 66, 68, 91, 98, 114, 242, 245
Gregory VII 240
Greens 118, 168
Guatemala 128

Habsburg empires 32-3, 90, 146, 148-9
Hall 134
Hallstein 159
Hamburg 28
Handel 90
Havel 33
Health care 180-1
Heath 168
Hébrard 42
Hegel 113
Heine 110
Heseltine 17, 22, 63
Hindus 196-7, 204, 208
Hitler 38, 45, 93, 146, 188, 208-9, 225
Holbach 110
Holmer 117
Holy Alliance 90
    Roman Empire 89
Homosexuality 220, 222
Honecker 117
Hugo 23
Human rights 49, 107-9, 192-3, 204
Humanae Vitae 235
Humanism 105-6, 109
Hungary 32-3, 70-1, 93
Hussites 97

Iceland 67
Ignatius 230
Iliescu 117
IMF 57, 129
Immaculate Conception 230
Immigration 20, 25, 149-50, 195-6
Imperialism 128-30, 143, 145, 147 *and see* Colonialism
Incas 140
India 86, 130, 134, 136, 138, 140, 142-5, 205, 208
Indo-China 137
Indonesia 135, 137, 143
Industrialization 144, 187
Infallibility 240-1

Inflation 63-4, 146, 149, 189
Innocent III 240
Inquisition 124, 233
Irenaeus, 240
Isaiah, Book of 83-4
Islam 69, 81, 85-6, 125-6, 130, 187, 204, 208
Israel 69
Italian attitudes to EC 14-15, 17, 19-20, 34-6, 38
    life 22, 41-2, 45, 54, 80-1, 91, 98, 111, 149, 156, 159, 219, 227

Japan 59, 86, 128, 131, 143, 167, 199
Jaruzelski 117
Jenkins 168
Jesus *see* Christ
    Prayer 103
JET 47, 182
Jeunesse 80
Jews 84, 196-7, 204, 208
John Paul II 33, 93, 117, 214, 230, 232, 235, 239
Joll 169
Jones 148
Justice 48-50, 107

Kadar 117
Kant 106, 111
Kaunda 58
Kennedy 158
Kierkegaard 90, 221
Kirchentag 96
Koenig 232
Kohl 31, 165
Koinonia 203-4
Korea 128
Krenz 117
Kubla Khan 130
Kurds 68

Laborem Exercens 239
Labour Party 16, 63, 158, 168, 183
Languages 20, 21, 41
Lash 113
Latin America 27, 50, 59, 115, 125, 129-30
League of Nations 154-5
Leibniz 43
Leipzig 93
Leo I 240
    XIII 238-9
Lefebvre 217
Lenin 114, 137, 247
Liberal Christianity 215-18, 228-9
Liénart 232
Lindsay 42

Index

Living Church 243
Locke 73-4, 110
Lomé 56, 59
London 28, 44, 149
Louis XIV 31, 74, 90
Luxembourg 35, 45, 178
                 Compromise 160
Lydia 27

Macao 126
Madrid 45
Maghreb 189
MacIntyre 107
Magyars 89, 130
Manchester 184
Mandela 142
Mansholt 59
Mao 115
Market 13-14, 39-40, 49, 112-13, 179-81, 185, 201-4, *and see* Capitalism
Marshall Aid 55, 157
Martin 176
Marx 72, 113-14, 142
Marxism *see* Communism
Mary 104, 123, 142, 237
Mergers 47-8
Messina 159
Methodius 89
Mezzogiorno 54
Michelangelo 110
Miesko 89
Milan 54, 166
Milton 90
Ming empire 133
Missionaries 126-7
Mitteleuropa 73
Mitterand 164-5, 194
Monetary union 61-5, 163-8
Monnet 154-60, 162, 168
Montaigne 106
Morocco 69
Morrow 156
Moscow 244
Mounier 40
Mouvement RP 91
Mughal empire 133-4, 136
Music 41
Muslims *see* Islam
Musset 43
Mussolini 45

Nairobi 210
Namibia 128
Napoleon 31, 45, 75, 90
Nationalism 44-6, 162, 173
NATO 157-8, 170-6

Nazism 11, 84, 91, 207, 224
Netherlands 22, 35-6, 41-2, 45, 52, 73, 99, 111, 118, 134-5, 148-9, 198, 227
Neutralism 67, 173-4
New Delhi 209-10
Newfoundland 134
Newman 229
Newton 43, 110
New Zealand 158
Nicaragua 128
Nicodemus 247
Nightingale 90
Non-Christian religions 135, 195-200
Northern Ireland 30, 44-5, 206
Norway 67, 102, 163
Novak 241
Nuclear power 14, 19, 21, 44, 47, 166, 182
        weapons 19, 44, 170-1, 175

Oil 21, 166, 185
Old Believers 217
Opus Dei 80
Orthodox Churches 83, 89, 97, 205-14, 217, 229, 236, 241-5
Orwell 34
Ottoman empire 32, 68, 131, 242

Palestrina 90
Papacy 89, 109, 126, 202, 205, 212, 222, 229-30, 239-41, 244
Parables 202
Parthenon 53
Pascal 90
Pasternak 94
Paul, St 83, 103-4, 110, 201, 207, 225, 239, 240, 242, 246
Paul VI 210, 230
Peace 29-34, 170-6
Péguy 100
Penn 33
Pentecostal churches 205, 219
Perestroika 71-2, 77-8, 86, 247
Permanent Representatives 35
Persian empire 83-4
Personalism 40
Peru 126, 148
Philip II 31
Philippines 107
Pius II 90
      IX 240-1
      XI 80, 214
      XII 80, 238-9
Plato 110
Pluralism 12-13, 85-7, 197
Poland 22, 25, 32-3, 40, 89, 93, 98, 115, 161, 214, 227, 235-6

Polaris 170
Police 20
Political co-operation 179
Pollution 52-3
Population 132, 141, 186-7, 235
Portugal 20, 35, 38, 55, 68, 98, 123, 126, 131, 134-5, 143, 148, 227
Poverty 29, 103, 167
Power 34-7, 176-9
Prague 81
Presidencies in EC 178
Priests 221, 231-2, 235-7
Protestantism 111, 130, 211-32, 237
Psalm 8, 107
Puritanism 220

Quadragesimo Anno 239

Rabelais 43
Racism 125, 150, 195-200
Rahner 232
Ramadier 157
Ratzinger 232-3
"Red Indians" 140
Reformation *see* Protestantism
Regional Fund 15, 54, 64, 185
Regionalism 44-6, 54-5, 185
Religion 24-8, 87, 105-6, 196, 221-2
Rembrandt 42, 90
Renaissance 109-10, 245
Rerum Novarum 238
Resistance 207-8, 213
Rhodesia 135
Rights of Man 74, 109
Road to Damascus 128-30, 139, 144
Roberts 87
Roman Catholicism 30, 78-81, 97, 99, 206-9, 212, 214, 217, 219-41, 243-5
Romania 23, 32, 72-3, 82, 93, 98, 115, 242
Rome 24, 230, 240, 246
Rural life 189-192 *and see* Agriculture
Rushdie 197
Russell 106
Russia 21, 31, 89, 131, 139, 146, 242
Ruysdael 42

Scammel 131
Scandinavia 101-2, 206, 224
Scepticism 105-13
Schillebeeckx 233
Schiller 26
Schuman 91, 156
Schumpeter 137
Scotland 41, 44, 46
Second Vatican Council 79, 99-100, 198, 207, 209, 217, 231-3, 237-8, 241

Security 21, 157-9, 170-6
Serbia 242
Shakespeare 43, 90
Shalom 27
Shipbuilding 132-3, 183
Sicily 54
Sieyés 109
Sikhs 195
Sikorski 161
Silver 134, 148-9
Single European Act 16, 18, 23, 50-1, 164, 192
    Market 13-14, 49, 162-8
Slave trade 125, 140
Smallness 46-7, 211
Smith 112, 133
Social Charter 19, 20, 50-2, 109, 183-4
    Democrats 16, 80, 114, 116, 146-7, 165
    Fund 15, 52, 55, 64, 185
Socialism 16-18, 39, 46, 70-2, 79-80, 90, 114-17, 180, 184, 238
Solidarity 40, 92, 214, 228
Solzhenitsyn 44
Songhay empire 140
South Africa 27, 128, 142, 198
Soviet Union 12, 31, 38, 40-2, 69-72, 77-8, 86, 93-6, 172, 193
Spaak 159
Spanish attitudes to EC 19-20, 35-6, 54-5
    empire 125-6, 134-5
    life 22, 31, 42, 45, 80-1, 89, 98, 114, 123, 148-9, 227
Spinelli 154, 160-2, 164, 168
Spinoza 110
Spirituality 102-5, chs. 8, 9
Sport 41
Stalin 38, 77, 95, 114, 155, 172, 208-9
State control of churches 126, 224, 242
Steel 50, 183 *and see* European CSC
Stephen 89
Stott 215
Strasbourg 12, 29, 36, 168, 177, 192-3
Stuttgart 127
Subsidiarity 239-40
Suenens 232
Sugar 58-9, 141
Sweden 67-8, 101, 118, 163, 173, 191
Switzerland 67-8, 99, 191, 207
Syllabus of Errors 240

Tartars 130
Tasmania 139
Tawney 111
Taxes 20
Teresa 90

Index 257

Texas 126
Thailand 141
Thatcher 11, 16, 19, 92, 101, 165, 168, 173, 184
Third World *see* Two-Thirds
Thomism 245
Timisoara 93
Tindemans 163
Tito 116-17
Togliatti 117
Tokes 93
Toleration 73, 78-9
Tolstoy 90, 94
Tornado 47
Tourism 42
Trade unions 36, 51, 183
Tradition and Truth 215-6
Traditionalism 217-18, 243
Transnational corporations 20, 47-8, 129, 182-3, 189
Transport policy 20, 168
Transubstantiation 221
Treaty of Rome 12, 23, 24, 34, 39, 52, 54-6, 60, 66, 68, 90, 164
    Tordesillas 134
    Versailles 146
Truth in Christianity 214-18, 233-4
Tugendhat 153-4
Tunisia 69
Turin 54
Turkey 33, 92, 244
TV 41, 100, 182
Twinning 181-2
Two-Thirds World 57 *and see* Aid, Development, World

Ukraine 206
Unam Sanctam 240
Unemployment 50, 167, 190
Union, idea of 152, 194 *and see* ch.6
Unitatis Redintegratio 237
Urban II 90
Urban life 189-91
USA 11, 41, 49, 55, 57-9, 86, 128, 138, 147, 157, 167, 170-4, 176, 184, 205

VAT 20, 49, 160
Venice 28, 42, 53, 131
Ventotene 161
Vespucci 126
Victoria 145
Vienna 68
Vietnam 143
Vikings 67, 88
Vincent 201
Visser 't Hooft 210
Vladimir 89
Vogel 165
Voltaire 43, 106, 110

Wales 44, 88
Warsaw Pact 171-2, 175
Water 53-4
Watteau 42
Wealth 24, 26-8, 102-3
Weber 111
Wesley 206
West European Union 158-9
Westminster Abbey 29
Wilson 154
Women 51, 104, 222, 230
    priests 237
Workers *see* Social Charter
World Bank 57, 129
    Council of Churches 13, 96, 200, 207, 245
    trade 55-9, 186-9
    wars 29, 38, 119, 146, 196, 199, 207-8, 213

Yalta 38
Yaoundé 56
Yeltsin 115
Youth culture 41
Yugoslavia 32, 174

Zürich 82